The Python Apprentice

A Practical and Thorough Introduction to the Python
Programming Language

Robert Smallshire
Austin Bingham

BIRMINGHAM - MUMBAI

The Python Apprentice

Copyright © 2017 Robert Smallshire, Austin Bingham

First published: June 2017

Production reference: 1160617

Published by Packt Publishing Ltd.
Livery Place
35 Livery Street
Birmingham
B3 2PB, UK.
ISBN 978-1-78829-318-1

www.packtpub.com

Credits

Authors
Robert Smallshire
Austin Bingham

Acquisition Editor
Frank Pohlmann

Project Coordinator
Suzanne Coutinho

Technical Editor
Joel Wilfred D'souza

Indexer
Rekha Nair

Layout Coordinator
Deepika Naik

About the Authors

Robert Smallshire is a founding director of Sixty North, a software consulting and training business in Norway providing services throughout Europe, and which uses Python extensively. Robert has worked in senior architecture and technical management roles for several software companies providing tools in the energy sector. He has dealt with understanding, designing, advocating and implementing effective architectures for sophisticated scientific and enterprise software in Python, C++, C# and F# and Javascript. Robert is a regular speaker at conferences, meetups and corporate software events and can be found speaking about topics as diverse as behavioural microeconomics in software development to implementing web services on 8-bit microcontrollers. He is organiser of the Oslo Python group and holds a Ph.D. in a natural science.

Austin Bingham is a founding director of Sixty North, a software consulting, training, and application development company. A native of Texas, in 2008 Austin moved to Stavanger, Norway where he helped develop industry-leading oil reservoir modeling software in C++ and Python. Prior to that he worked at National Instruments developing LabVIEW, at Applied Research Labs (Univ. of Texas at Austin) developing sonar systems for the U.S. Navy, and at a number of telecommunications companies. He is an experienced presenter and teacher, having spoken at numerous conferences, software groups, and internal corporate venues. Austin is also an active member of the open source community, contributing regularly to various Python and Emacs projects, and he's the founder of Stavanger Software Developers, one of the largest and most active social software groups in Stavanger. Austin holds a Master of Science in Computer Engineering from the University of Texas at Austin.

www.PacktPub.com

For support files and downloads related to your book, please visit www.PacktPub.com.

Did you know that Packt offers eBook versions of every book published, with PDF and ePub files available? You can upgrade to the eBook version at www.PacktPub.com and as a print book customer, you are entitled to a discount on the eBook copy. Get in touch with us at service@packtpub.com for more details.

At www.PacktPub.com, you can also read a collection of free technical articles, sign up for a range of free newsletters and receive exclusive discounts and offers on Packt books and eBooks.

https://www.packtpub.com/mapt

Get the most in-demand software skills with Mapt. Mapt gives you full access to all Packt books and video courses, as well as industry-leading tools to help you plan your personal development and advance your career.

Why subscribe?

- Fully searchable across every book published by Packt
- Copy and paste, print, and bookmark content
- On demand and accessible via a web browser

Customer Feedback

Thanks for purchasing this Packt book. At Packt, quality is at the heart of our editorial process. To help us improve, please leave us an honest review on this book's Amazon page at `www.amazon.com/dp/1788293185`.

If you'd like to join our team of regular reviewers, you can e-mail us at `customerreviews@packtpub.com`. We award our regular reviewers with free eBooks and videos in exchange for their valuable feedback. Help us be relentless in improving our products!

Table of Contents

Preface — 1

Chapter 1: Getting started — 11

  Obtaining and installing Python 3 — 11
    Windows — 12
    macOS — 13
    Linux — 14
  Starting Python command line REPL — 15
  Leaving the REPL — 16
    Windows — 17
    Unix — 17
  Code structure and significant indentation — 17
  Python culture — 21
  Importing standard library modules — 23
  Getting help() — 23
    Counting fruit with math.factorial() — 25
    Different types of numbers — 26
  Scalar data types: integers, floats, None and bool — 27
    int — 27
    float — 29
      Special floating point values — 30
      Promotion to float — 30
    None — 30
    bool — 31
  Relational operators — 32
    Rich comparison operators — 33
  Control flow: if-statements and while-loops — 33
    Conditional control flow: The if-statement — 33
    if...else — 34
    if...elif...else — 35
    Conditional repetition: the while-loop — 36
      Exiting loops with break — 38
  Summary — 39

Chapter 2: Strings and Collections — 41

  str – an immutable sequence of Unicode code points — 41

String quoting styles   42

Moment of zen   43

Concatenation of adjacent strings   44

Multiline strings and newlines   44

Raw strings   46

The str constructor   46

Strings as sequences   47

String methods   47

Strings with Unicode   49

The bytes type – an immutable sequence of bytes   50

Literal bytes   50

Converting between bytes and str   51

list – a sequence of objects   54

The dict type – associating keys with values   55

The For-loops – iterating over series of items   56

Putting it all together   57

Summary   61

Chapter 3: Modularity   65

Organizing code in a .py file   66

Running Python programs from the operating system shell   66

Importing modules into the REPL   67

Defining functions   68

Organizing our module into functions   69

The __name__ type and executing modules from the command line   70

The Python execution model   72

The difference between modules, scripts, and programs   73

Setting up a main function with command line argument   73

Accepting command line arguments   77

Moment of zen   79

Docstrings   79

Comments   82

Shebang   83

Executable Python programs on Linux and Mac   83

Executable Python programs on Windows   83

Summary   84

Chapter 4: Built-in types and the object model   87

The nature of Python object references   87

Reassigning a reference   88

Assigning one reference to another	89
Exploring value vs. identity with id()	90
Testing for equality of identity with is	91
Mutating without mutating	91
References to mutable objects	94
Equality of value (equivalence) versus equality of identity	96
Argument passing semantics – pass by object-reference	**97**
Modifying external objects in a function	97
Binding new objects in a function	99
Argument passing is reference binding	101
Python return semantics	**102**
Function arguments in detail	**102**
Default parameter values	103
Keyword arguments	103
When are default arguments evaluated?	104
The Python type system	**107**
Dynamic typing in Python	107
Strong typing in Python	108
Variable declaration and scoping	**108**
The LEGB rule	108
Scopes in action	**109**
Identical names in global and local scope	110
The global keyword	111
Moment of zen	**112**
Everything is an object	**112**
Inspecting a function	113
Summary	**114**
Chapter 5: Exploring Built-in Collection types	**119**
tuple – an immutable sequence of objects	**120**
Literal tuples	120
Tuple element access	120
The length of a tuple	120
Iterating over a tuple	121
Concatenating and repetition of tuples	121
Nested tuples	121
Single-element tuples	122
Empty tuples	122
Optional parentheses	122
Returning and unpacking tuples	123

Swapping variables with tuple unpacking   124

The tuple constructor   124

Membership tests   124

Strings in action   125

The length of a string   125

Concatenating strings   125

Joining strings   127

Splitting strings   127

Moment of zen   128

Partitioning strings   128

String formatting   129

Other string methods   130

range – a collection of evenly spaced integers   130

Starting value   131

Step argument   131

Not using range: enumerate()   132

list in action   133

Negative indexing for lists (and other sequences)   134

Slicing lists   135

Copying lists   138

Shallow copies   139

Repeating lists   144

Finding list elements with index()   146

Membership testing with count() and in   147

Removing list elements by index with del   147

Removing list elements by value with remove()   148

Inserting into a list   148

Concatenating lists   149

Rearranging list elements   149

Out-of-place rearrangement   150

Dictionaries   151

Copying dictionaries   153

Updating dictionaries   154

Iterating over dictionary keys   154

Iterating over dictionary values   155

Iterating over key-value pairs   156

Membership testing for dictionary keys   156

Removing dictionary items   157

Mutability of dictionaries   157

Pretty printing	158
set – an unordered collection of unique elements	**158**
The set constructor	160
Iterating over sets	160
Membership testing of sets	160
Adding elements to sets	161
Removing elements from sets	162
Copying sets	162
Set algebra operations	162
Union	163
Intersection	164
Difference	164
Symmetric difference	164
Subset relationships	165
Collection protocols	**166**
Container protocol	167
Sized protocol	167
Iterable protocol	167
Sequence protocol	168
Other protocols	168
Summary	**168**
Chapter 6: Exceptions	**171**
Exceptions and control flow	**172**
Handling exceptions	173
Handling multiple exceptions	**174**
Programmer errors	**175**
Empty blocks – the pass statement	**176**
Exception objects	**177**
Imprudent return codes	**178**
Re-raising exceptions	**179**
Exceptions are part of your function's API	**180**
Exceptions raised by Python	181
Catching exceptions	182
Raising exceptions explicitly	182
Guard clauses	**184**
Exceptions, APIs, and protocols	**185**
IndexError	186
ValueError	186
KeyError	186

Choosing not to guard against TypeError	187
Pythonic style – EAFP versus LBYL	188
Clean-up actions	190
Moment of zen	191
Platform-specific code	191
Summary	193
Chapter 7: Comprehensions, iterables, and generators	195
Comprehensions	195
List comprehensions	196
List comprehension syntax	196
Elements of a list comprehension	196
Set comprehensions	197
Dictionary comprehensions	198
Comprehension complexity	199
Filtering comprehensions	199
Combining filtering and transformation	200
Moment of zen	201
Iteration protocols	202
An example of the iteration protocols	202
A more practical example of the iteration protocols	203
Generator functions	204
The yield keyword	204
Generators are iterators	205
When is generator code executed?	206
Maintaining explicit state in the generator function	207
The first stateful generator: take()	207
The second stateful generator: distinct()	208
Understand these generators!	209
Lazy generator pipelines	209
Laziness and the infinite	210
Generating the Lucas series	210
Generator expressions	211
Generator objects only run once	212
Iteration without memory	213
Optional parentheses	213
Using an if-clause in generator expressions	213
Batteries included iteration tools	213
Introducing itertools	214
Sequences of booleans	215
Merging sequences with zip	215
More than two sequences with zip()	216

Lazily concatenating sequences with chain()   217
Pulling it all together   217
Summary   218
Generators   219
Iteration tools   219

Chapter 8: Defining new types with classes   221

Defining classes   222
Instance methods   223
Instance initializers   224
A lack of access modifiers   225
Validation and invariants   226
Adding a second class   227
Collaborating classes   229
Moment of zen   231
Booking seats   231
Allocating seats to passengers   235
Naming methods for implementation details   238
Implementing relocate_passenger()   239
Counting available seats   241
Sometimes the only object you need is a function   242
Making Flight create boarding cards   243
Polymorphism and duck-typing   244
Refactoring Aircraft   245
Inheritance and implementation sharing   248
A base class for aircraft   248
Inheriting from Aircraft   249
Hoisting common functionality into a base class   250
Summary   251

Chapter 9: Files and Resource Management   255

Files   256
Binary and text modes   256
The important of encoding   256
Opening a file for writing   257
Writing to files   258
Closing files   259
The file outside of Python   259
Reading files   260
Readline line by line   261
Reading multiple lines at once   261

Appending to files	262
File objects as iterators	262
Context Managers	264
Managing resources with finally	266
The with-blocks	267
Moment of zen	268
Binary files	269
The BMP file format	269
Bitwise operators	274
Writing a BMP file	274
Generating fractal images	275
Reading binary files	276
File-like objects	278
You've already seen file-like objects!	278
Using file-like objects	278
Other resources	280
Summary	282

Chapter 10: Unit testing with the Python standard library — 285

Test cases	285
Fixtures	286
Assertions	286
Unit testing example: text analysis	286
Running the initial tests	288
Making the test pass	288
Using fixtures to create temporary files	289
Using the new fixtures	290
Using assertions to test behavior	292
Counting lines	293
Counting characters	293
Testing for exceptions	296
Testing for file existence	296
Moment of zen	297
Summary	298

Chapter 11: Debugging with PDB — 299

Debugging commands	300
Palindrome debugging	300
Bug hunting with PDB	302
Finding infinite loops with sampling	304
Setting explicit breaks	305

Stepping through execution	307
Fixing the bug	308
Summary	309
Afterword: Just the Beginning	311
Appendix A: Virtual Environments	313
Creating a virtual environment	314
Activating a virtual environment	314
Deactivating a virtual environment	315
Other tools for working with virtual environments	315
Appendix B: Packaging and Distribution	317
Configuring a package with distutils	317
Installing with distutils	320
Packaging with distutils	321
Appendix C: Installing Third-Party Packages	325
Installing pip	325
The Python Package Index	326
Installing with pip	326
Installing Local Packages with pip	328
Uninstalling Packages	328
Index	329

Preface

Welcome to *The Python Apprentice*! Our goal with this book is to give you a practical and thorough introduction to the Python programming language, providing you with the tools and insight you need to be a productive member of nearly any Python project. Python is a big language, and its not our intention with this book to cover everything there is to know. Rather we want to help you build solid foundations, orient you in the sometimes bewildering universe of Python, and put you in a position to direct your own continued learning.

This book is primarily aimed at people with some experience programming in another language. If you're currently programming in any of the mainstream imperative or object-oriented languages like C++, C#, or Java, then you'll have the background you need to get the most out of this book. If you have experience in other types of languages – for example, functional or actor-based – then you may have a bit steeper learning curve with Python, but you won't encounter any serious difficulties. Most programmers find Python very approachable and intuitive, and with just a little practice they quickly become comfortable with it.

On the other hand, if you don't have *any* experience with programming this book may be a bit daunting. You'll be learning not just a programming language but many of the topics and issues common to all languages at the same time. And to be fair, we don't spend a lot of time trying to explain these areas of "assumed knowledge". **This doesn't mean you can't learn from this book!** It just means that you might have to work a bit harder, read sections multiple times, and perhaps get guidance from others. The reward for this effort, though, is that you'll start to develop the knowledge and instincts for approaching other languages, and this is a critical skill for the professional programmer.

In this first chapter we'll take a quick tour of the Python language. We'll cover what Python is (hint: it's more than just a language!), take a look at how it was – and still is – developed, and get a sense of what makes it so appealing to so many programmers. We'll also give a brief preview of how the rest of the book is structured.

Python Promo

To start with, what's so great about Python? Why do you want to learn it? There are lots of good answers to those questions. One is that Python is powerful. The Python language is expressive and productive, it comes with a `great standard library`, and it's the center of a `huge universe of wonderful third-party libraries`. With Python you can build everything from simple scripts to complex applications, you can do it quickly, you can do it safely, and you can do it with fewer lines of code than you might think possible.

But that's just one part of what makes Python great. Another is that Python is wonderfully open. Its open-source, so you can `get to know every aspect of it` if you want. At the same time, Python is hugely popular and has a `great community to support you` when you run into trouble. This combination of openness and large userbase means that almost anyone – from casual programmers to professional software developers – can engage with the language at the level they need.

Another benefit of a large user base is that Python is showing up in more and more places. You may be wanting learn Python simply because it's the language of some technology you want to use, and this is not surprising – many of the most popular web and scientific packages in the world are written in Python.

But for many people those reasons take back-seat to something more important: Python is fun! Python's expressive, readable style, quick edit-and-run development cycle, and "batteries included" philosophy mean that you can sit down and enjoy writing code rather than fighting compilers and thorny syntax. And Python will grow with you. As your experiments become prototypes and your prototypes become products, Python makes the experience of writing software not just easier but truly enjoyable.

In the `words of Randall Munroe`, "Come join us! Programming is fun again!"

Overview

This book comprises 10 chapters (not including this one). The chapters build on one another, so unless you've already had some exposure to Python you'll need to follow them in order. We'll start with getting Python installed into your system and orienting you a bit.

We'll then cover language elements, features, idioms, and libraries, all driven by working examples that you'll be able to build along with the text. We're firm believers that you'll learn more by doing than by just reading, so we encourage you to run the examples yourself.

By the end of the book you'll know the fundamentals of the Python language. You'll also know how to use third-party libraries, and you'll know the basics of developing them yourself. We'll even cover the basics of testing so that you can ensure and maintain the quality of the code you develop.

The chapters are:

1. **Getting started:** We go through installing Python, look at some of the basic Python tools, and cover the core elements of the language and syntax.

2. **Strings and Collections:** We look at some of the fundamental complex data types: strings, byte sequences, lists, and dictionaries.

3. **Modularity:** We look at the tools Python has for structuring your code, such as functions and modules.

4. **Built-in types and the object model:** We examine Python's type system and object system in detail, and we develop a strong sense of Python's reference semantics.

5. **Exploring Built-in Collection Types:** We go into more depth on some of the Python collection types, as well as introduce a few more.

6. **Exceptions:** We learn about Python's exception-handling system and the central role that exceptions play in the language.

7. **Comprehensions, iterables, and generators:** We explore the elegant, pervasive, and powerful sequence-oriented parts of Python such as comprehensions and generator functions.

8. **Defining new types with classes:** We cover developing your own complex data types in Python using classes to support object-oriented programming.

9. **Files and Resource Management:** We look at how to work with files in Python, and we cover the tools Python has for Resource Management.

10. **Unit testing with the Python standard library:** We show you how to use Python's unittest package to produce defect-free code that works as expected.

What is Python?

It's a programming language!

So what is Python? Simply put, Python is a programming language. It was initially developed by Guido van Rossum in the late 1980's in the Netherlands. Guido continues to be actively involved in guiding the development and evolution of the language, so much so that he's been given the title "Benevolent Dictator for Life", or, more commonly, *BDFL*. Python is developed as an open-source project and is free to download and use as you wish. The non-profit `Python Software Foundation` manages Python's intellectual property, plays a strong role in promoting the language, and in some cases funds its development.

On a technical level, Python is a strongly typed language. This means that every object in the language has a definite type, and there's generally no way to circumvent that type. At the same time, Python is dynamically typed, meaning that there's no type-checking of your code prior to running it. This is in contrast to statically typed languages like C++ or Java where a compiler does a lot of type-checking for you, rejecting programs which misuse objects. Ultimately, the best description of the Python type system is that it uses *duck-typing* where an object's suitability for a context is only determined at runtime. We'll cover this in more detail in `Chapter 8`, *Defining new types with classes*.

Python is a general-purpose programming language. It's not intended for use in any particular domain or environment, but instead can be fruitfully used for a wide variety of tasks. There are, of course, some areas where it's less suitable than others – for example in extremely time-sensitive or memory-constrained environments – but for the most part Python is as flexible and adaptable as many modern programming language, and more so than most.

Python is an interpreted language. This is a bit of a misstatement, technically, because Python *is* normally compiled into a form of byte-code before it's executed. However, this compilation happens invisibly, and the experience of using Python is normally one of immediately executing code without a noticeable compilation phase. This lack of an interruption between editing and running is one of the great joys of working with Python.

The syntax of Python is designed to be clear, readable, and expressive. Unlike many popular languages, Python uses white-space to delimit code blocks, and in the process does away with reams of unnecessary parentheses while enforcing a universal layout. This means that all Python code looks alike in important ways, and you can learn to read Python very quickly. At the same time, Python's expressive syntax means that you can get a lot of meaning into a single line of code. This expressive, highly-readable code means that Python maintenance is relatively easy.

There are multiple implementations of the Python language. The original – and still by far the most common – implementation is written in C. This version is commonly referred to as *CPython*. When someone talks about "running Python", it's normally safe to assume that they are talking about CPython, and this is the implementation that we'll be using for this book.

Other implementations of Python include:

- `Jython`, written to target the Java Virtual Machine

- `IronPython`, written to target the .NET platform

- `PyPy`, written (somewhat circularly) in a language called RPython which is designed for developing dynamic languages like Python

These implementations generally trail behind CPython, which is considered to be the "standard" for the language. Much of what you will learn in this book will apply to all of these implementations.

Versions of the Python language

There are two important versions of the Python language in common use right now: Python 2 and Python 3. These two versions represent changes in some key elements of the language, and code written for one will not generally work for the other unless you take special precautions. Python 2 is older and more well-established than Python 3, but Python 3 addresses some known shortcomings in the older version. Python 3 is the definite future of Python, and you should use it if at all possible.

While there are some critical differences between Python 2 and 3, most of the fundamentals of the two version are the same. If you learn one, most of what you know transfers cleanly to the other. In this book we'll be teaching Python 3, but we'll point out important differences between the versions when necessary.

It's a standard library!

Beyond being a programming language, Python comes with a powerful and broad standard library. Part of the Python philosophy is "batteries included", meaning that you can use Python for many complex, real-world tasks out-of-the box, with no need to install third-party packages. This is not only extremely convenient, but it means that it's easier to get started learning Python by using interesting, engaging examples – something we aim for in this book!

Another great effect of the "batteries included" approach is that it means that many scripts – even non-trivial ones – can be run immediately on any Python installation. This removes a common, annoying barrier to installing software that you can face with other languages.

The standard library has a generally high level of good documentation. The APIs are well documented, and the modules often have good narrative descriptions with quick start guides, best practice information, and so forth. `The standard library documentation is always available online`, and you can also install it locally if you want to.

Since the standard library is such an important part of Python, we'll be covering parts of it throughout this book. Even so, we won't be covering more than a small fraction of it, so you're encouraged to explore it on your own.

It's a philosophy

Finally, no description of Python would be complete with mentioning that, to many people, Python represents a philosophy for writing code. Principles of clarity and readability are part of what it means to write correct or *pythonic* code. It's not always clear what *pythonic* means in all circumstances, and sometimes there may be no single correct way to write something. But the fact that the Python community is concerned about issues like simplicity, readability, and explicitness means that Python code tends to be more...well...beautiful!

Many of Python's principles are embodied in the so-called `Zen of Python`. The "zen" isn't a hard-and-fast set of rules, but rather a set of guidelines or touchstones to keep in mind when coding. When you find yourself trying to decide between several courses of action, these principles can often give you a nudge in the right direction. We'll be highlighting elements from the "Zen of Python" throughout this book.

The journey of a thousand miles...

We think Python is a great language, and we're excited to help you get started with it. By the time you get through this book, you will be able to write substantial Python programs, and you'll be able to read even more complex ones. More importantly, you'll have the foundation you need to go out and discover all of the more advanced topics in the language, and hopefully we'll get you excited enough about Python to actually do so. Python is a big language with a huge eco-system of software built in and around it, and it can be a real adventure to discover everything it has to offer.

Welcome to Python!

Though more and more projects are starting to be "primarily Python 3" or even "Python 3 only".

This book came about by circuitous means. In 2013, when we incorporated our Norway-based sofware consultancy and training business *Sixty North*, we were courted by *Pluralsight*, a publisher of online video training material, to produce Python training videos for the rapidly growing MOOC market. At the time, we had no experience of producing video training material, but we were sure we wanted to carefully structure our introductory Python content to respect certain constraints. For example, we wanted an absolute minimum of forward references since those would be very inconvenient for our viewers. We're both men of words who live by Turing Award winner Leslie Lamport's maxim *"If you're thinking without writing you only think you're thinking"*, so it was natural for us to attack video course production by first writing a script.

In short order our online video course was written, recorded, and published by *Pluralsight* as `Python Fundamentals`, to a hugely positive reception which has sustained for several years now. From the earliest days we had in mind that the script could form the basis of a book, although it's fair to say we underestimated the effort required to transform the content from a good script into a better book.

The Python Apprentice is the result of that transformation. It can be used either as a standalone Python tutorial, or as the companion volume to our video course, depending on which style of learning suits you best. *The Python Apprentice* is the first in a trilogy of three books, comprising in addition `The Python Journeyman` and `The Python Master`. The two later books correspond to our subsequent *Pluralsight* courses `Python - Beyond the Basics` and *Advanced Python* (coming soon!).

Errata and Suggestions

All the material in this book has been thoroughly reviewed and tested; nevertheless, it's inevitable that some mistakes have crept in. If you do spot a mistake, we'd really appreciate it if you'd let us know via the *Leanpub* Python Apprentice Discussion page so we can make amends and deploy a new version.

Conventions Used in This Book

Code examples in this book are shown in a lucida console text:

```
>>> def square(x):
...     return x * x
...
```

Some of our examples show code saved in files, and others — such as the one above — are from interactive Python sessions. In such interactive cases, we include the prompts from the Python session such as the triple-arrow >>> and triple-dot ... prompts. You don't need to type these arrows or dots. Similarly, for operating system shell-commands we will use a dollar prompt $ for Linux, macOS and other Unixes, or where the particular operating system is unimportant for the task at hand:

```
$ python3 words.py
```

In this case, you don't need to type the $ character.

For Windows-specific commands we will use a leading greater-than prompt:

```
> python words.py
```

Again, there's no need to type the > character. For code blocks which need to be placed in a file, rather than entered interactively, we show code without any leading prompts:

```
def write_sequence(filename, num):
    """Write Recaman's sequence to a text file."""
    with open(filename, mode='wt', encoding='utf-8') as f:
        f.writelines("{0}\n".format(r)
            for r in islice(sequence(), num + 1))
```

We've worked hard to make sure that our lines of code are short enough so that each single logical line of code corresponds to a single physical line of code in your book. However, the vagaries of publishing e-books to different devices and the very genuine need for occasional long lines of code mean we can't guarantee that lines don't wrap. What we can guarantee, however, is that where a line does wrap, the publisher has inserted a backslash character \ in the final column. You need to use your judgement to determine whether this character is legitimate part of the code or has been added by the e-book platform.

```
>>> print("This is a single line of code which is very long. Too long, in
fact, to fit on a single physical line of code in the book.")
```

If you see a backslash at the end of the line within the above quoted string, it is *not* part of the code, and should not be entered.

Occasionally, we'll number lines of code so we can refer to them easily from the narrative next. These line numbers should not be entered as part of the code. Numbered code blocks look like this:

```python
def write_grayscale(filename, pixels):
    height = len(pixels)
    width = len(pixels[0])

    with open(filename, 'wb') as bmp:
        # BMP Header
        bmp.write(b'BM')

        # The next four bytes hold the filesize as a 32-bit
        # little-endian integer. Zero placeholder for now.
        size_bookmark = bmp.tell()
        bmp.write(b'\x00\x00\x00\x00')
```

Sometimes we need to present code snippets which are incomplete. Usually this is for brevity where we are adding code to an existing block, and where we want to be clear about the block structure without repeating all existing contents of the block. In such cases we use a Python comment containing three dots # ... to indicate the elided code:

```python
class Flight:

    # ...

    def make_boarding_cards(self, card_printer):
        for passenger, seat in sorted(self._passenger_seats()):
            card_printer(passenger, seat, self.number(),
                self.aircraft_model())
```

Here it is implied that some other code already exists within the `Flight` class block before the `make_boarding_cards()` function.

Finally, within the text of the book, when we are referring to an identifier which is also a function we will use the identifier with empty parentheses, just as we did with `make_boarding_cards()` in the preceding paragraph.

Downloading the example code

You can download the example code files for this book from your account at `http://www.packtpub.com`. If you purchased this book elsewhere, you can visit `http://www.packtpub.com/support` and register to have the files e-mailed directly to you.

You can download the code files by following these steps:

1. Log in or register to our website using your e-mail address and password.
2. Hover the mouse pointer on the **SUPPORT** tab at the top.
3. Click on **Code Downloads & Errata**.
4. Enter the name of the book in the **Search** box.
5. Select the book for which you're looking to download the code files.
6. Choose from the drop-down menu where you purchased this book from.
7. Click on **Code Download**.

Once the file is downloaded, please make sure that you unzip or extract the folder using the latest version of:

- WinRAR / 7-Zip for Windows
- Zipeg / iZip / UnRarX for Mac
- 7-Zip / PeaZip for Linux

The code bundle for the book is also hosted on GitHub at `https://github.com/PacktPublishing/The-Python-Apprentice`. We also have other code bundles from our rich catalog of books and videos available at `https://github.com/PacktPublishing/`. Check them out!

Downloading the color images of this book

We also provide you with a PDF file that has color images of the screenshots/diagrams used in this book. The color images will help you better understand the changes in the output. You can download this file from `https://www.packtpub.com/sites/default/files/downloads/ThePythonApprentice_ColorImages.pdf`.

1
Getting started

In this chapter we'll cover obtaining and installing Python on your system for Windows, Ubuntu Linux, and macOS. We'll also write our first basic Python code and become a acquainted with the essentials Python programming culture, such as the Zen of Python, while never forgetting the comical origins of the name of the language.

Obtaining and installing Python 3

There are two major versions of the Python language, *Python 2* which is the widely deployed legacy language and *Python 3* which is the present and future of the language. Much Python code will work without modification between the last version of Python 2 (which is *Python 2.7* (`https://www.python.org/download/releases/2.7/`)) and recent versions of *Python 3*, such as *Python 3.5* (`https://www.python.org/download/releases/3.5.1/`). However, there are some key differences between the major versions, and in a strict sense the languages are incompatible. We'll be using Python 3.5 for this book, but we'll point out key differences with Python 2 as we go. It's also very likely that, this being a book on Python fundamentals, everything we present will apply to future versions of Python 3, so don't be afraid to try those as they become available.

Before we can start programming in Python we need to get hold of a Python environment. Python is a highly portable language and is available on all major operating systems. You will be able to work through this book on Windows, Mac or Linux, and the only major section where we diverge into platform specifics is coming right up — as we install Python 3. As we cover the three platforms, feel free to skip over the sections which aren't relevant for you.

Windows

The following are the steps to be performed for Windows platform:

1. For Windows you need to visit the `official Python website`, and then head to the **Downloads** page by clicking the link on the left. For Windows you should choose one of the MSI installers depending on whether you're running on a 32- or 64-bit platform.

2. Download and run the installer.

3. In the installer, decide whether you only want to install Python for yourself, or for all users of your machine.

4. Choose a location for the Python distribution. The default will be in `C:\Python35` in the root of the `C:` drive. We don't recommended installing Python into Program Files because the virtualized file store used to isolate applications from each other in Windows Vista and later can interfere with easily installing third-party Python packages.

5. On the **Customize Python** page of the wizard we recommend keeping the defaults, which use less than 40 MB of space.

6. In addition to installing the Python runtime and standard library, the installer will register various file types, such as `*.py` files, with the Python interpreter.

7. Once Python has been installed, you'll need to add Python to your system PATH environment variable. To do this, from the Control Panel choose **System and Security**, then **System**. Another way to get here easily is to hold down your Windows key and press the *Break* key on your keyboard. Using the task pane on the left choose **Advanced System Settings** to open the **Advanced** tab of the **System Properties** dialog. Click **Environment variables** to open the child dialog.

8. If you have Administrator privileges you should be able to add the paths `C:\Python35` and `C:\Python35\Scripts` to the semicolon separated list of entries associated with the PATH system variable. If not, you should be able to create, or append to, a PATH variable specific to your user containing the same value.

9. Now open a *new* console window — either Powershell or cmd will work fine — and verify that you can run python from the command line:

```
> python
Python 3.5.0 (v3.5.0:374f501f4567, Sep 13 2015, 02:27:37) [MSC v.1900 64
bit (AMD64)] on win32
Type "help", "copyright", "credits" or "license" for more information.
>>>
```

Welcome to Python!

The triple arrow prompt shows you that Python is waiting for your input.

At this point you might want to skip forward whilst we show how to install Python on Mac and Linux.

macOS

1. For macOS you need to visit the official Python website at `http://python.org`. Head to the `Download` page by clicking the link on the left. On the `Download` page, find the macOS installer matching your version of macOS and click the link to download it.

2. A DMG Disk Image file downloads, which you open from your Downloads stack or from the Finder.

3. In the Finder window that opens you will see the file `Python.mpkg` multipackage installer file. Use the "secondary" click `action` to open the context menu for that file. From that menu, select **Open**.

4. On some versions of macOS you will now be told that the file is from an unidentified developer. Press the **Open** button on this dialog to continue with the installation.

5. You are now in the Python installer program. Follow the directions, clicking through the wizard.

6. There is no need to customize the install, and you should keep the standard settings. When it's available, click the `Install` button to install Python. You may be asked for your password to authorize the installation. Once the installation completes click `Close` to close the installer.

7. Now that Python 3 is installed, open a terminal window and verify that you can run Python 3 from the command line:

```
> python
Python 3.5.0 (default, Nov 3 2015, 13:17:02)
[GCC 4.2.1 Compatible Apple LLVM 6.1.0 (clang-602.0.53)] on darwin
Type "help", "copyright", "credits" or "license" for more information.
>>>
```

Welcome to Python!

The triple arrow prompt shows that Python is waiting for your input.

Linux

1. To install Python on Linux you will want to use your system's package manager. We'll show how to install Python on a recent version of Ubuntu, but the process is very similar on most other modern Linux distributions.

2. On Ubuntu, first start the Ubuntu Software Center. This can usually be run by clicking on it's icon in the launcher. Alternatively, you can run it from the dashboard by searching on Ubuntu Software Center and clicking the selection.

3. Once you're in the software center, enter the search term *python 3.5* in the search bar in the upper right-hand corner and press return.

4. One of the results you'll get will say *Python (v3.5)* with *Python Interpreter (v3.5)* in smaller type beneath it. Select this entry and click the `Install` button that appears.

5. You may need to enter your password to install the software at this point.

6. You should now see a progress indicator appear, which will disappear when installation is complete.

7. Open a terminal (using *Ctrl+Alt+T*) and verify that you can run Python 3.5 from the command line:

```
$ python3.5
Python 3.5.0+ (default, Oct 11 2015, 09:05:38)
[GCC 5.2.1 20151010] on linux
Type "help", "copyright", "credits" or "license" for more information.
>>>
```

Welcome to Python!

The triple arrow prompt shows you that Python is waiting for your input.

Starting Python command line REPL

Now that Python is installed and running, you can immediately start using it. This is a good way to get to know the language, as well as a useful tool for experimentation and quick testing during normal development.

This Python command line environment is a *Read-Eval-Print-Loop*. Python will **READ** whatever input we type in, **EVAL**uate it, **PRINT** the result and then **LOOP** back to the beginning. You'll often hear it referred to simply as the "REPL".

When started, the REPL will print some information about the version of Python you're running, and then it will give you a triple-arrow prompt. This prompt tells you that Python is waiting for you to type something.

Within an interactive Python session you can enter fragments of Python programs and see instant results. Let's start with some simple arithmetic:

```
>>> 2 + 2
4
>>> 6 * 7
42
```

As you can see, Python reads our input, evaluates it, prints the result, and loops around to do the same again.

We can assign to variables in the REPL:

```
>>> x = 5
```

Print their contents simply by typing their name:

```
>>> x
5
```

Refer to them in expressions:

```
>>> 3 * x
15
```

Within the REPL you can use the special underscore variable to refer to the most recently printed value, this being one of very few obscure shortcuts in Python:

```
>>> _
15
```

Or you can use the special underscore variable in an expression:

```
>>> _ * 2
30
```

Remember that this useful trick only works at the REPL; the underscore doesn't have any special behavior in Python scripts or programs.

Notice that not all statements have a return value. When we assigned 5 to x there was no return value, only the side-effect of bringing the variable x into being. Other statements have more visible side-effects.

Try the following command:

```
>>> print('Hello, Python')
Hello, Python
```

You'll see that Python immediately evaluates and executes this command, printing the string Hello, Python and returning you to another prompt. It's important to understand that the response here is not the result of the expression evaluated and displayed by the REPL, but is a side-effect of the print() function.

As an aside, print is one of the biggest differences between Python 2 and Python 3. In Python 3, the parentheses are required, whereas is Python 2 they were not. This is because in Python 3, print() is a function call. More on functions later.

Leaving the REPL

At this point, we should show you how to exit the REPL and get back to your system shell prompt. We do this by sending the *end-of-file* control character to Python, although unfortunately the means of sending this character varies across platforms.

Windows

If you're on Windows, press *Ctrl+Z* to exit.

Unix

If you're on Mac or Linux, press *Ctrl+D* to exit.

If you regularly switch between platforms and you accidentally press `Ctrl+Z` on a Unix-a-like system, you will inadvertently suspend the Python interpreter and return to your operating system shell. To reactivate Python by making it a foreground process again, simply run the `fg` command:

```
$ fg
```

Now press *Enter* and couple of times to get the triple arrow Python prompt back:

```
>>>
```

Code structure and significant indentation

Start your Python 3 interpreter:

```
> python
```

If on Windows or:

```
$ python3
```

On Mac or Linux.

The control flow structures of Python, such as `for`-loops, `while`-loops, and `if`-statements, are all introduced by statements which are terminated by a colon, indicating that the body of the construct is to follow. For example, `for`-loops require a body, so if you enter:

```
>>> for i in range(5):
...
```

Python will present you with a prompt of three dots to request that you provide the body. One distinctive (and sometimes controversial) aspect of Python is that leading whitespace is syntactically significant.

What this means is that Python uses indentation levels, rather the braces used by other languages, to demarcate code blocks.By convention, contemporary Python code is indented by four spaces for each level.

So when Python present us with the three dot prompt, we provide those four spaces and a statement to form the body of the loop:

```
...      x = i * 10
```

Our loop body will contain a second statement, so after pressing Return at the next three dot prompt we'll enter another four spaces followed by a call to the built-in `print()` function:

```
...      print(x)
```

To terminate our block, we must enter a blank line into the REPL:

```
...
```

With the block complete, Python executes the pending code, printing out the multiples of 10 less than 50:

```
0
10
20
30
40
```

Looking at at screenful of Python code, we can see how the indentation clearly matches —
and in fact *must* match — the structure of the program which is as follows:

```
"""Class model for aircraft flights."""


class Flight:
    """A flight with a particular aircraft."""

    def __init__(self, number, aircraft):
        if not number[:2].isalpha():
            raise ValueError("No airline code in '{}'".format(number))

        if not number[:2].isupper():
            raise ValueError("Invalid airline code '{}'".format(number))

        if not (number[2:].isdigit() and int(number[2:]) <= 9999):
            raise ValueError("Invalid route number '{}'".format(number))

        self._number = number
        self._aircraft = aircraft

        rows, seats = self._aircraft.seating_plan()
        self._seating = [None] + [ {letter:None for letter in seats} for _ in rows ]


    def _passenger_seats(self):
        """An iterable series of passenger seating allocations."""
        row_numbers, seat_letters = self._aircraft.seating_plan()
        for row in row_numbers:
            for letter in seat_letters:
                passenger = self._seating[row][letter]
                if passenger is not None:
                    yield (passenger, "{}{}".format(row, letter))
```

Figure 1.1: Whitespaces in the code

Even if we replace the code by gray lines, the structure of the program is clear as shown in the following image:

Figure 2.2 : Replaced code with grey lines

Each statement terminated by a colon starts a new line and introduces an additional level of indentation, which continues until a dedent restores the indentation to a previous level. Each level of indent is typically four spaces, although we'll cover the rules in more detail in a moment.

Python's approach to significant whitespace has three great advantages:

1. It forces developers to use a single level of indentation in a code-block. This is generally considered good practice in any language because it makes code much more readable.
2. Code with significant whitespace doesn't need to be cluttered with unnecessary braces, and you never need to have code-standard debates about where the braces should go. All code-blocks in Python code are easily identifiable and everyone writes them the same way.

3. Significant whitespace requires that a consistent interpretation must be given to the structure of the code by the author, the Python runtime system and future maintainers who need to read the code. As a result you can never have code that contains a block from Python's point of view, but which doesn't look like it contains a block from a cursory human perspective.

The rules for Python indentation can seem complex, but they are quite straightforward in practice:

- The whitespace you use can be either spaces or tabs. The general consensus is that *spaces are preferable to tabs*, and *four spaces has become a standard in the Python community*.

- One essential rule is *NEVER* to mix spaces and tabs. The Python interpreter will complain, and your colleagues will hunt you down.

- You are allowed to use different amounts of indentation at different times if you wish. The essential rule is that *consecutive lines of code at the same indentation level are considered to be part of the same code block*.

- There are some exceptions to these rules, but they almost always have to do with improving code readability in other ways, for example by breaking up necessarily long statements over multiple lines.

This rigorous approach to code formatting is *Programming as Guido intended it* or, perhaps more appropriately, as Guido *indented* it! A philosophy of placing a high value on code qualities such as readability gets to the very heart of Python culture, something we'll take a short break to explore now.

Python culture

Many programming languages are at the center of a cultural movement. They have their own communities, values, practices, and philosophy, and Python is no exception. The development of the Python language itself is managed through a series of documents called *Python Enhancement Proposals*, or *PEPs*. One of the PEPs, called PEP 8, explains how you should format your code, and we follow its guidelines throughout this book. For example, it is PEP 8 which recommends that we use four spaces for indentation in new Python code.

Another of these PEPs, called PEP 20 is called "The Zen of Python". It refers to 20 aphorisms describing the guiding principles of Python, only 19 of which have been written down. Conveniently, the Zen of Python is never further away than the nearest Python interpreter, as it can always be accessed from the REPL by typing:

```
>>> import this
The Zen of Python, by Tim Peters
Beautiful is better than ugly.
Explicit is better than implicit.
Simple is better than complex.
Complex is better than complicated.
Flat is better than nested.
Sparse is better than dense.
Readability counts.
Special cases aren't special enough to break the rules.
Although practicality beats purity.
Errors should never pass silently.
Unless explicitly silenced.
In the face of ambiguity, refuse the temptation to guess.
There should be one-- and preferably only one --obvious way to do it.
Although that way may not be obvious at first unless you're Dutch.
Now is better than never.
Although never is often better than *right* now.
If the implementation is hard to explain, it's a bad idea.
If the implementation is easy to explain, it may be a good idea.
Namespaces are one honking great idea -- let's do more of those!
```

Throughout this book we'll be highlighting particular nuggets of wisdom from the Zen of Python in *moments of zen* to understand how they apply to what we have learned. As we've just introduced Python significant indentation, this is a good time for our first *moment of zen*:

Figure 1.1: Moment of zen

In time, you'll come to appreciate Python's significant whitespace for the elegance it brings to *your* code, and the ease with which you can read *other's*.

Importing standard library modules

As mentioned earlier, Python comes with an extensive standard library, an aspect of Python that is often referred to as *batteries included*. The standard library is structured as *modules*, a topic we'll discuss in depth later. What's important at this stage is to know that you gain access to standard library modules by using the import keyword.

The basic form of importing a module is simply the import keyword followed by a space and the name of the module. For example, lets see how we can use the standard library's math module to compute square roots. At the triple-arrow prompt we type the following command:

```
>>> import math
```

Since import is a statement which doesn't return a value, Python doesn't print anything if the import succeeds, and we're immediately returned to the prompt. We can access the contents of the imported module by using the name of the module, followed by a dot, followed by the name of the attribute in the module that you need. Like many object oriented languages the dot operator is used to drill down into object structures. Being expert Pythonistas, we have inside knowledge that the math module contains a function called sqrt(). Let's try to use the following command:

```
>>> math.sqrt(81)
9.0
```

Getting help()

But how can we find out what other functions are available in the math module?

The REPL has a special function help() which can retrieve any embedded documentation from objects for which documentation has been provided, such as standard library modules.

To get help, simply type help at the prompt:

```
>>> help
Type help() for interactive help, or help(object) for help about object.
```

We'll leave you to explore the first form — for interactive help — in your own time. Here we'll go for the second option and pass the math module as the object for which we want help:

```
>>> help(math)
Help on module math:

NAME
 math

MODULE REFERENCE
        http://docs.python.org/3.3/library/math

    The following documentation is automatically generated from the
    Python source files. It may be incomplete, incorrect or include
    features that are considered implementation detail and may vary
    between Python implementations. When in doubt, consult the module
    reference at the location listed above.

DESCRIPTION
 This module is always available. It provides access to the
 mathematical functions defined by the C standard.

FUNCTIONS
 acos(...)
 acos(x)

    Return the arc cosine (measured in radians) of x.
```

You can use the space-bar to page through the help, and if you're on Mac or Linux use the arrow keys to scroll up and down.

Browsing through the functions, you'll can see that there's a math function, factorial, for computing factorials. Press *Q* to exit the help browser, and return us to the Python REPL.

Now practice using `help()` to request specific help on the factorial function:

```
>>> help(math.factorial)
Help on built-in function factorial in module math:

factorial(...)
 factorial(x) -> Integral

    Find x!. Raise a ValueError if x is negative or non-integral.
```

Press *Q* to return to the REPL.

Let's use `factorial()` a bit. The function accepts an integer argument and return an integer value:

```
>>> math.factorial(5)
120
>>> math.factorial(6)
720
```

Notice how we need to qualify the function name with the module namespace. This is generally good practice, as it makes it abundantly clear where the function is coming from. That said, it can result in code that is excessively verbose.

Counting fruit with math.factorial()

Let's use factorials to compute how many ways there are to draw three fruit from a set of five fruit using some math we learned in school:

```
>>> n = 5
>>> k = 3
>>> math.factorial(n) / (math.factorial(k) * math.factorial(n - k))
10.0
```

This simple expression is quite verbose with all those references to the `math` module. The Python import statement has an alternative form that allows us to bring a specific function from a module into the current namespace by using the from keyword:

```
>>> from math import factorial
>>> factorial(n) / (factorial(k) * factorial(n - k))
10.0
```

This is a good improvement, but is still a little long-winded for such a simple expression.

A third form of the `import` statement allows us to rename the imported function. This can be useful for reasons of readability, or to avoid a namespace clash. Useful as it is, though, we recommend that this feature be used infrequently and judiciously:

```
>>> from math import factorial as fac
>>> fac(n) / (fac(k) * fac(n - k))
10.0
```

Different types of numbers

Remember that when we used `factorial()` alone it returned an integer. But our more complex expression above for calculating combinations is producing a floating point number. This is because we've used /, Python's floating-point division operator. Since we know our operation will only ever return integral results, we can improve our expression by using //, Python's integer division operator:

```
>>> from math import factorial as fac
>>> fac(n) // (fac(k) * fac(n - k))
10
```

What's notable is that many other programming languages would fail on the above expression for even moderate values of n. In most programming languages, regular garden variety signed integers can only store values less than 2×10^{31}:

```
>>> 2**31 - 1
2147483647
```

However, factorials grow so fast that the largest factorial you can fit into a 32-bit signed integer is 12! since 13! is too large:

```
>>> fac(13)
6227020800
```

In most widely used programming languages you would need either more complex code or more sophisticated mathematics merely to compute how many ways there are to draw 3 fruits from a set of 13!. Python encounters no such problems and can compute with arbitrarily large integers, limited only by the memory in your computer. To demonstrate this further, let's try the larger problem of computing how many different pairs of fruit we can pick from 100 different fruits (assuming we can lay our hands on so many fruit!):

```
>>> n = 100
>>> k = 2
>>> fac(n) // (fac(k) * fac(n - k))
4950
```

Just to emphasize how large the size of the first term of that expression is, calculate 100! on it's own:

```
>>> fac(n)
93326215443944152681699238856266700490715968264381621468592963895217599993229
915608941463976156518286253697920827223758251185210916864000000000000000000
00000000
```

This number is vastly larger even than the number of atoms in the known universe, with an awful lot of digits. If, like us, you're curious to know exactly how many digits, we can convert our integer to a text string and count the number of characters in it like this:

```
>>> len(str(fac(n)))
158
```

That's definitely a lot of digits. And a lot of fruit. It also starts to show how Python's different data types — in this case, integers, floating point numbers, and text strings — work together in natural ways. In the next section we'll build on this experience and look at integers, strings, and other built-in types in more detail.

Scalar data types: integers, floats, None and bool

Python comes with a number of built-in datatypes. These include primitive scalar types like integers as well as collection types like dictionaries. These built-in types are powerful enough to be used alone for many programming needs, and they can be used as building blocks for creating more complex data types.

The basic built-in scalar types we'll look at are:

- int — signed, unlimited precision integers
- float — IEEE 754 floating-point numbers
- None — a special, singular null value
- bool — true/false boolean values

For now we'll just be looking at their basic details, showing their literal forms and how to create them.

int

We've already seen Python integers in action quite a lot. Python integers are signed and have, for all practical purposes, unlimited precision. This means that there is no pre-defined limit to the magnitude of the values they can hold.

Integer literals in Python are typically specified in decimal:

```
>>> 10
10
```

They may also be specified in binary with a 0b prefix:

```
>>> 0b10
2
```

There may also be a octal, with a 0o prefix:

```
>>> 0o10
8
```

If its a hexadecimal we use the 0x prefix:

```
>>> 0x10
16
```

We can also construct integers by a call to the int constructor which can convert from other numeric types, such as floats, to integers:

```
>>> int(3.5)
3
```

Note that, when using the int constructor, the rounding is always towards zero:

```
>>> int(-3.5)
-3
>>> int(3.5)
3
```

We can also convert strings to integers as follows:

```
>>> int("496")
496
```

Be aware, though, that Python will throw an exception (much more on those later!) if the string doesn't represent an integer.

You can even supply an optional number base when converting from a string. For example, to convert from base 3 simply pass 3 as the second argument to the constructor:

```
>>> int("10000", 3)
81
```

float

Floating point numbers are supported in Python by the float type. Python floats are implemented as `IEEE-754 double-precision floating point numbers` with 53 bits of binary precision. This is equivalent to between 15 and 16 significant digits in decimal.

Any literal number containing a decimal point is interpreted by Python as a `float`:

```
3.125
```

Scientific notation can be used, so for large numbers — such as 3×10^8, the approximate speed of light in metres per second — we can write:

```
>>> 3e8
300000000.0
```

and for small numbers like Planck's constant 1.616×10^{-35} we can enter:

```
>>> 1.616e-35
1.616e-35
```

Notice how Python automatically switches the display representation to the most readable form.

As for integers, we can convert to floats from other numeric or string types using the `float` constructor. For example, the constructor can accept an `int`:

```
>>> float(7)
7.0
```

The `float` constructor can also accept a string as follows:

```
>>> float("1.618")
1.618
```

Special floating point values

By passing certain strings to the float constructor, we can create the special floating point value NaN (short for **N**ot **a N**umber) and also positive and negative infinity:

```
>>> float("nan")
nan
>>> float("inf")
inf
>>> float("-inf")
-inf
```

Promotion to float

The result of any calculation involving int and float is promoted to a float:

```
>>> 3.0 + 1
4.0
```

You can read more about Python's number types in the Python documentation.

None

Python has a special null value called None, spelled with a capital N. None is frequently used to represent the absence of a value. The Python REPL never prints None results, so typing None into the REPL has no effect:

```
>>> None
>>>
```

The null value None can be bound to variable names just like any other object:

```
>>> a = None
```

and we can test whether an object is None by using Python's is operator:

```
>>> a is None
True
```

We can see here that the response is True, which brings us conveniently on to the bool type.

bool

The `bool` type represents logical states and plays an important role in several of Python's control flow structures, as we'll see shortly. As you would expect there are two `bool` values, `True` and `False`, both spelled with initial capitals:

```
>>> True
True
>>> False
False
```

There is also a `bool` constructor which can be used to convert from other types to `bool`. Let's look at how it works. For `int`s, zero is considered *falsey* and all other values *truthy*:

```
>>> bool(0)
False
>>> bool(42)
True
>>> bool(-1)
True
```

We see the same behavior with floats where only zero is considered *falsey*:

```
>>> bool(0.0)
False
>>> bool(0.207)
True
>>> bool(-1.117)
True
>>> bool(float("NaN"))
True
```

When converting from collections, such as strings or lists, only empty collections are treated as falsey. When converting from lists — which we'll look at shortly — we see that only the empty list (shown here in it's literal form of `[]`) evaluates to `False`:

```
>>> bool([])
False
>>> bool([1, 5, 9])
True
```

Similarly, with strings only the empty string, `""`, evaluates to `False` when passed to `bool`:

```
>>> bool("")
False
>>> bool("Spam")
True
```

In particular, you cannot use the bool constructor to convert from string representations of `True` and `False`:

```
>>> bool("False")
True
```

Since the string `False` is not empty, it will evaluate to `True`. These conversions to `bool` are important because they are widely used in Python `if`-statements and `while`-loops which accept `bool` values in their condition.

Relational operators

Boolean values are commonly produced by Python's relational operators which can be used for comparing objects. Two of the most widely used relational operators are Python's equality and inequality tests, which actually test for equivalence or inequivalence of values. That is, two objects are *equivalent* if one could use used in place of the other. We'll learn more about the notion of object equivalence later in the book. For now, we'll compare simple integers.

Let's start by assigning — or binding — a value to a variable g:

```
>>> g = 20
```

We test for equality with == as shown in the following command:

```
>>> g == 20
True
>>> g == 13
False
```

For inequality we use !=:

```
>>> g != 20
False
>>> g != 13
True
```

Rich comparison operators

We can also compare the order of quantities using the rich comparison operators. Use < to determine if the first argument is less than the second:

```
>>> g < 30
True
```

Likewise, use > to determine if the first is greater than the second:

```
>>> g > 30
False
```

You can test less-than or equal-to with <=:

```
>>> g <= 20
True
```

We can use the greater-than or equal-to with >= ,shown as follows:

```
>>> g >= 20
True
```

If you have experience with relational operators from other languages, then Python's operators are probably not surprising at all. Just remember that these operators are comparing equivalence, not identity, a distinction we'll cover in detail in coming chapters.

Control flow: if-statements and while-loops

Now that we've examined some basic built-in types, let's look at two important control flow structures which depend on conversions to the `bool` type: `if`-statements and `while`-loops.

Conditional control flow: The if-statement

Conditional statements allow us to branch execution based on the value of an expression. The form of the statement is the `if` keyword, followed by an expression, terminated by a colon to introduce a new block. Let's try this at the REPL:

```
>>> if True:
```

Remembering to indent four spaces within the block, we add some code to be executed if the condition is `True`, followed by a blank line to terminate the block:

```
...        print("It's true!")
...
It's true!
```

At this point the block will execute, because self-evidently the condition is True. Conversely, if the condition is `False`, the code in the block does not execute:

```
>>> if False:
...        print("It's true!")
...
>>>
```

The expression used with the `if`-statement will be converted to a `bool` just as if the `bool()` constructor had been used, so:

```
>>> if bool("eggs"):
...        print("Yes please!")
...
Yes please!
```

If the value is exactly equivalent to something, we then use the `if` command as follows:

```
>>> if "eggs":
...        print("Yes please!")
...
Yes please!
```

Thanks to this useful shorthand, explicit conversion to `bool` using the `bool` constructor is rarely used in Python.

if...else

The `if`-statement supports an optional `else` clause which goes in a block introduced by the `else` keyword (followed by a colon) which is indented to the same level as the `if` keyword. Let's start by creating (but not finishing) an `if`-block:

```
>>> h = 42
>>> if h > 50:
...        print("Greater than 50")
```

To start the `else` block in this case, we just omit the indentation after the three dots:

```
... else:
...     print("50 or smaller")
...
50 or smaller
```

if...elif...else

For multiple conditions you might be tempted to do something like this:

```
>>> if h > 50:
...     print("Greater than 50")
... else:
...     if h < 20:
...         print("Less than 20")
...     else:
...         print("Between 20 and 50")
...
Between 20 and 50
```

Whenever you find yourself with an `else`-block containing a nested `if` statement, like this, you should consider using Python's `elif` keyword which is a combined `else-if`.

As the Zen of Python reminds us, *Flat is better than nested*:

```
>>> if h > 50:
...     print("Greater than 50")
... elif h < 20:
...     print("Less than 20")
... else:
...     print("Between 20 and 50")
...
Between 20 and 50
```

This version is altogether easier to read.

Conditional repetition: the while-loop

Python has two types of loop: `for`-loops and `while`-loops. We've already briefly encountered `for`-loops back when we introduced significant whitespace, and we'll return to them soon, but right now we'll cover `while`-loops.

The `While`-loops in Python are introduced by the while keyword, which is followed by a boolean expression. As with the condition for `if`-statements, the expression is implicitly converted to a boolean value as if it has been passed to the `bool()` constructor. The `while` statement is terminated by a colon because it introduces a new block.

Let's write a loop at the REPL which counts down from five to one. We'll initialize a counter variable called c to five, and keep looping until we reach zero. Another new language feature here is the use of an augmented-assignment operator, `-=`, to subtract one from the value of the counter on each iteration. Similar augmented assignment operators exist for the other basic math operations such as addition and multiplication:

```
>>> c = 5
>>> while c != 0:
...     print(c)
...     c -= 1
...
5
4
3
2
1
```

Because the condition — or predicate — will be implicitly converted to `bool`, just as if a call to the `bool()` constructor were present, we could replace the above code with the following version:

```
>>> c = 5
>>> while c:
...     print(c)
...     c -= 1
...
5
4
3
2
1
```

This works because the conversion of the integer value of c to `bool` results in `True` until we get to zero which converts to `False`. That said, to use this short form in this case might be described as un-Pythonic, because, referring back to the Zen of Python, explicit is better than implicit. We place higher value of the readability of the first form over the concision of the second form.

The `while`-loops are often used in Python where an infinite loop is required. We achieve this simply by passing `True` as the predicate expression to the while construct:

```
>>> while True:
...     print("Looping!")
...
Looping!
Looping!
Looping!
Looping!
Looping!
Looping!
Looping!
Looping!
```

Now you're probably wondering how we get out of this loop and regain control of our REPL! Simply press *Ctrl+C*:

```
Looping!
Looping!
Looping!
Looping!
Looping!
Looping!^C
Traceback (most recent call last):
File "<stdin>", line 2, in <module>
KeyboardInterrupt
>>>
```

Python intercepts the key stroke and raises a special exception which terminates the loop. We'll be talking much more about what exceptions are, and how to use them, later in Chapter 6, *Exceptions*.

Exiting loops with break

Many programming languages support a loop construct which places the predicate test at the end of the loop rather than at the beginning. For example, C, C++, C# and Java support the do-while construct. Other languages have repeat-until loops instead or as well. This is not the case in Python, where the idiom is to use while True together with an early exit, facilitated by the break statement.

The break statement jumps out of the loop — and only the innermost loop if severals loops have been nested — continuing execution immediately after the loop body.

Let's look at an example of break, introducing a few other Python features along the way, and examine it line-by-line:

```
>>> while True:
...         response = input()
...         if int(response) % 7 == 0:
...             break
...
```

We start with a while True: for an infinite loop. On the first statement of the while block we use the built-in input() function to request a string from the user. We assign that string to a variable called response.

We now use an if-statement to test whether the value provided is divisible by seven. We convert the response string to an integer using the int() constructor and then use the modulus operator, %, to divide by seven and give the remainder. If the remainder is equal to zero, the response was divisible by seven, and we enter the body of the if-block.

Within the if-block, now two levels of indentation deep, we start with eight spaces and use the break keyword. break terminates the inner-most loop — in this case the while-loop — and causes execution to jump to the first statement after the loop.

Here, that *statement* is the end of the program. We enter a blank line at the three dots prompt to close both the if-block and the while-block. Our loop will start executing, and will pause at the call to input() waiting for us to enter a number. Let's try a few:

```
12
67
34
28
>>>
```

As soon as we enter a number divisible by seven the predicate becomes True, we enter the `if`-block, and then we literally `break` out of the loop to the end of program, returning us to the REPL prompt.

Summary

- Starting out with Python
    - Obtaining and installing Python 3

    - Starting the Read-Eval-Print-Loop or REPL

    - Simple arithmetic

    - Creating variables by binding objects to names

    - Printing with the built-in `print()` function

    - Exiting the REPL with *Ctrl+Z* (Windows) or *Ctrl+D* (Unix)

- Being Pythonic

    - Significant indentation

    - PEP 8 - The Style Guide for Python Code

    - PEP 20 - The Zen of Python

- Importing modules with the import statement in various forms

- Finding and browsing `help()`

- Basic types and control flow

    - `ints`, `floats`, `None`, and `bool`, plus conversions between them

    - Relational operators for equality and ordering tests

- The `if`-statements with else and `elif` blocks

- The `while`-loops with implicit conversion to bool

- Interrupting infinite loops with *Ctrl+C*

- Breaking out of loops with break

- Requesting text from the user with `input ()`

- Augmented assignment operators

2

Strings and Collections

Python includes a rich selection of built-in collection types which are often completely sufficient for even quite intricate programs without resorting to defining our own data structures. We'll give an overview of some of these fundamental collection types now – enough to allow us to write some interesting code – although we'll be revisiting each of these collection types, together with a few additional ones, in later chapters.

Let's start with these types:

- `str` – immutable strings of Unicode code points
- `bytes` – immutable strings of bytes
- `list` – mutable sequences of objects
- `dict` – mutable mappings from keys to values

Along the way, we'll also cover Python's `for`-loops.

str – an immutable sequence of Unicode code points

Strings in Python have the datatype `str` and we've been using them extensively already. A string is a sequence of Unicode code-points, and for the most part you can think of code-points as being like characters, although they aren't strictly equivalent. The sequence of code-points in a Python string is immutable, so once you've constructed a string, you can't modify its contents.

The difference between code points, letters, characters, and glyphs can be confusing. Let's try to clarify with an example: The Greek capital letter Σ (sigma), which is of course used widely in the writing of Greek text, is also used by mathematicians to signify summation of a series. These two uses of the letter sigma are represented by distinct Unicode characters called GREEK CAPITAL LETTER SIGMA and N-ARY SUMMATION respectively. Typically, where the same letter is used to convey different information, a different Unicode character is used. Another example would be the GREEK CAPITAL LETTER OMEGA and OHM SIGN, the symbol for the unit of electrical resistance. A code point is any one member of the set of of numerical values which make up the code space. Each character is associated with a single code point, so GREEK CAPITAL LETTER SIGMA is assigned to U+03A3 and N-ARY SUMMATION is assigned to U+2211. As we have done here, code points are often written in U+nnnn form where nnnn is a four, five or six digit hexadecimal number. Not all code points have yet been allocated to characters. For example, U+0378 is an unassigned code point, and there's nothing to stop you including this code point in a Python `str` using the `\u0378` escape sequence; hence, `str` really is a sequence of code points and not a sequence of characters. Although the term in not used in the context of Python, for completeness we feel we should point out that a glyph is the visual representation of a character. Different characters, such as GREEK CAPITAL LETTER SIGMA and N-ARY SUMMATION may be rendered using the same glyph, or indeed different glyphs, depending on the font in use.

String quoting styles

Literal strings in Python are delimited by quotes:

```
>>> 'This is a string'
```

You can use single quotation marks, as we have above. Or you can use double quotation marks, as shown below:

```
>>> "This is also a string"
```

You must, however, be consistent. For example, you can't use a double quotation mark paired with a single quotation mark:

```
>>> "inconsistent'
  File "<stdin>", line 1
    "inconsistent'
                 ^
SyntaxError: EOL while scanning string literal
```

Supporting both quoting styles allows you to easily incorporate the other quote character into the literal string without resorting to ugly escape character gymnastics:

```
>>> "It's a good thing."
"It's a good thing."
>>> '"Yes!", he said, "I agree!"'
'"Yes!", he said, "I agree!"'
```

Notice that the REPL exploits the same quoting flexibility when echoing the strings back to us.

Moment of zen

The text in the following image Moment of zen: Practicality beats purity – Beautiful text strings, Rendered in literal form. Simple elegance:

Figure 2.1: Moment of zen: Practicality beats purity Moment of zen

At first sight support for both quoting styles seems to violate an important principle of Pythonic style. From the Zen of Python:

> There should be one – and preferably only one – obvious way to do it.

In this case, however, another aphorism from the same source takes precedence:

> **Practicality beats purity**

The utility of supporting two quoting styles is valued more highly than the alternative:a single quoting style combined with more frequent use of ugly escape sequences, which we'll encounter shortly.

Concatenation of adjacent strings

Adjacent literal strings are concatenated by the Python compiler into a single string:

```
>>> "first" "second"
'firstsecond'
```

Although at first this seems rather pointless, it can be useful for nicely formatting code as we'll see later.

Multiline strings and newlines

If you want a literal string containing newlines, you have two options:

- Use multiline strings,
- Use escape sequences.

First, let's look at multiline strings. Multiline strings are delimited by three quote characters rather than one. Here's an example using three double-quotes:

```
>>> """This is
... a multiline
... string"""
'This is\na multiline\nstring'
```

Notice how, when the string is echoed back to us, the newlines are represented by the \n escape sequence.

We can also use three single-quotes:

```
>>> '''So
... is
... this.'''
'So\nis\nthis.'
```

As an alternative to using multiline quoting, we can just embed the control characters ourselves:

```
>>> m = 'This string\nspans mutiple\nlines'
>>> m
'This string\nspans mutiple\nlines'
```

To get a better sense of what we're representing in this case, we can use the built-in print() function to see the string:

```
>>> print(m)
This string
spans mutiple
lines
```

If you're working on Windows, you might be thinking that newlines should be represented by the carriage-return, newline couplet \r\n rather than just the newline character, \n. There's no need to do that with Python, since Python 3 has a feature called *universal newline support* which translates from the simple \n to the native newline sequence for your platform on input and output. You can read more about Universal Newline Support in PEP 278.

We can use the escape sequences for other purposes, too, such as incorporating tabs with \t or using quote characters inside strings with \:

```
>>> "This is a \" in a string"
'This is a " in a string'
```

The other way around:

```
>>> 'This is a \' in a string'
"This is a ' in a string"
```

As you can see, Python is smarter than we are at using the most convenient quote delimiters, although Python will also resort to escape sequences when we use both types of quotes in a string:

```
>>> 'This is a \" and a \' in a string'
'This is a " and a \' in a string'
```

Because the backslash has special meaning, to place a backslash in a string we must escape the backslash with itself:

```
>>> k = 'A \\ in a string'
'A \\ in a string'
```

To reassure ourselves that there really is only one backslash in that string, we can print() it:

```
>>> print(k)
A \ in a string
```

You can read more about `escape sequences in the Python documentation`.

Raw strings

Sometimes, particularly when dealing with strings such as Windows filesystem paths or regular expression patterns which use backslashes extensively, the requirement to double-up on backslashes can be ugly and error prone. Python comes to the rescue with its raw strings. Raw strings don't support any escape sequences and are very much what-you-see-is-what-you-get. To create a raw string, precede the opening quote with a lower-case r:

```
>>> path = r'C:\Users\Merlin\Documents\Spells'
>>>
>>> path
'C:\\Users\\Merlin\\Documents\\Spells'
>>> print(path)
C:\Users\Merlin\Documents\Spells
```

> Although it's common to store and manipulate filesystem paths as strings, for anything but the most straightforward path handling, you should investigate the Python Standard Library `pathlib` module.

The str constructor

We can use the `str` constructor to create strings representations of other types, such as integers:

```
>>> str(496)
>>> '496'
```

Or `floats`:

```
>>> str(6.02e23)
'6.02e+23'
```

Strings as sequences

The Strings in Python are what are called *sequence* types, which means they support certain common operations for querying ordered series of elements. For example, we can access individual characters using square brackets with an zero-based integer index:

```
>>> s = 'parrot'
>>> s[4]
'o'
```

In contrast to many other programming languages, there is no separate character type distinct from the string type. The indexing operation returns a full-blown string that just contains a single code point element, a fact we can demonstrate using Python's built-in `type()` function:

```
>>> type(s[4])
<class 'str'>
```

We'll be looking at types and classes much more later in this book.

String methods

The `String` objects also support a wide variety of operations implemented as methods. We can list those methods by using `help()` on the string type:

```
>>> help(str)
```

When you press *Enter*, you should see a display like this:

```
Help on class str in module builtins:

class str(object)
 |  str(object='') -> str
 |  str(bytes_or_buffer[, encoding[, errors]]) -> str
 |
 |  Create a new string object from the given object. If encoding or
 |  errors is specified, then the object must expose a data buffer
 |  that will be decoded using the given encoding and error handler.
 |  Otherwise, returns the result of object.__str__() (if defined)
```

```
|   or repr(object).
|   encoding defaults to sys.getdefaultencoding().
|   errors defaults to 'strict'.
|
|   Methods defined here:
|
|   __add__(self, value, /)
|       Return self+value.
|
|   __contains__(self, key, /)
|       Return key in self.
|
|   __eq__(self, value, /)
:
```

On any platform you can browse through the help page by pressing the spacebar to advance one page at a time until you see the documentation for the capitalize() method, skipping over all the methods that begin and end with double underscores:

```
|       Create and return a new object.  See help(type) for accurate
|       signature.
|
|   __repr__(self, /)
|       Return repr(self).
|
|   __rmod__(self, value, /)
|       Return value%self.
|
|   __rmul__(self, value, /)
|       Return self*value.
|
|   __sizeof__(...)
|       S.__sizeof__() -> size of S in memory, in bytes
|
|   __str__(self, /)
|       Return str(self).
|
|   capitalize(...)
|       S.capitalize() -> str
|
|       Return a capitalized version of S, i.e. make the first
|       character have upper case and the rest lower case.
|
:
```

Press *Q* to quit the help browser, and we'll try to use `captialize()`. Let's make a string that deserves capitalization – the name of a capital city no less!

```
>>> c = "oslo"
```

To call methods on objects in Python we use the dot after the object name and before the method name. Methods are functions, so we must use the parentheses to indicate that the method should be called.

```
>>> c.capitalize()
'Oslo'
```

Remember that strings are immutable, so the `capitalize()` method didn't modify c in place. Rather, it returned a new string. We can verify this, by displaying c, which remains unchanged:

```
>>> c
'oslo'
```

You might like to spend a little time familiarizing yourself with the various useful methods provided by the string type by browsing the help.

Strings with Unicode

Strings are fully Unicode capable, so you can use them with international characters easily, even in literals, because the default source code encoding for Python 3 is UTF-8. For example, if you have access to Norwegian characters, you can simply enter this:

```
>>> "Vi er så glad for å høre og lære om Python!"
'Vi er så glad for å høre og lære om Python!'
```

Alternatively, you can use the hexadecimal representations of Unicode code points as an escape sequence prefixed by \u:

```
>>> "Vi er s\u00e5 glad for \u00e5 h\xf8re og l\u00e6re om Python!"
'Vi er så glad for å høre og lære om Python!'
```

We're sure you'll agree, though, that this is somewhat more unwieldy.

Similarly, you can use the \x escape sequence followed by a 2-character hexadecimal string to include one-byte Unicode code points in a `string` literal:

```
>>> '\xe5'
'å'
```

You can even an use an escaped octal string using a single backlash followed by three digits in the range zero to seven, although we confess we've never seen this used in practice, except inadvertently as a bug:

```
>>> '\345'
'å'
```

There are no such Unicode capabilities in the otherwise similar bytes type, which we'll look at next.

The bytes type – an immutable sequence of bytes

The bytes type is similar to the `str` type, except that rather than each instance being a sequence of Unicode code points, each instance is a sequence of, well, `bytes`. As such, `bytes` objects are used for raw binary data and fixed-width, single-byte character encodings, such as ASCII.

Literal bytes

As with strings they have a simple, literal form delimited by either single or double quotes, although for literal bytes the opening quote must be preceded by a lower-case `b`:

```
>>> b'data'
b'data'
>>> b"data"
b'data'
```

There is also a `bytes` constructor, but it has fairly complex behavior and we defer coverage of it to the second book in this series, *The Python Journeyman*. At this point in our journey, it's sufficient for us to recognize the `bytes` literals and understand that they support many of the same operations as `str`, such as indexing and splitting:

```
>>> d = b'some bytes'
>>> d.split()
[b'some', b'bytes']
```

You'll see that the `split()` method returns a list of of bytes objects.

Converting between bytes and str

To convert between bytes and `str` we must know the encoding of the byte sequence used to represent the string's Unicode code points as bytes. Python supports a wide-variety of so-called *codecs* such as UTF-8, UTF-16, ASCII, Latin-1, Windows-1251, and so on – consult the Python documentation for a current list of codecs

In Python we can *encode* a Unicode `str` into a `bytes` object, and going the other way we can *decode* a `bytes` object into a Unicode `str`. In either direction it's up to us to specify the encoding. Python won't — and generally speaking can't do anything to prevent you erroneously decoding UTF-16 data stored in a bytes object using, say, a CP037 codec for handling strings on legacy IBM mainframes.

If you're lucky the decoding will fail with a `UnicodeError` at runtime; if you're unlucky you'll wind up with a `str` full of garbage that will go undetected by your program.

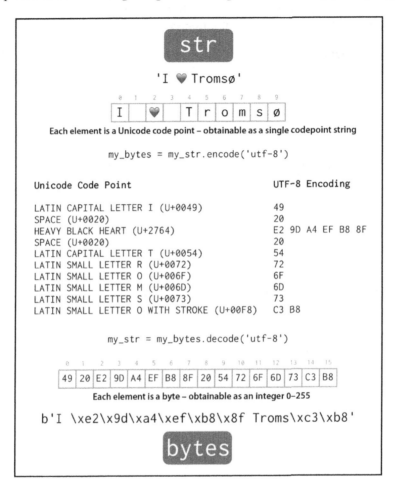

Figure 2.2: Encoding and Decoding.

Let's kick off an interactive session looking at strings, with an interesting Unicode string which contains all the characters of the 29 letter Norwegian alphabet – a pangram:

```
>>> norsk = "Jeg begynte å fortære en sandwich mens jeg kjørte taxi på vei
til quiz"
```

We'll now encode that using the UTF-8 codec into a `bytes` object using the `encode()` method of the `str` object:

```
>>> data = norsk.encode('utf-8')
>>> data
b'Jeg begynte \xc3\xa5 fort\xc3\xa6re en sandwich mens jeg kj\xc3\xb8rte
taxi p\xc3\xa5 vei til quiz'
```

See how each of the Norwegian letters has been rendered as a pair of bytes.

We can reverse the process using the `decode()` method of the bytes object. Again, it is up to us to supply the correct encoding:

```
>>> norwegian = data.decode('utf-8')
```

We can check that the encoding/decoding round-trip gives us a result equal to what we started with:

```
>>> norwegian == norsk
True
```

Let's try to display it for good measure:

```
>>> norwegian
'Jeg begynte å fortære en sandwich mens jeg kjørte taxi på vei til quiz'
```

All this messing about with encodings may seem like unnecessary detail at this juncture – especially if you operate in an anglophone environment – but it's crucial to understand since files and network resources such as HTTP responses are transmitted as byte streams, whereas we prefer to work with the convenience of Unicode strings.

String differences between Python 3 and Python 2
The biggest difference between contemporary Python 3 and legacy Python 2 is the handling of strings. In versions of Python up to and including Python 2 the `str` type was a so-called byte string, where each character was encoded as a single `byte`. In this sense, Python 2 `str` was similar to the Python 3 `bytes`, however, the interface presented by `str` and `bytes` is in fact different in significant ways. In particular their constructors are completely different and indexing into a `bytes` object returns an integer rather than a single code point string. To confuse matters further, there is also a `bytes` type in Python 2.6 and Python 2.7, but this is just a synonym for `str` and as such has an identical interface. If you're writing text handling code intended to be portable across Python 2 and Python 3 – which is perfectly possible – tread carefully!

list – a sequence of objects

Python lists, such as those returned by the string `split()` method, are sequences of objects. Unlike strings lists are mutable, insofar as the elements within them can be replaced or removed, and new elements can be inserted or appended. lists are the workhorse of Python data structures.

Literal lists are delimited by square brackets, and the items within the list are separated by commas. Here is a list of three numbers:

```
>>> [1, 9, 8]
[1, 9, 8]
```

And here is a list of three strings:

```
>>> a = ["apple", "orange", "pear"]
```

We can retrieve elements by using square brackets with a zero-based index:

```
>>> a[1]
"orange"
```

We can replace elements by assigning to a specific element:

```
>>> a[1] = 7
>>> a
['apple', 7, 'pear']
```

See how lists can be heterogeneous with respect to the type of the contained objects. We now have a list containing an `str`, an `int`, and another `str`.

It's often useful to create an empty list, which we can do using empty square brackets:

```
>>> b = []
```

We can modify the list in other ways. Let's add some floats to the end of the list using the `append()` method:

```
>>> b.append(1.618)
>>> b
[1.618]
>>> b.append(1.414)
[1.618, 1.414]
```

There are many other useful methods for manipulating lists, which we'll cover in a later chapter. Right now, we just need to be able to perform rudimentary list operations.

There is also a `list` constructor, which can be used to create lists from other collections, such as strings:

```
>>> list("characters")
['c', 'h', 'a', 'r', 'a', 'c', 't', 'e', 'r', 's']
```

Although the significant whitespace rules in Python can, at first, seem very rigid, there is a lot of flexibility. For example, if you have unclosed brackets, braces, or parentheses at the end of a line, you can continue on the next line. This can be very useful for representing long literal collections, or improving the readability of even short collections:

```
>>> c = ['bear',
...      'giraffe',
...      'elephant',
...      'caterpillar',]
>>> c
['bear', 'giraffe', 'elephant', 'caterpillar']
```

See also how we're allowed to use an additional comma after the last element, an handy feature that improves the maintainability of the code.

The dict type – associating keys with values

Dictionaries – embodied in the `dict` type – are completely fundamental to the way the Python language works, and are very widely used. A dictionary maps keys to values, and in some languages it is known as a map or associative array. Let's look at how to create and use dictionaries in Python.

Literal dictionaries are created using curly braces containing key-value pairs. Each pair is separated by a comma, and each key is separated from its corresponding value by a colon. Here we use a dictionary to create a simple telephone directory:

```
>>> d = {'alice': '878-8728-922', 'bob': '256-5262-124',
...      'eve': '198-2321-787'}
```

We can retrieve items by key using the square brackets operator:

```
>>> d['alice']
'878-8728-922'
```

And we can update the value associated with a particular key by assigning through the square brackets:

```
>>> d['alice'] = '966-4532-6272'
>>> d
{'bob': '256-5262-124', 'eve': '198-2321-787',
 'alice': '966-4532-6272'}
```

If we assign to a key that has not yet been added, a new entry is created:

```
>>> d['charles'] = '334-5551-913'
>>> d
{'bob': '256-5262-124', 'eve': '198-2321-787',
'charles': '334-5551-913', 'alice': '966-4532-6272'}
```

Be aware that the entries in the dictionary can't be relied upon to be stored in any particular order, and in fact the order that Python chooses may even change between runs of the same program. Similarly to lists, empty dictionaries can be created using empty curly braces:

```
>>> e = {}
```

This has been a *very* cursory look at dictionaries, but we'll be revisiting them in much more detail in Chapter 5, *Exploring built-in Collection types*.

The For-loops – iterating over series of items

Now that we have the tools to make some interesting data structures, we'll look at Python's other type of loop construct, the for-loop. The for-loops in Python correspond to what are called for-each loops in many other programming languages. They request items one-by-one from a collection – or more strictly from an iterable series (but more of that later) – and assign them in turn to the a variable we specify. Let's create a list collection, and use a for-loop to iterate over it, remembering to indent the code within the for-loop by four spaces:

```
>>> cities = ["London", "New York", "Paris", "Oslo", "Helsinki"]
>>> for city in cities:
...     print(city)
...
London
New York
Paris
Oslo
Helsinki
```

So iterating over a list yields the items one-by-one. If you iterate over a dictionary, you get just the keys in seemingly random order, which can then be used within the `for`-loop body to retrieve the corresponding values. Let's define a dictionary which maps color name strings to hexadecimal integer color codes stored as integers:

```
>>> colors = {'crimson': 0xdc143c, 'coral': 0xff7f50,
              'teal': 0x008080}
>>> for color in colors:
...     print(color, colors[color])
...
coral 16744272
crimson 14423100
teal 32896
```

Here we use the ability of the built-in `print()` function to accept multiple arguments, passing the key and the value for each color separately. See also how the color codes returned to us are in decimal.

Now, before we put some of what we've learned together into a useful program, practice exiting the Python REPL with *Ctrl+Z* on Windows or *Ctrl+D* on Mac or Linux.

Putting it all together

Let's take a short detour to try out some of the tools we've introduced on a slightly larger example. Textbooks typically avoid such pragmatism, especially in the early chapters, but we think it's fun to apply new ideas to practical situations. To avoid getting off the the wrong stylistic foot, we'll need to introduce a few "black-box" components to get the job done, but you'll learn about them in detail later, so don't worry.

We're going to write a longer snippet at the REPL, and briefly introduce the with statement. Our code will fetch some text data for some classic literature from the web using a Python standard library function called `urlopen()`. Here's the code entered at the REPL in full. We've annotated this code snippet with line numbers to facilitate referring to lines from the explanation:

```
>>> from urllib.request import urlopen
>>> with urlopen('http://sixty-north.com/c/t.txt') as story:
...     story_words = []
...     for line in story:
...         line_words = line.split()
...         for word in line_words:
...             story_words.append(word)
...
```

We'll work through this code, explaining each line in turn.

1. To get access to `urlopen()` we need to import the function from the `request` module, which itself resides within the standard library `urllib` package.

2. We're going to call `urlopen()` with the URL to the story text. We use a Python construct called a `with`-block to manage the resource obtained from the URL, since fetching the resource from the web requires operating system sockets and suchlike. We'll be talking more about with statements in a later chapter, but for now it's enough to know that using a with statement with objects which use external resources is good practice to avoid so-called *resource leaks*. The with statement calls the `urlopen()` function and binds the response object to a variable named story.

3. Notice that the with statement is terminated by a colon, which introduces a new block, so within the block we must indent four spaces. We create an empty list which ultimately will hold all of the words from the retrieved text.

4. We open a `for`-loop which will iterate through the story. Recall that for-loops request items one-by-one from the expression on the right of the in keyword — in this case story — and assign them in turn to the the name on the left — in this case line. It so happens that that type of the HTTP response object referred to by story yields successive lines of text from the response body when iterated over in this way, so the `for`-loop retrieves one line of text at a time from the story. The for statement is also terminated by a colon because it introduces the body of the `for`-loop, which is a new block and hence a further level of indentation.

5. The `for` each line of text, we use the `split()` method to divide it into words on whitespace boundaries, resulting in a list of words we call `line_words`.

6. Now we use a second `for`-loop nested inside the first to iterate over this list of words.

7. We `append()` each word in turn to the accumulating `story_words` list.

8. Finally, we enter a blank line at the three dots prompt to close all open blocks — in this case the inner `for`-loop , the outer `for`-loop, and the with-block will all be terminated. The block will be executed, and after a short delay, Python now returns us to the regular triple-arrow prompt. At this point if Python gives you an error, such as a `SyntaxError` or `IndentationError`, you should go back, review what you entered, and carefully re-enter the code until Python accepts the whole block without complaint. If you get an `HTTPError`, then you were unable to fetch the resource over the Internet, and you should check your network connection or try again later, although it's worth checking that you typed the URL correctly.

We can look at the words we've collected by asking Python to evaluate the valueof `story_words`:

```
>>> story_words
[b'It', b'was', b'the', b'best', b'of', b'times', b'it', b'was', b'the',
b'worst', b'of', b'times',b'it', b'was', b'the', b'age', b'of', b'wisdom',
b'it', b'was', b'the', b'age', b'of', b'foolishness', b'it', b'was',
b'the', b'epoch', b'of', b'belief', b'it', b'was', b'the', b'epoch', b'of',
b'incredulity', b'it', b'was', b'the', b'season', b'of', b'Light', b'it',
b'was', b'the', b'season', b'of', b'Darkness', b'it', b'was', b'the',
b'spring', b'of', b'hope', b'it', b'was', b'the', b'winter', b'of',
b'despair', b'we', b'had', b'everything', b'before', b'us', b'we', b'had',
b'nothing', b'before', b'us', b'we', b'were', b'all', b'going', b'direct',
b'to', b'Heaven', b'we', b'were', b'all', b'going', b'direct', b'the',
b'other', b'way', b'in', b'short', b'the', b'period', b'was', b'so',
b'far', b'like', b'the', b'present', b'period', b'that', b'some', b'of',
b'its', b'noisiest',b'authorities', b'insisted', b'on', b'its', b'being',
b'received', b'for', b'good', b'or', b'for', b'evil', b'in', b'the',
b'superlative', b'degree', b'of', b'comparison', b'only']
```

This sort of exploratory programming at the REPL is very common for Python, as it allows us to figure out what bits of code do before we decide to use them. In this case notice that each of the single-quoted words is prefixed by a lower-case letter b meaning that we have a list of `bytes` objects where we would have preferred a list of `str` objects. This is because the HTTP request transferred raw bytes to us over the network.

To get a list of strings we should decode the byte stream in each line from UTF-8 into Unicode strings. We can do this by inserting a call to the `decode()` method of the `bytes` object, and then operating on the resulting Unicode string. The Python REPL supports a simple command history, and by careful use of the up and down arrow keys, we can re-enter our snippet, although there's no need to re-import `urlopen`, so we can skip the first line:

```
>>> with urlopen('http://sixty-north.com/c/t.txt') as story:
... story_words = []
... for line in story:
... line_words = line.decode('utf-8').split()
... for word in line_words:
... story_words.append(word)
...
```

It is the fourth line here we have changed – you can just edit it using the left and right arrow keys to insert the requisite call to `decode()` when you get to that part of the command history. When we re-run the block and take a fresh look at `story_words`, we should see we have a list of strings:

```
>>> story_words
['It', 'was', 'the', 'best', 'of', 'times', 'it',
'was', 'the', 'worst', 'of', 'times', 'it', 'was', 'the', 'age', 'of',
'wisdom', 'it', 'was', 'the', 'age', 'of', 'foolishness', 'it', 'was',
'the', 'epoch', 'of', 'belief', 'it', 'was', 'the', 'epoch', 'of',
'incredulity', 'it', 'was', 'the', 'season', 'of', 'Light', 'it',
'was', 'the', 'season', 'of', 'Darkness', 'it', 'was', 'the',
'spring', 'of', 'hope', 'it', 'was', 'the', 'winter', 'of', 'despair',
'we', 'had', 'everything', 'before', 'us', 'we', 'had', 'nothing',
'before', 'us', 'we', 'were', 'all', 'going', 'direct', 'to',
'Heaven', 'we', 'were', 'all', 'going', 'direct', 'the', 'other',
'way', 'in', 'short', 'the', 'period', 'was', 'so', 'far', 'like',
'the', 'present', 'period', 'that', 'some', 'of', 'its', 'noisiest',
'authorities', 'insisted', 'on', 'its', 'being', 'received', 'for',
'good', 'or', 'for', 'evil', 'in', 'the', 'superlative', 'degree',
'of', 'comparison', 'only']
```

We've just about reached the limit of what's comfortable to enter and revise at the Python REPL, so in the next chapter we'll look at how to move this code into a file where it can be more easily worked with in a text editor.

Summary

- The `str` Unicode strings and `bytes` strings:

    - We looked at the various forms of quotes (single or double quotation marks) for quoting strings, useful for incorporating quote marks themselves into strings. Python is flexible over which quoting style you use, but you must be consistent when delimiting a particular string.

    - We demonstrated that so-called triple quotes, consisting of three consecutive quotation mark characters can be used to delimit a multi-line string. Traditionally, each quote character is itself a double quotation mark, although single quotation marks can also be used.

    - We saw how adjacent string literals are implicitly concatenated.

    - Python has support for universal newlines, so no matter what platform
    you're using it's sufficient to use a single \n character, safe in the knowledge that is will be appropriately translated from and to the native
    newline during I/O.

    - Escape sequences provide an alternative means of incorporating newlines and other control characters into literal strings.

    - The backslashes used for escaping can be a hindrance for Windows filesystem paths or regular expressions, so raw strings with an `r` prefix can be used to suppress the escaping mechanism.

    - Other types, such as integers, can be converted to strings using the `str()` constructor.

    - Individual characters, returned as one character strings, can be retrieved using square brackets with integer zero-based indices.

    - Strings support a rich variety of operations, such as splitting, through their methods.

- In Python 3, literal strings can contain any Unicode character directly in the source, which is interpreted as UTF-8 by default.

- The `bytes` type has many of the capabilities of strings, but it is a sequence as `bytes` rather than a sequence of Unicode code points.

- The `bytes` literals are prefixed with a lowercase `b`.

- To convert between string and bytes instances we use the `encode()` method of `str` or the `decode()` method of `bytes`, in both cases passing the name of the codec, which we must know in advance.

- The `list` literal

  - Lists are mutable, heterogeneous sequences of objects.

  - The list literals are delimited by square brackets and the items are separated by commas.

  - Individual elements can be retrieved by indexing into a list with square brackets containing a zero-based integer index.

  - In contrast to strings individual list elements can be replaced by assigning to the indexed item.

  - Lists can be grown by `append()`-ing to them, and can be constructed from other sequences using the `list()` constructor.

- `dict`

  - Dictionaries associate keys with values.

  - Literal dictionaries are delimited by curly braces. The key-value pairs are separated from each other by commas, and each key is associated with its corresponding value with a colon.

- The `for` loops

  - The `for`-loops take items one-by-one from an `iterable` object such as a list, and bind the same name to the current item.

- They correspond to what are called `for`-each loops in other languages.

We don't cover *regular expressions* – also known as *regexes* – in this book. See the documentation for the Python Standard Library `re` module for more information. `https://docs.python.org/3/library/re.html`.

3
Modularity

Modularity is an important property for anything but trivial software systems as it gives us the power to make self-contained, reusable pieces which can be combined in new ways to solve different problems. In Python, as with most programming languages, the most fine-grained modularization facility is the definition of reusable functions. But Python also gives us several other powerful modularization mechanisms.

Collections of related functions are themselves grouped together a form modularity called *modules*. Modules are source code files that can be referenced by other modules, allowing the functions defined in one module to be re-used in another. So long as you take care to avoid any circular dependencies, modules are a simple and flexible way to organize programs.

In previous chapters we've seen that we can import modules into the REPL. We'll also show you how modules can be executed directly as programs or scripts. As part of this we'll investigate the Python execution model, to ensure that you have a good understanding of exactly *when* code is evaluated and executed. We'll round off this chapter by showing you how to use command-line arguments to get basic configuration data into your program and make your program executable.

To illustrate this chapter, we'll start with the code snippet for retrieving words from a web-hosted text document that we developed at the end of the previous chapter. We'll elaborate on that code by organizing it into a fully-fledged Python module.

Organizing code in a .py file

Let's start with the snippet we worked with in Chapter 2, *Strings and Collections*. Open a text editor – preferably one with syntax highlighting support for Python – and configure it to insert four spaces per indent level when you press the tab key. You should also check that your editor saves the file using the UTF 8 encoding as that's what the Python 3 runtime expects by default.

Create a directory called pyfund in your home directory. This is where we'll put the code for the chapter.

All Python source files use the .py extension, so let's get the snippet we wrote at the REPL at end of the previous module into a text file called pyfund/words.py. The file's contents should looks like this:

```python
from urllib.request import urlopen

with urlopen('http://sixty-north.com/c/t.txt') as story:
    story_words = []
    for line in story:
        line_words = line.decode('utf-8').split()
        for word in line_words:
            story_words.append(word)
```

You'll notice some minor differences between the code above and what we wrote previously at the REPL. Now that we're using a text file for our code we can pay a little more attention to readability, so, for example, we've put a blank line after the import statement.

Save this file before moving on.

Running Python programs from the operating system shell

Switch to a console with your operating system's shell prompt and change to the new pyfund directory:

```
$ cd pyfund
```

We can execute our module simply by calling Python and passing the module's filename:

```
$ python3 words.py
```

The command would be as follows if on Mac or Linux:

```
> python words.py
```

When on Windows.

When you press *Enter*, after a short delay you'll be returned to the system prompt. Not very impressive, but if you got no response then the program is running as expected. If, on the other hand, you saw some error out, then something it wrong. An HTTPError, for example, indicates there's a network problem, whilst other types of errors probably mean you have mistyped the code.

Let's add another for-loop to the end of the program to print out one word per line. Add this code to the end of your Python file:

```
for word in story_words:
    print(word)
```

If you go to your command prompt and execute the code again, you should see some output. Now we have the beginnings of a useful program!

Importing modules into the REPL

Our module can also be imported into the REPL. Let's try that and see what happens. Start the REPL and import your module. When importing a module, you use import <module-name>, omitting the .py extension from the module name. In our case, it looks something like this:

```
$ python
Python 3.5.0 (default, Nov 3 2015, 13:17:02)
[GCC 4.2.1 Compatible Apple LLVM 6.1.0 (clang-602.0.53)] on darwin
Type "help", "copyright", "credits" or "license" for more information.
>>> import words
It
was
the
best
of
times
. . .
```

The code in your module is executed immediately when imported! That's maybe not what you expected, and it's certainly not very useful. To give us more control over when our code is executed, and to allow it to be reused, we'll need to put our code in a function.

Defining functions

Functions are defined using the def keyword followed by the function name, an argument list in parentheses, and a colon to start a new block. Let's quickly define a few functions at the REPL to get the idea:

```
>>> def square(x):
...     return x * x
...
```

We use the return keyword to return a value from the function.

As we've seen previously, we call functions by providing the actual arguments in parentheses after the function name:

```
>>> square(5)
5
```

Functions aren't required to explicitly return a value though — perhaps they produce side effects:

```
>>> def launch_missiles():
...     print("Missiles launched!")
...
>>> launch_missiles()
Missiles launched!
```

You can return early from a function by using the return keyword with no parameter:

```
>>> def even_or_odd(n):
...     if n % 2 == 0:
...         print("even")
...         return
...     print("odd")
...
>>> even_or_odd(4)
even
>>> even_or_odd(5)
odd
```

If you don't have an explicit return in your function, Python will implicitly add one at the end if your function. This implicit return, or a return without a parameter, actually causes the function to return None. Remember, though, that the REPL doesn't display None results, so we don't see them. By capturing the returned object into a named variable we can test for None:

```
>>> w = even_or_odd(31)
```

```
odd
>>> w is None
True
```

Organizing our module into functions

Let's organize our words module using functions.

First we'll move all the code except the import statement into a function called fetch_words(). You do that simply by adding the def statement and indenting the code below it by one extra level:

```
from urllib.request import urlopen


def fetch_words():
    with urlopen('http://sixty-north.com/c/t.txt') as story:
        story_words = []
        for line in story:
            line_words = line.decode('utf-8').split()
            for word in line_words:
            story_words.append(word)

 for word in story_words:
 print(word)
```

Save the module, and reload the module using a fresh Python REPL:

```
$ python3
Python 3.5.0 (default, Nov  3 2015, 13:17:02)
[GCC 4.2.1 Compatible Apple LLVM 6.1.0 (clang-602.0.53)] on darwin
Type "help", "copyright", "credits" or "license" for more information.
>>> import words
```

The module imports, but the words are not fetched until we call the fetch_words() function:

```
>>> words.fetch_words()
It
was
the
best
of
times
```

Alternatively we can import our specific function:

```
>>> from words import fetch_words
>>> fetch_words()
It
was
the
best
of
times
```

So far so good, but what happens when we try to run our module directly from the operating system shell?

Exit from the REPL with *Ctrl+D* from Mac or Linux or *Ctrl+Z* for Windows, and run Python 3 passing the module filename:

```
$ python3 words.py
```

No words are printed. This is because all the module does now is to define a function and then immediately exit. To make a module from which we can usefully import functions into the REPL *and* which can be run as a script, we need to learn a new Python idiom.

The __name__ type and executing modules from the command line

The Python runtime system defines some special variables and attributes, the names of which are delimited by double underscores. One such special variable is called __name__, and it gives us the means for our module to determine whether it has been run as a script or, instead, imported into another module or the REPL. To see how, add:

```
print(__name__)
```

Add the end of your module, outside of the fetch_words() function.

Speaking Python aloud

You will from time to time need to talk about Python aloud, and you'll invariably find that — like any programming language — Python has elements which don't lend themselves to human speech. The special names denoted by double underscores are a prime example because they're ubiquitous in Python and, frankly, you can only say "double underscore name double underscore" so many times before you start to think about changing careers. To help alleviate this situation, a common practice among Pythonistas is to use the term "dunder" as short hand for "surrounded by double underscores". So, for example, __name__ would be pronounced "dunder name". As an added bonus, saying "dunder" is fun! Try it and I guarantee you'll feel better.

First of all, let's import the modified words module back into the REPL:

```
$ python3
Python 3.5.0 (default, Nov  3 2015, 13:17:02)
[GCC 4.2.1 Compatible Apple LLVM 6.1.0 (clang-602.0.53)] on darwin
Type "help", "copyright", "credits" or "license" for more information.
>>> import words
words
```

We can see that when imported __name__ does indeed evaluate to the module's name.

As a brief aside, if you import the module again, the print statement will *not* be executed; module code is only executed once, on first import:

```
>>> import words
>>>
```

Now let's try running the module as a script:

```
$ python3 words.py
__main__
```

In this case the special __name__ variable is equal to the string main which is also delimited by double underscores. Our module can use this behavior to detect how it is being used. We replace the print statement with an if-statement which tests the value of __name__. If the value is equal to main then our function is executed:

```
if __name__ == '__main__':
    fetch_words()
```

Now we can safely import our module without unduly executing our function:

```
$ python3
```

```
>>> import words
>>>
```

If we can usefully run our function as a script:

```
$ python3 words.py
It
was
the
best
of
times
```

The Python execution model

In order to have a really solid foundation in Python, it's important to understand the Python *execution model*. By this, we mean the rules defining precisely when function definitions and other important events occur during module import and execution. To help you develop this understanding, we'll focus on the def keyword since you're already familiar with it. Once you have an understanding of how def is processed by Python, you'll know most of what you need to know about Python's execution model.

What's important to understand is this: **def isn't merely a declaration, it's a** *statement*. What this means is that def is actually executed at runtime along with the rest of the top-level module-scope code. What def does is to bind the code in the function's body to the name following def. When modules are imported or run, all of the top-level statements are run, and this is the means by which the functions within the module namespace are defined.

To reiterate, def is executed at runtime. This is very different from how function definitions are handled in many other languages, especially compiled languages like C++, Java, and C#. In those languages, function definitions are processed by the compiler at *compile time*, not at runtime. By the time the program is actually executing, those function definitions are fixed. In Python there is no compiler, and functions don't exist in any form — except that of source code — until execution. In fact, since a function is only defined when its def is processed on import, a function in a module which is never imported will never be defined.

Understanding this dynamic nature of Python function definitions is critical to understanding important concepts later in this book, so make sure you're comfortable with it. If you've access to a Python debugger, For Example, in an IDE, you might spend some time stepping through your words.py module as it's imported.

The difference between modules, scripts, and programs

We're sometimes asked about the differences between Python modules, Python scripts, and Python programs. Any `.py` file constitutes a Python module, but as we have seen modules can be written for convenient import, convenient execution, or, using the `if __name__ == "__main__"` idiom, both.

We strongly recommend making even simple scripts importable since it eases development and testing so much if you can access your code from the Python REPL. Likewise, even modules which are only ever meant to be imported in production settings benefit from having executable test code. For this reason nearly all modules we create have this form of defining one or more importable functions with a postscript to facilitate execution.

Whether you consider a module to be a Python script or Python program is a matter of context and usage. It's certainly wrong to consider Python to be merely a scripting tool — in the vein of Windows batch files or Unix shell scripts — as many large and complex applications have been built exclusively with Python.

Setting up a main function with command line argument

Let's refine our word fetching module a little further. First, we'll perform a small refactoring and separate the word retrieval and collection on the one hand from the word printing on the other:

```python
from urllib.request import urlopen

# This fetches the words and returns them as a list.
def fetch_words():
    with urlopen('http://sixty-north.com/c/t.txt') as story:
        story_words = []
        for line in story:
            line_words = line.decode('utf-8').split()
            for word in line_words:
                story_words.append(word)
    return story_words


# This prints a list of words
def print_words(story_words):
```

```
        for word in story_words:
            print(word)


    if __name__ == '__main__':
        words = fetch_words()
        print_words(words)
```

We do this because it separates two important concerns: when importing we'd rather get the words as a list, but when running directly, we'd prefer the words to be printed.

Next, we'll extract the code from our if __name__ == '__main__' block into a function called main():

```
    def main():
        words = fetch_words()
        print_words(words)
    if __name__ == '__main__':
        main()
```

By moving this code into a function we can test it from the REPL, something which isn't possible while it's in the module scope if-block.

We can now try these functions from the REPL:

```
    >>> from words import (fetch_words, print_words)
    >>> print_words(fetch_words())
```

We've used this opportunity to introduce a couple of new forms of the import statement. The first new form imports multiple objects from a module using a comma separated list. The parentheses are optional, but they do allow you to break this list over multiple lines if it gets long. This form is perhaps the most widely used form of the import statement.

A second new form imports everything from a module using an asterisk wildcard:

```
    >>> from words import *
```

This latter form is recommended only for casual use at the REPL. It can wreak havoc in programs since what is imported is now potentially beyond your control, opening yourself up to potential namespace clashes at some future time.

Having done this, we can fetch words from the URL:

```
    >>> fetch_words()
    ['It', 'was', 'the', 'best', 'of', 'times', 'it', 'was', 'the',
    'worst','of', 'times', 'it', 'was', 'the', 'age', 'of', 'wisdom', 'it',
```

```
'was','the', 'age', 'of', 'foolishness', 'it', 'was', 'the', 'epoch',
'of','belief', 'it', 'was', 'the', 'epoch', 'of', 'incredulity', 'it',
'was','the', 'season', 'of', 'Light', 'it', 'was', 'the', 'season',
'of','Darkness', 'it', 'was', 'the', 'spring', 'of', 'hope', 'it', 'was',
'the','winter', 'of', 'despair', 'we', 'had', 'everything', 'before', 'us',
'we','had', 'nothing', 'before', 'us', 'we', 'were', 'all', 'going',
'direct','to', 'Heaven', 'we', 'were', 'all', 'going', 'direct', 'the',
'other','way', 'in', 'short', 'the', 'period', 'was', 'so', 'far', 'like',
'the','present', 'period', 'that', 'some', 'of', 'its', 'noisiest',
'authorities','insisted', 'on', 'its', 'being', 'received', 'for', 'good',
'or', 'for','evil', 'in', 'the', 'superlative', 'degree', 'of',
'comparison', 'only']
```

Since we've separated the fetching code from the printing code, we can also print *any* list of words:

```
>>> print_words(['Any', 'list', 'of', 'words'])
Any
list
of
words
```

Indeed, we can even run the main program:

```
>>> main()
It
was
the
best
of
times
```

Notice that the print_words() function isn't fussy about the type items in the list. It's perfectly happy to print a list of numbers:

```
>>> print_words([1, 7, 3])
1
7
3
```

So perhaps print_words() isn't the best name. In fact, the function doesn't mention lists either - it will happily print any collection that the for-loop is capable of iterating over, such as a string:

```
>>> print_words("Strings are iterable too")
S
t
r
```

i
n
g
s

a
r
e

i
t
e
r
a
b
l
e

t
o
o

So let's perform a minor refactoring and rename this function to `print_items()`, changing the variable names within the function to suit:

```python
def print_items(items):
    for item in items:
        print(item)
```

 We'll talk more about the dynamic typing in Python which allows this degree of flexibility in the next module.

Finally, one obvious improvement to our module would be to replace the hard-coded URL with a value we can pass in. Let's extract that value into an argument of the `fetch_words()` function:

```python
def fetch_words(url):
    with urlopen(url) as story:
        story_words = []
        for line in story:
            line_words = line.decode('utf-8').split()
            for word in line_words:
                story_words.append(word)
    return story_words
```

Accepting command line arguments

That last change actually breaks our `main()` since it's not passing the new `url` argument. When running our module as a standalone program, we'll need to accept the URL as a command line argument. Access to command line arguments in Python is through an attribute of the `sys` module called `argv` which is a list of strings. To use it we must first import the `sys` module at the top of our program:

```
import sys
```

We then get the second argument (with an index of one) from the list:

```
def main():
    url = sys.argv[1]
    words = fetch_words(url)
    print_items(words)
```

And of course this works as expected:

```
$ python3 words.py http://sixty-north.com/c/t.txt
It
was
the
best
of
times
```

This looks fine until we realize that we can't usefully test `main()` any longer from the REPL because it refers to `sys.argv[1]` which is unlikely to have a useful value in that environment:

```
$ python3
Python 3.5.0 (default, Nov 3 2015, 13:17:02)
[GCC 4.2.1 Compatible Apple LLVM 6.1.0 (clang-602.0.53)] on darwin
Type "help", "copyright", "credits" or "license" for more information.
>>> from words import *
>>> main()
Traceback (most recent call last):
  File "<stdin>", line 1, in <module>
  File "/Users/sixtynorth/projects/sixty-north/the-python-
  apprentice/manuscript/code/pyfund/words.py", line 21, in main
  url = sys.argv[1]
IndexError: list index out of range
>>>
```

The solution is to allow the argument list to be passed as a formal argument to the `main()` function, using `sys.argv` as the actual parameter in the `if __name__ == '__main__'` block:

```
def main(url):
    words = fetch_words(url)
    print_items(words)


if __name__ == '__main__':
    main(sys.argv[1])
```

Testing from the REPL again, we can see that everything works as expected:

```
>>> from words import *
>>> main("http://sixty-north.com/c/t.txt")
It
was
the
best
of
times
```

Python is a great tool for developing command line tools, and you'll likely find that you need to handle command line arguments for many situations. For more sophisticated command line processing we recommend you look at the `Python Standard Library` `argparse` module or `the inspired third-party docopt module`.

Moment of zen

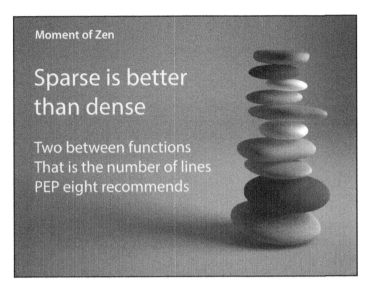

Figure 3.1: Moment of zen: Two between functions

You'll notice that our top level functions have two blank lines between them. This is conventional for modern Python code.

According to `the PEP 8 style-guide` it's customary to use two blank lines between module-level functions. We find this convention has served us well, making code easier to navigate. Similarly, we use single blank lines for logical breaks within functions.

Docstrings

We saw previously how it was possible to ask at the REPL for help on Python functions. Let's look at how to add this self-documenting capability to our own module.

API documentation in Python uses a facility called *docstrings*. Docstrings are literal strings which occur as the first statement within a named block, such as a function or module. Let's document the `fetch_words()` function:

```python
def fetch_words(url):
    """Fetch a list of words from a URL."""
    with urlopen(url) as story:
        story_words = []
        for line in story:
            line_words = line.decode('utf-8').split()
            for word in line_words:
                story_words.append(word)
    return story_words
```

We use triple-quoted strings even for single-line docstrings because they can be easily expanded to add more detail.

One Python convention for docstrings is documented in PEP 257, although it is not widely adopted. Various tools, such as Sphinx, are available to build HTML documentation from Python docstrings, and each tool mandates its preferred docstring format. Our preference is to use the form presented in Google's Python style-guide, since it is amenable to being machine parsed whilst still remaining readable at the console:

```python
def fetch_words(url):
    """Fetch a list of words from a URL.

    Args:
        url: The URL of a UTF-8 text document.

    Returns:
        A list of strings containing the words from
        the document.
    """
    with urlopen(url) as story:
        story_words = []
        for line in story:
            line_words = line.decode('utf-8').split()
            for word in line_words:
                story_words.append(word)
    return story_words
```

Now we'll access this `help()` from the REPL:

```
$ python3
Python 3.5.0 (default, Nov 3 2015, 13:17:02)
[GCC 4.2.1 Compatible Apple LLVM 6.1.0 (clang-602.0.53)] on darwin
Type "help", "copyright", "credits" or "license" for more information.
```

```
>>> from words import *
>>> help(fetch_words)
```

Help on function fetch_words in module words:

```
fetch_words(url)
    Fetch a list of words from a URL.

    Args:
        url: The URL of a UTF-8 text document.

    Returns:
        A list of strings containing the words from
        the document.
```

We'll add similar docstrings for our other functions:

```
def print_items(items):
    """Print items one per line.

    Args:
        items: An iterable series of printable items.
    """
    for item in items:
        print(item)


def main(url):
    """Print each word from a text document from at a URL.

    Args:
        url: The URL of a UTF-8 text document.
    """
    words = fetch_words(url)
    print_items(words)
```

And one for the module itself. Module docstrings should be placed at the beginning of the module, before any statements:

```
"""Retrieve and print words from a URL.

Usage:

  python3 words.py <URL>
"""
import sys
from urllib.request import urlopen
```

Now when we request `help()` on the module as a whole, we get quite a lot of useful information:

```
$ python3
Python 3.5.0 (default, Nov 3 2015, 13:17:02)
[GCC 4.2.1 Compatible Apple LLVM 6.1.0 (clang-602.0.53)] on darwin
Type "help", "copyright", "credits" or "license" for more information.
>>> import words
>>> help(words)

Help on module words:

NAME
    words - Retrieve and print words from a URL.

DESCRIPTION
    Usage:
        python3 words.py <URL>

FUNCTIONS
    fetch_words(url)
        Fetch a list of words from a URL.

        Args:
            url: The URL of a UTF-8 text document.

        Returns:
            A list of strings containing the words from
            the document.

    main(url)
        Print each word from a text document from at a URL.

        Args:
        url: The URL of a UTF-8 text document.

    print_items(items)
        Print items one per line.

        Args:
        items: An iterable series of printable items.

FILE
    /Users/sixtynorth/the-python-apprentice/words.py

(END)
```

Comments

We believe docstrings are the right place for most documentation in Python code. They explain how to consume the facilities your module provides rather than how it works. Ideally your code should be clean enough that ancillary explanation is not required. Nevertheless, it's sometimes necessary to explain *why* a particular approach has be chosen or a particular technique used, and we can do that using Python comments. Comments in Python begin with # and continue to the end of the line.

As a demonstration, let's document the fact that it might not be immediately obvious why we're using `sys.argv[1]` rather than `sys.argv[0]` in our call to `main()`:

```
if __name__ == '__main__':
    main(sys.argv[1])   # The 0th arg is the module filename.
```

Shebang

It's common on Unix-like systems to have the first line of a script include a special comment, #!, called a *shebang*. This allows the program loader to identify which interpreter should be used to run the program. Shebangs have an additional purpose of conveniently documenting at the top of a file whether the Python code therein is Python 2 or Python 3.

The exact details of your shebang command depend on the location of Python on your system. Typical Python 3 shebangs use the Unix env program to locate Python 3 on your PATH environment variable, which importantly is compatible with Python virtual environments:

```
#!/usr/bin/env python3
```

Executable Python programs on Linux and Mac

On Mac or Linux, we must mark our script as executable using the chmod command before the shebang will have any effect:

```
$ chmod +x words.py
```

Having done that, we can now run our script directly:

```
$ ./words.py http://sixty-north.com/c/t.txt
```

Executable Python programs on Windows

Starting with Python 3.3, Python on Windows also supports the use of the shebang to make Python scripts directly executable with the correct version of the Python interpreter, even to the extent that shebangs that look like they should only work on Unix-like systems will work as expected on Windows. This works because Windows Python distributions now use a program called *PyLauncher*. PyLauncher, the executable for which is called simply `py.exe`, will parse the shebang and locate the appropriate version of Python.

For example, on Windows at the `cmd` prompt, this command will be sufficient to run your script with Python 3 (even if you also have Python 2 installed):

```
> words.py http://sixty-north.com/c/t.txt
```

In Powershell the equivalent is:

```
PS> .\words.py http://sixty-north.com/c/t.txt
```

You can read more about PyLauncher in `PEP 397`.

Summary

- Python modules:

    - Python code is placed in `*.py` files called modules.

    - Modules can be executed directly by passing them as the first argument to the Python interpreter.

    - Modules can also be imported into the REPL, at which point all top-level statements in the module are executed in order.

- Python functions:

    - Named functions are defined using the def keyword followed by the function name and the argument list in parentheses.

    - We can return objects from functions using the return statement.

    - Return statements without a parameter return None, as does the implicit return at the end of every function body.

- Module execution:

    - We can detect whether a module has been imported or executed by examining
      the value of the special __name__ variable. If it is equal to the string
      "__main__" our module has been executed directly as a program. By executing a function if this condition is met using the top-level
      `if __name__ == '__main__'` idiom at the end of our module,
      we can make our module both usefully importable and executable,
      an important testing technique even for short scripts.

    - Module code is only executed once, on first import.

    - The `def` keyword is a statement which binds executable code to a function name.

    - Command line arguments can be accessed as a list of strings accessible through the `argv` attribute of the `sys` module. The `zero-th` command line argument is the script filename, so the item at index one is the first true argument.

    - Python's dynamic typing means our functions can be very generic with respect to the type of their arguments.

- Docstrings:

    - A literal string as the first line of a function's definition forms the function's docstring. They are typically triple-quoted multiline strings containing usage information.

    - Function documentation provided in docstrings can be retrieved using `help()` in the REPL.

    - Module docstrings should be placed near the beginning of the module prior to any Python statements such as import statements.

- Comments:

    - Comments in Python commence with a hash character and continue to the end of the line.

- The first line of the module can contain a special comment called a shebang, allowing the program loader to launch the correct Python interpreter on all major platforms.

1. Technically modules don't have to be simple source code files, but for the purposes of this book that is a sufficient definition.

2. Technically some of these compiled languages *do* provide mechanisms for defining functions dynamically at runtime. However, these methods are by far the exception rather than the rule in almost all situations.

3. Python code is actually compiled to byte-code, so in that sense Python has a compiler. But the compiler is doing substantially different kinds of work than what you might be used to from popular compiled, statically-typed languages.

4

Built-in types and the object model

One of the most fundamental design elements of the Python language is its use of objects. Objects are the central data structure not only of user-level constructs but also many of the inner workings of the language itself. In this chapter we'll start to to develop a sense of what this means, both in principle and in practice, and hopefully you'll start to appreciate just how pervasive objects are throughout Python.

We'll take a look at what objects are, how you use them, and how you manage references to them. We'll also start to explore the notion of *types* in Python, and we'll see how Python's types are both similar to and different from those in many other popular languages. As part this exploration we'll take a more in-depth look at some collection types we've met already, and introduce a few more collection types as well.

The nature of Python object references

In previous chapters we've already talked about and used "variables" in Python, but what exactly is a variable? Consider something as straightforward as assigning an integer to a variable:

```
>>> x = 1000
```

What's really happening when we do this? First, Python creates an int *object* with a value of 1000. This object is anonymous in the sense that it doesn't, in and of itself, have a name (x or otherwise). It's simply an object allocated and tracked by the Python runtime system.

After creating the object, Python then creates an *object reference* with the name x and arranges for x to refer to the int(1000) object:

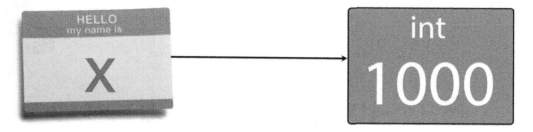

Figure 4.1: Assign the name 'x' to an integer object with the value 1000

Reassigning a reference

Now we'll modify the value of x with another assignment:

```
>>> x = 500
```

This does **not** result any sort of change to the int(1000) object we previously constructed. Integer objects in Python are immutable and cannot be changed. In fact, what happens here is that Python first creates a new immutable integer object with the value 500 and then redirects the x reference to point at the new object:

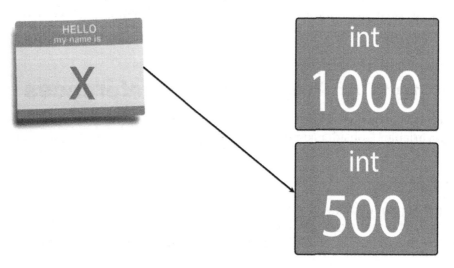

Figure 4.2: Reassign the name 'x' to a new integer object with the value 500

Since we have no other references to the original int (1000) object, we now have no way of reaching it from our code. As a result, the Python garbage collector is free to collect it when and if it chooses.

Assigning one reference to another

When we assign from one variable to another, what we're really doing is assigning from one object reference to another object reference, so that both references then refer to the same object. For example, let's assign our existing variable x to a new variable y:

```
>>> y = x
```

That gives us this resulting reference-object diagram:

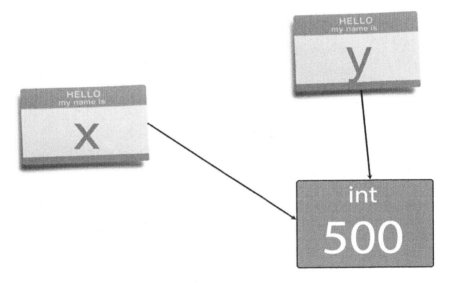

Figure 4.3: Assign the existing name 'x' to the name 'y'

Now both references refer to the same object. We now reassign x to another new integer:

```
>>> x = 3000
```

Doing this gives us a reference-object diagram showing our two references and our two objects:

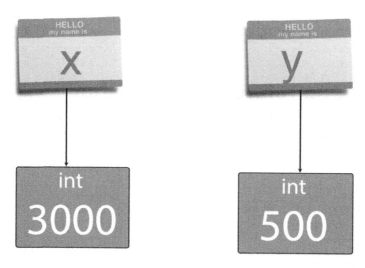

Figure 4.4: Assign a new integer 3000 to 'x'

In this case there is no work for the garbage collector to do because all of the objects are reachable from live references.

Exploring value vs. identity with id()

Let's dig a little deeper into the relationship between objects and references using the built-in id() function. id() accepts any object as an argument and returns an integer identifier which is unique and constant for the lifetime of the object. Let's re-run the previous experiment using id():

```
>>> a = 496
>>> id(a)
4302202064
>>> b = 1729
>>> id(b)
4298456016
>>> b = a
>>> id(b)
4302202064
>>> id(a) == id(b)
True
```

Here we see that initially a and b refer to different objects and, thus, id() gives us different values for each variable. However, when we then assign a to b, both names refer to the same object so id() gives the same value for both. The main lesson here is that id() can be used to establish the *identity* of an object independent of any particular reference to it.

Testing for equality of identity with is

In reality, the id() function is seldom used in production Python code. Its main use is in object model tutorials (such as this one!) and as a debugging tool. Much more commonly used than the id() function is the is operator which tests for equality of identity. That is, is tests whether two references refer to the same object:

```
>>> a is b
True
```

We've already met the is operator earlier, in Chapter 1, *Getting started*, when we tested for None:

```
>>> a is None
False
```

It's critical to remember that is is always testing *identity equality*, that is, whether two references refer to the exact same object. We'll look in-depth at the other primary type of equality, *value equality*, in just a bit.

Mutating without mutating

Even operations which seem naturally mutating in nature are not necessarily so. Consider the augmented assignment operator:

```
>>> t = 5
>>> id(t)
4297261280
>>> t += 2
>>> id(t)
4297261344
```

At first glance, it appears that we're asking Python to increment the integer value t by two. But the id() results here clearly show that t refers to two different objects before and after the augmented assignment.

Rather than modifying integer objects, here's a depiction of what's actually happening. Initially, we have the name t referring to an int(5) object:

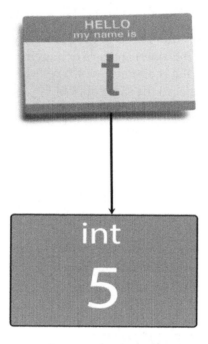

Figure 4.5: 'x' refers to the integer 5

Next, to perform the augmented assignment of 2 to t, Python create an int(2) object behind the scenes. Note that we never have a named reference to this object; it's managed completely by Python on our behalf:

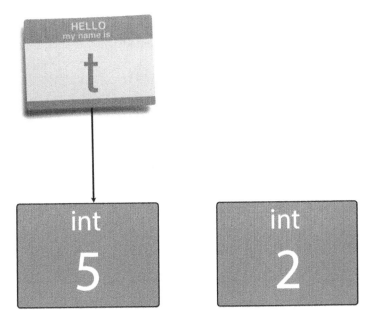

Figure 4.6: Python creates an integer 2 behind the scenes

Python then performs the addition operation between t and the anonymous int(2) giving us — you guessed it! — another integer object, this time an int(7):

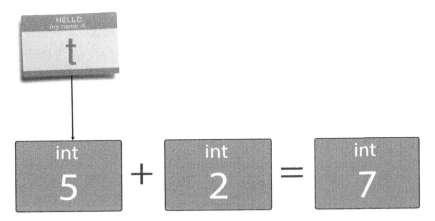

Figure 4.7: Python creates a new integer as the result of the addition

Finally, Python's augmented assignment operator simply reassigns the name t to the `new int(7)` object, leaving the other integer objects to be handled by the garbage collector:

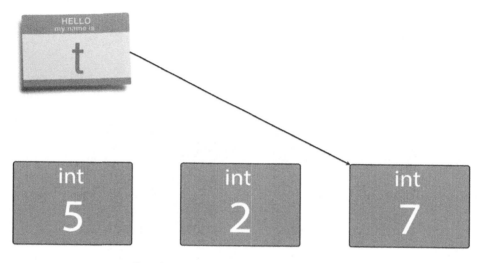

Figure 4.8: Python reassigned the name 't' to the result of the addition

References to mutable objects

Python objects show this name-binding behavior for all types. *The assignment operator only ever binds object to names, it never copies an object by value.* To help make this point crystal clear, let's look at another example using mutable objects: Lists. Unlike the immutable `int`s that we just looked at, list objects have mutable state, meaning that the value of a `list` object can change over time.

To illustrate this, we first create an `list` object with three elements, binding the list object to a reference named r:

```
>>> r = [2, 4, 6]
>>> r
[2, 4, 6]
```

We then assign the reference r to a new reference s:

```
>>> s = r
>>> s
[2, 4, 6]
```

The reference-object diagram for this situation makes it clear that we have two names referring to a single list instance:

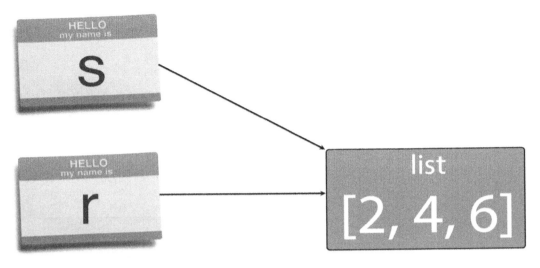

Figure 4.9: 's' and 'r' refer to the same list object

When we modify the list referred to by s by changing the middle element, we see that the list referred to by r has changed as well:

```
>>> s[1] = 17
>>> s
[2, 17, 6]
>>> r
[2, 17, 6]
```

Again, this is because the names s and r refer to the same *mutable* object , a fact that we can verify by using the is keyword which we learned about earlier:

```
>>> s is r
True
```

The main point of this discussion is that Python doesn't really have variables in the metaphorical sense of a box holding a value. It only has named references to objects, and these references behave more like labels which allow us to retrieve objects. That said, it's still common to talk about variables in Python because it's convenient. We will continue to do so throughout this book, secure in the knowledge that you now understand what's *really* going on behind the scenes.

Equality of value (equivalence) versus equality of identity

Let's contrast that behavior with a test for value-equality, or equivalence. We'll create two identical lists:

```
>>> p = [4, 7, 11]
>>> q = [4, 7, 11]
>>> p == q
True
>>> p is q
False
```

Here we see that p and q refer to different objects, but that the objects they refer to have the same value:

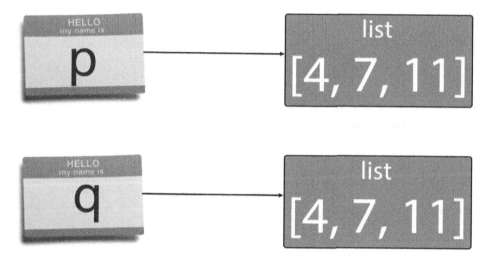

Figure 4.10: 'p' and 'q' different list objects with identical values

As you would expect when testing for value-equality, an object should always be equivalent to itself:

```
>>> p == p
True
```

Value-equality and identity are fundamentally different notions of "equality", and it's important to keep them separate in your mind.

It's also worth noting that value comparison is something that is defined programatically. When you define types, you can control how that class determines value-equality. In contrast, identity comparison is defined by the language and you can't change that behavior.

Argument passing semantics – pass by object-reference

Now let's look at how all this relates to function arguments and return values. When we call a function, we literally create new name bindings — those declared in the function definition — to existing objects — those passed in at the call itself. As such, it's important to really understand Python reference semantics if you want to know how your functions work.

Modifying external objects in a function

To demonstrate Python's argument passing semantics, we'll define a function at the REPL which appends a value to a list and prints the modified list. First we'll create a list and give it the name m:

```
>>> m = [9, 15, 24]
```

Then we'll define a function `modify()` which appends to, and prints, the list passed to it. The function accepts a single formal argument named k:

```
>>> def modify(k):
...     k.append(39)
...     print("k =", k)
...
```

We then call `modify()`, passing our list m as the actual argument:

```
>>> modify(m)
k = [9, 15, 24, 39]
```

This indeed prints the modified list with four elements. But what does our list reference m outside the function now refer to?

```
>>> m
[9, 15, 24, 39]
```

The list referred to by m has been modified because it is the self-same list referred to by k inside the function. As we mentioned at the beginning of the section, when we pass an object-reference to a function we're essentially assigning from the actual argument reference, in this case m, to the formal argument reference, in this case k.

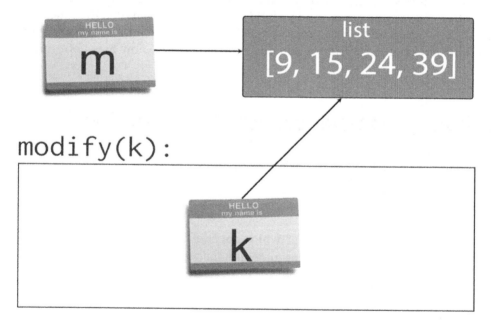

Figure 4.11: Referring to the same list in and out of a function

As we have seen, assignment causes the assigned-to reference to refer to the same object as the assigned-from reference. This is exactly what's going on here. If you want a function to modify a copy of an object, it's the responsibility of the function to do the copying.

Binding new objects in a function

Let's look at another instructive example. First, we'll create a new list f:

```
>>> f = [14, 23, 37]
```

Then we'll create new a function replace(). As the name suggests, rather than modifying its arguments replace() will change the object that its parameter refers to:

```
>>> def replace(g):
...     g = [17, 28, 45]
...     print("g =", g)
...
```

We now call replace() with actual argument f:

```
>>> replace(f)
g = [17, 28, 45]
```

This is much as we'd expect. But what's the value of the external reference f now?

```
>>> f
[14, 23, 37]
```

The object reference f still refers to the original, unmodified list. This time, the function did not modify the object that was passed in. What's going on?

The answer is this: The object reference f was assigned to the formal argument named g, so g and f did indeed refer to the same object, just as in the previous example:

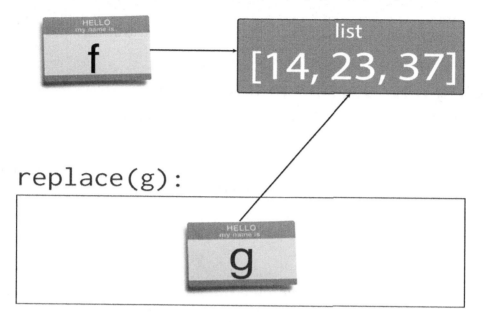

Figure 4.12 : Initially 'f' and 'g' refer to the same list object

However, on the first line the of the function we re-assigned the reference g to point to a newly constructed list **[17, 28, 45]**, so within the function the reference to the original **[14, 23, 37]** list was overwritten, although the unmodified object itself was still pointed to by the f reference outside the function:

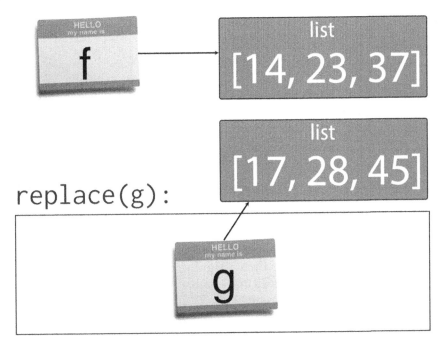

Figure 4.13 : After reassignment, 'f' and 'g' refer to different objects

Argument passing is reference binding

So we've seen that it's quite possible to modify the objects through function argument references, but also that it's possible to rebind the argument references to new values. If you want to change the contents of a list parameter and have the changes seen outside the function, you could modify the contents of the list like this:

```
>>> def replace_contents(g):
...     g[0] = 17
...     g[1] = 28
...     g[2] = 45
...     print("g =", g)
...
>>> f
[14, 23, 37]
>>> replace_contents(f)
g = [17, 28, 45]
```

And indeed, if you check the contents of f you'll see that they have been modified:

```
>>> f
[17, 28, 45]
```

Function arguments are transferred by what is called "pass by object reference". This means that the value of the *reference* is copied into the function argument, not the value of the referred to object; no objects are copied.

Python return semantics

Python's return statement uses the same pass-by-object-reference semantics as function arguments. When you return an object from a function in Python, what you're really doing is passing an object reference back to the caller. If the caller assigns the return value to a reference, they are doing nothing more than assigning a new reference to the returned object. This uses the exact same semantics and mechanics that we saw with explicit reference assignment and argument passing.

We can demonstrate this by writing a function which simply returns its only argument:

```
>>> def f(d):
...     return d
...
```

If we create an object such as a list and pass it through this simple function, we see that it returns the very same object that we passed in:

```
>>> c = [6, 10, 16]
>>> e = f(c)
>>> c is e
True
```

Remember that is only returns True when two names refer to the exact same objects, so example this shows that no copies of the list were made.

Function arguments in detail

Now that we understand the distinction between object references and objects, we'll look at some more capabilities of function arguments.

Default parameter values

The formal function arguments specified when a function is defined with the `def` keyword are a comma-separated list of the argument names. These arguments can be made optional by providing default values. Consider a function which prints a simple banner to the console:

```
>>> def banner(message, border='-'):
...     line = border * len(message)
...     print(line)
...     print(message)
...     print(line)
...
```

This function takes two arguments, and we provide a default value — in this case `'-'` — in a literal string. When we define functions using default arguments, the parameters with default arguments must come after those without defaults, otherwise we will get a `SyntaxError`.

On line 2 of the function we multiply our border string by the length of the message string. This line shows two interesting features. First, it demonstrates how we can determine the number of items in a Python collection using the `built-in len()` function. Secondly, it shows how multiplying a string (in this case the single character string border) by an integer results in a new string containing the original string repeated a number of times. We use that feature here to make a string equal in length to our message.

On lines 3 through 5 we print the full-width border, the message, and the border again.

When we call our `banner()` function, we don't need to supply the border string because we've provided a default value:

```
>>> banner("Norwegian Blue")
--------------
Norwegian Blue
--------------
```

However, if we do provide the optional argument, it is used:

```
>>> banner("Sun, Moon and Stars", "*")
*******************
Sun, Moon and Stars
*******************
```

Keyword arguments

In production code, this function call is not particularly self documenting. We can improve that situation by naming the border argument at the call site:

```
>>> banner("Sun, Moon and Stars", border="*")
********************
Sun, Moon and Stars
********************
```

In this case the message string is called a "positional argument" and the border string a "keyword argument". In a call, the positional arguments are matched up in sequence with the formal arguments declared in the function definition. The keyword arguments, on the other hand, are matched by name. If we use keyword arguments for both of our parameters, we have the freedom to supply them in any order:

```
>>> banner(border=".", message="Hello from Earth")
. . . . . . . . . . . . . . .
Hello from Earth
. . . . . . . . . . . . . . .
```

Remember, though, that all keyword arguments must be specified after any positional arguments.

When are default arguments evaluated?

When you supply a default parameter value for a function, you do so by providing an *expression*. This expression can be a simple literal value, or it can be a more complex function call. In order to actually use the default value that you provide, Python has to at some point evaluate that expression.

It's crucial, then, to have an appreciation of exactly *when* Python evaluates the default value expression. This will help you to avoid a common pitfall which frequently ensnares newcomers to Python. Let's examine this question closely using the Python standard library time module:

```
>>> import time
```

We can easily get the current time as a readable string by using the ctime() function of the time module:

```
>>> time.ctime()
'Sat Feb 13 16:06:29 2016'
```

Let's write a function which uses a value retrieved from `ctime()` as a default argument value:

```
>>> def show_default(arg=time.ctime()):
...     print(arg)
...
>>> show_default()
Sat Feb 13 16:07:11 2016
```

So far so good, but notice what happens when you call `show_default()` again a few seconds later:

```
>>> show_default()
Sat Feb 13 16:07:11 2016
```

And again:

```
>>> show_default()
Sat Feb 13 16:07:11 2016
```

As you can see, the displayed time never progresses.

Recall how we said that `def` is a statement that when executed binds a function definition to a function name? Well, the default argument expressions are evaluated only once, when the `def` statement is executed. In many cases the default value is a simple immutable constant like and integer or a string, so this does not cause any problems. But it can be a confusing trap for the unwary that usually shows up when you use mutable collections like lists as argument defaults.

Let's take a closer look. Consider this function which uses an empty list as a default argument. It accepts a menu as a list of strings, appends the item `"spam"` to the list, and returns the modified menu:

```
>>> def add_spam(menu=[]):
...     menu.append("spam")
...     return menu
...
```

Let's create a simple breakfast of `bacon` and `eggs`:

```
>>> breakfast = ['bacon', 'eggs']
```

Naturally, we'll add spam to it:

```
>>> add_spam(breakfast)
['bacon', 'eggs', 'spam']
```

We'll do something similar for lunch:

```
>>> lunch = ['baked beans']
>>> add_spam(lunch)
['baked beans', 'spam']
```

Nothing unexpected so far. But look what happens when you rely on the default argument by not passing an existing menu:

```
>>> add_spam()
['spam']
```

When we append 'spam' to an empty menu we get just spam. This is probably still what you expected, but if we do that again we get two spams added to our menu:

```
>>> add_spam()
['spam', 'spam']
```

And three:

```
>>> add_spam()
['spam', 'spam', 'spam']
```

And four:

```
>>> add_spam()
['spam', 'spam', 'spam', 'spam']
```

What's happening here is this. First, the empty list used for the default argument is created exactly once, when the def statement is executed. This is a normal list like any other we've seen so far, and Python will use this exact list for the entire execution of your program.

The first time we actually use the default, then, we end up adding spam directly to the default list object. When we use the default a second time, we're using the same default list object — the one to which we just added spam – and we end up adding a second instance of "spam" to it. The third call adds a third spam, *ad infinitum*. Or perhaps *ad nauseum*.

The solution to this is straightforward, but perhaps not obvious: **Always use immutable objects such as integers or strings for default values**. Following this advice, we can solve this particular case by using the immutable None object as a sentinel:

```
>>> def add_spam(menu=None):
...         if menu is None:
...             menu = []
...         menu.append('spam')
...         return menu
```

```
...
>>> add_spam()
['spam']
>>> add_spam()
['spam']
>>> add_spam()
['spam']
```

Our add_spam() function works as expected.

The Python type system

Programming languages can be distinguished by several characteristics, but one of the most important is the nature of their type systems. Python can be characterized as having a *dynamic* and *strong* type system. Let's investigate what that means.

Dynamic typing in Python

Dynamic typing means that the type of an object-reference isn't resolved until the program is running, and it needn't be specified up front when the program is written. Take a look at this simple function for adding two objects:

```
>>> def add(a, b):
...     return a + b
...
```

Nowhere in this definition do we mention any types. We can use add() with integers:

```
>>> add(5, 7):
12
```

And we can use it for floats:

```
>>> add(3.1, 2.4)
5.5
```

You might be surprised to see that it even works for strings:

```
>>> add("news", "paper")
'newspaper'
```

Indeed, this function works for any types, like list, for which the addition operator has been defined:

```
>>> add([1, 6], [21, 107])
[1, 6, 21, 107]
```

These examples illustrate the dynamism of the type system: The two arguments, a and b, of the add() function can reference any types of object.

Strong typing in Python

The strength of the type system, on the other hand, can be demonstrated by attempting to add() types for which addition has not been defined, such as strings and floats:

```
>>> add("The answer is", 42)
Traceback (most recent call last):
  File "<stdin>", line 1, in <module>
  File "<stdin>", line 2, in add
TypeError: Can't convert 'int' object to str implicitly
```

Trying to do this results in a TypeError because Python will not, in general, perform implicit conversions between object types or otherwise attempt to coerce one type to another. The primary exception to this is the conversion to bool used for if statement and while-loop predicates.

Variable declaration and scoping

As we have seen, no type declarations are necessary in Python, and variables are essentially just untyped name bindings to objects. As such, they can be rebound – or reassigned – as often as necessary, even to object of different types.

But when we bind a name to an object, where is that binding stored? To answer that question, we must look at scopes and scoping rules in Python.

The LEGB rule

There are four types of *scope* in Python, and they are arranged in a hierarchy. Each scope is a context in which names are stored and in which they can be looked up. The four scopes from narrowest to broadest are:

- **Local** - names defined inside the current function.

- **Enclosing** - names defined inside any and all enclosing functions. (This scope isn't important for the contents of this book.)

- **Global** - names defined at the top-level of a module. Each module brings with it a new global scope.

- **Built-in** - names built-in to the Python language through the special builtins module.

Together, these scopes comprise the LEGB rule:

The LEGB Rule

Names are looked up in the narrowest relevant context.

It's important to note that scopes in Python do not, in general, correspond to the source-code blocks as demarcated by indentation. For-loops, with-blocks, and the like do not introduce new nested scopes.

Scopes in action

Consider our words.py module. It contains the following global names:

- main - bound by def main()
- sys - bound by import sys
- __name__ - provided by the Python runtime
- urlopen - bound by from urllib.request import urlopen
- fetch_words - bound by def fetch_words()
- print_items - bound by def print_items()

Module scope name bindings are typically introduced by import statements and function or class definitions. It is possible to use other objects at module scope, and this is typically used for constants, although it can also be used for variables.

Within the fetch_words() function we have the six local names:

- word - bound by the inner for-loop
- line_words - bound by assignment

- `line` - bound by the outer `for`-loop
- `story_words` - bound by assignment
- `url` - bound by the formal function argument
- `story` - bound by the with-statement

Each of these bindings is brought into existence at first use and continues to live within the function scope until the function completes, at which point the references will be destroyed.

Identical names in global and local scope

Very occasionally we need to rebind a global name at module scope from within a function. Consider the following simple module:

```
count = 0

def show_count():
    print(count)

def set_count(c):
    count = c
```

If we save this module in `scopes.py`, we can import it into the REPL for experimentation:

```
$ python3
Python 3.5.0 (default, Nov  3 2015, 13:17:02)
[GCC 4.2.1 Compatible Apple LLVM 6.1.0 (clang-602.0.53)] on darwin
Type "help", "copyright", "credits" or "license" for more information.
>>> from scopes import *
>>> show_count()
count =  0
```

When `show_count()` is called Python looks up the name count in the local namespace (`L`). It doesn't find it so looks in the next most outer namespace, in this case the global module namespace (`G`), where it finds the name count and prints the referred-to object.

Now we call `set_count()` with a new value:

```
>>> set_count(5)
```

We then call `show_count()` again:

```
>>> show_count()
count =  0
```

You might be surprised that `show_count()` displays 0 after the call to `set_count(5)`, so let's work through what's happening.

When we call `set_count()`, the assignment `count = c` creates a *new* binding for the name count in the *local* scope. This new binding refers, of course, to the object passed in as `c`. Critically, no lookup is performed for the global count defined at module scope. We have created a new variable which shadows, and thereby prevents access to, the global of the same name.

The global keyword

To avoid this shadowing of names in the global scope, we need to instruct Python to resolve the name count in the `set_count()` function to the count defined in the module namespace. We can do this by using the global keyword. Let's modify `set_count()` to do so:

```
def set_count(c):
    global count
    count = c
```

The `global` keyword simply introduces a binding in the local scope to a name from the global scope.

Quit and restart the Python interpreter to exercise our revised module:

```
>>> from scopes import *
>>> show_count()
count =  0
>>> set_count(5)
>>> show_count()
count =  5
```

It now demonstrates the required behaviour.

Moment of zen

Special cases aren't special enough to break the rules – We follow patterns not to kill complexity but to master it :

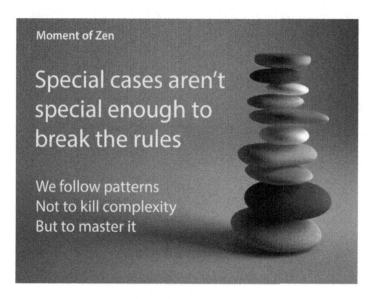

Figure 4.14: Moment of zen

As we have shown, all variables in Python are references to objects, even in the case of basic types such as integers. This thorough approach to object orientation is a strong theme in Python and practically everything in Python is an object, including functions and modules.

Everything is an object

Let's go back to our words module and experiment with it further at the REPL. On this occasion we'll import just the module:

```
$ python3
Python 3.5.0 (default, Nov  3 2015, 13:17:02)
[GCC 4.2.1 Compatible Apple LLVM 6.1.0 (clang-602.0.53)] on darwin
Type "help", "copyright", "credits" or "license" for more information.
>>> import words
```

The `import` statement binds a `module` object to the name `words` in the current namespace. We can determine the type of any object by using the `type()` built-in function:

```
>>> type(words)
<class 'module'>
```

If we want to see the attributes of an object, we can use the `dir()` built-in function in a Python interactive session to introspect an object:

```
>>> dir(words)
['__builtins__', '__cached__', '__doc__', '__file__', '__initializing__',
'__loader__', '__name__', '__package__', 'fetch_words', 'main',
'print_items', 'sys', 'urlopen']
```

The `dir()` function returns a sorted list of the module attribute names, including:

- The ones we defined such as the function `fetch_words()`
- Any imported names such as `sys` and `urlopen`
- Various special *dunder* attributes such as `__name__` and `__doc__` which reveal the inner-workings of Python

Inspecting a function

We can use the `type()` function on any of these attributes to learn more about them. For instance, we can see that `fetch_words` is a function object:

```
>>> type(words.fetch_words)
<class 'function'>
```

We can in turn use `dir()` on the function to reveal its attributes:

```
>>> dir(words.fetch_words)
['__annotations__', '__call__', '__class__', '__closure__', '__code__',
'__defaults__', '__delattr__', '__dict__', '__dir__', '__doc__', '__eq__',
'__format__', '__ge__', '__get__', '__getattribute__', '__globals__',
'__gt__', '__hash__', '__init__', '__kwdefaults__', '__le__', '__lt__',
'__module__', '__name__', '__ne__', '__new__', '__qualname__',
'__reduce__',
'__reduce_ex__', '__repr__', '__setattr__', '__sizeof__', '__str__',
'__subclasshook__']
```

We can see here that function objects have *many* special attributes to do with how Python functions are implemented behind the scenes. For now, we'll just look at a couple of simple attributes.

As you might expect, its __name__ attribute is the name of the function object as a string:

```
>>> words.fetch_words.__name__
'fetch_words'
```

Likewise, __doc__ is the docstring we provided, giving us some clues about how the built-in help() function might be implemented:

```
>>> words.fetch_words.__doc__
'Fetch a list of words from a URL.\n\n    Args:\n        url: The URL of a
UTF-8 text document.\n\n    Returns:\n        A list of strings containing
the words from\n        the document.\n    '
```

This is just a small example of how you can introspect Python objects at runtime, and there are many more powerful tools that you can use to learn more about the objects you're using. Perhaps the most instructive part of the example is that we were dealing with a *function object*, demonstrating that Python's pervasive object orientation includes elements of the language that may not be accessible at all in other languages.

Summary

- Python object references

  - Think of Python working in terms of named references to objects rather
    than variables and values.

  - Assignment doesn't put a value in a box. It attaches a name tag to an
    object.

  - Assigning from one reference to another puts two name tags on the same object.

  - The Python garbage collector will reclaim unreachable objects - those
    objects with no name tag.

- Object identity and equivalence

    - The `id()` function returns a unique and constant identifier but should rarely, if ever, be used in production.

    - The is operator determines equality of identity. That is, whether two
    names refer to the same object.

    - We can test for equivalence using the double-equals operator.

- Function arguments and return values

    - Function arguments are passed by object-reference, so functions can modify their arguments if they are mutable objects.

    - If a formal function argument is rebound through assignment, the reference to the passed-in object is lost. To change a mutable argument you should replace its *contents* rather than replacing the whole object.

    - The return statement also passes by object-reference. No copies are made.

    - Function arguments can be specified with defaults.

    - Default argument expressions are evaluated only once when the `def`
    statement is executed.

- The Python type system

    - Python uses dynamic typing, so we don't need to specify reference types in advance.

    - Python uses strong typing. Types are not coerced to match.

- Scopes

    - Python reference names are looked up in one of four nested scopes according to the LEGB rule: Local to functions, in Enclosing functions, in the Global (or module) namespace and Built-ins.

- Global references can be read from a local scope

- Assigning to global references from a local scope requires that the reference be declared global using the global keyword.

- Objects and introspection

  - Everything in Python is an object, including modules and functions. They can be treated just like other objects.

  - The import and `def` keywords result in binding to named references.

  - The built-in `type()` function can be used to determine the type of an object.

  - The built-in `dir()` function can be used to introspect an object and return a list of its attribute names.

  - The name of a function or module object can be accessed through its
    `__name__` attribute.

  - The docstring for a function or module object can be accessed through its `__doc__` attribute.

- Miscellaneous

  - We can use `len()` to measure the length of a string.

  - If we "multiply" a string by an integer we get a new string with multiple copies of the operand string. This is called the "repetition" operation.

1. You'll notice that here we've referred to the *object reference* with the name x as x. This is admittedly a bit sloppy since, of course, x will generally mean *the object referred to by the object reference with the name x*. But that's a mouthful and a bit overly pedantic. Generally speaking, the context of the use of reference names will be sufficient to tell you whether we mean the object or the reference.

2. Garbage collection is an advanced topic that we won't cover in this book. In short, though, it's the system by which Python deallocates and reclaims resources (that is, objects) which it determines are no longer in use.

3. Since assigning a list reference to another name doesn't copy the list, you may be wondering how you *could* make copy if you wanted. This requires other techniques which we'll look at later when we cover lists in more detail.

4. Note, however, that Python does not enforce this behavior. It is entirely possible to create an object which reports that it is not value-identical to itself. We'll look at how to do this — should you for some reason feel the urge — in later chapters.

5. Though there's no universally accepted terminology, you'll often see the term *parameters* or *formal parameters* used to mean the names declared at the function definition. Likewise, the term *arguments* is often used to mean the actual objects passed into a function (and, thus, bound to the parameters). We'll use this terminology as needed throughout this book.

6. And this behavior is part of the syntax implementation, not the type system.

5

Exploring Built-in Collection types

We've already encountered some of the built-in collections

- `str` – the immutable string sequence of Unicode code points
- `list` – the mutable sequence of objects
- `dict` – the mutable dictionary mapping from immutable keys to mutable objects

We've only scratched the surface of how these collections work, so we'll explore their powers in greater depth in this chapter. We'll also introduce three new built-in collections types:

- `tuple` - the immutable sequence of objects

- `range` - for arithmetic progressions of integers

- `set` - a mutable collection of unique, immutable objects

We won't cover the `bytes` type any further here. We've already discussed its essential differences with `str`, and most of what we learn about `str` can also be applied to `bytes`.

This is not an exhaustive list of Python collection types, but it's completely sufficient for the overwhelming majority of Python 3 programs you'll encounter in the wild or are likely to write yourself.

In this chapter we'll be covering these collections in the order mentioned above, rounding things off with an overview of the *protocols* that unite these collections and which allow them to be used in consistent and predictable ways.

tuple – an immutable sequence of objects

Tuples in Python are immutable sequences of arbitrary objects. Once created, the objects within them cannot be replaced or removed, and new elements cannot be added.

Literal tuples

Tuples have a similar literal syntax to lists, except that they are delimited by parentheses rather than square brackets. Here is a literal tuple containing a `string`, a `float` and an integer:

```
>>> t = ("Norway", 4.953, 3)
>>> t
('Norway', 4.953, 3)
```

Tuple element access

We can access the elements of a tuple by zero-based index using square brackets:

```
>>> t[0]
'Norway'
>>> t[2]
3
```

The length of a tuple

We can determine the number of elements in the tuple using the built-in `len()` function:

```
>>> len(t)
3
```

Iterating over a tuple

We can iterate over it using a `for`-loop:

```
>>> for item in t:
>>>     print(item)
Norway
4.953
3
```

Concatenating and repetition of tuples

We can concatenate tuples using the plus operator:

```
>>> t + (338186.0, 265E9)
('Norway', 4.953, 3, 338186.0, 265000000000.0)
```

Similarly, we can repeat them using the multiplication operator:

```
>>> t * 3
('Norway', 4.953, 3, 'Norway', 4.953, 3, 'Norway', 4.953, 3)
```

Nested tuples

Since tuples can contain any object, it's perfectly possible to have nested tuples:

```
>>> a = ((220, 284), (1184, 1210), (2620, 2924), (5020, 5564), (6232,
6368))
```

We use repeated application of the indexing operator to get to the inner elements:

```
>>> a[2][1]
2924
```

Single-element tuples

Sometimes a single element tuple is required. To write this, we can't just use a simple object in parentheses. This is because Python parses that as an object enclosed in the precedence controlling parentheses of a math expression:

```
>>> h = (391)
>>> h
391
>>> type(h)
<class 'int'>
```

To create a single-element tuple we make use of the trailing comma separator which, you'll recall, we're allowed to use when specifying literal tuples, lists, and dictionaries. A single element with a trailing comma is parsed as a single element tuple:

```
>>> k = (391,)
>>> k
(391,)
>>> type(k)
<class 'tuple'>
```

Empty tuples

This leaves us with the problem of how to specify an empty tuple. In actuality the answer is simple, we just use empty parentheses:

```
>>> e = ()
>>> e
>>> type(e)
<class 'tuple'>
```

Optional parentheses

In many cases, the parentheses of literal tuples may omitted:

```
>>> p = 1, 1, 1, 4, 6, 19
>>> p
(1, 1, 1, 4, 6, 19)
>>> type(p)
<class 'tuple'>
```

Returning and unpacking tuples

This feature is often used when returning multiple values from a function. Here we make a function to return the minimum and maximum values of a sequence, the hard work being done by two built-in functions `min()` and `max()`:

```
>>> def minmax(items):
...     return min(items), max(items)
...
>>> minmax([83, 33, 84, 32, 85, 31, 86])
(31, 86)
```

Returning multiple values as a tuple is often used in conjunction with a wonderful feature of Python called *tuple unpacking*. Tuple unpacking is a so-called *destructuring operation* which allows us to unpack data structures into named references. For example, we can assign the result of our `minmax()` function to two new references like this:

```
>>> lower, upper = minmax([83, 33, 84, 32, 85, 31, 86])
>>> lower
31
>>> upper
86
```

This also works with nested tuples:

```
>>> (a, (b, (c, d))) = (4, (3, (2, 1)))
>>> a
4
>>> b
3
>>> c
2
>>> d
1
```

Swapping variables with tuple unpacking

Tuple unpacking leads to the beautiful Python idiom for swapping two (or more) variables:

```
>>> a = 'jelly'
>>> b = 'bean'
>>> a, b = b, a
>>> a
bean
>>> b
jelly
```

The tuple constructor

Should you need to create a tuple from an existing collection object, such as a list, you can use the `tuple()` constructor. Here we create a tuple from a list:

```
>>> tuple([561, 1105, 1729, 2465])
(561, 1105, 1729, 2465)
```

And here we create a tuple containing the characters of a string:

```
>>> tuple("Carmichael")
('C', 'a', 'r', 'm', 'i', 'c', 'h', 'a', 'e', 'l')
```

Membership tests

Finally, as with most collection types in Python, we can test for membership using the in operator:

```
>>> 5 in (3, 5, 17, 257, 65537)
True
```

Also non-membership with the not in operator:

```
>>> 5 not in (3, 5, 17, 257, 65537)
False
```

Strings in action

We covered the `str` type at some length already in chapter two, but we'll take time now to explore its capabilities in a more depth.

The length of a string

As with any other Python sequence, we can determine the length of a string with the built-in `len()` function.

```
>>> len("llanfairpwllgwyngyllgogerychwyrndrobwllllantysiliogogogoch")
58
```

The sign for the railway station at **Llanfairpwllgwyngyllgogerychwyrndrobwllllantysiliogo gogoch** on the Welsh island of Anglesey – the longest place name in Europe:

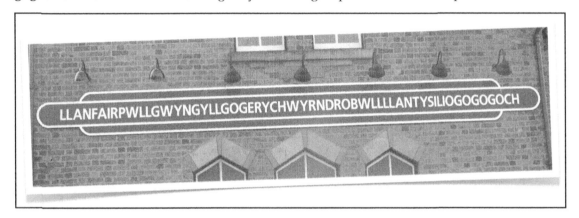

Figure 5.1: The longest place name in Europe

Concatenating strings

Concatenation of strings is supported using the plus operator:

```
>>> "New" + "found" + "land"
Newfoundland
```

Also the related augmented assignment operator:

```
>>> s = "New"
>>> s += "found"
>>> s += "land"
>>> s
'Newfoundland'
```

Newfoundland, the sixteenth largest island in the world, is one of relative few closed, triple-compound words in English:

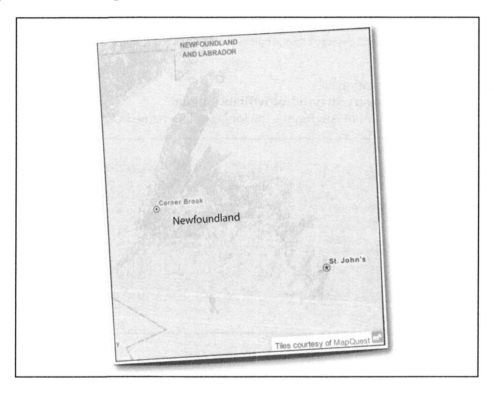

Figure 5.2: Newfoundland

Remember that strings are immutable, so here the augmented assignment operator is binding a new string object to s on each use. The illusion of modifying s in place is achievable because s is a reference to an object, not an object itself. That is, although the string itself is immutable, the reference to it is mutable.

Joining strings

For joining large numbers of strings, avoid using the + or += operators. Instead, the join() method should be preferred because it is substantially more efficient. This is because concatenation using the addition operator or it's augmented assignment version can lead to the generation of large numbers of temporaries, with consequent costs for memory allocation and copies. Let's see how join() is used.

The join() is a method on str which takes a collection of strings as an argument and produces a new string by inserting a separator between each of them. An interesting aspect of join() is how the separator is specified: it is the string on which join() is called.

As with many parts of Python, an example is the best explanation. To join a list of HTML color code strings into a semicolon separated string:

```
>>> colors = ';'.join(['#45ff23', '#2321fa', '#1298a3', '#a32312'])
>>> colors
'#45ff23;#2321fa;#1298a3;#a32312'
```

Here, we call join() on the separator we wish to use – the semicolon – and pass in the list of strings to be joined.

A widespread and fast Python idiom for concatenating together a collection of strings is to join() using an empty string as the separator:

```
>>> ''.join(['high', 'way', 'man'])
highwayman
```

Splitting strings

We can then split strings up again using the split() method (which we've already encountered, but this time we're going to provide it's optional argument):

```
>>> colors.split(';')
['#45ff23', '#2321FA', '#1298A3', '#A32912']
```

The optional argument lets you specify the string — not just the character — on which to split the string. So, for example, you could parse a hasty breakfast order by splitting on the word 'and':

```
>>> 'eggsandbaconandspam'.split('and')
['eggs', 'bacon', 'spam']
```

Moment of zen

Moment of zen: The way not be obvious at first – To concatenate, Invoke join on empty text. Something for nothing:

Figure 5.3: Moment of zen

This use of `join()` is often confusing to the uninitiated, but with use, the approach taken by Python will be appreciated as natural and elegant.

Partitioning strings

Another very useful string method is `partition()` which divides a string into three sections; the part before a separator, the separator itself, and the part after the separator:

```
>>> "unforgettable".partition('forget')
('un', 'forget', 'table')
```

The `partition()` method returns a tuple, so this is commonly used in conjunction with tuple unpacking:

```
>>> departure, separator, arrival = "London:Edinburgh".partition(':')
>>> departure
London
>>> arrival
Edinburgh
```

Often, we're not interested in capturing the separator value, so you might see the underscore variable name used. This is not treated in a special way by the Python language, but there's an unwritten convention that the underscore variable is for unused or dummy values:

```
>>> origin, _, destination = "Seattle-Boston".partition('-')
```

This convention is supported by many Python-aware development tools which will suppress unused variable warnings for underscore.

String formatting

One of the most interesting and frequently used string methods is `format()`. This supersedes, although does not replace, the string interpolation technique used in older versions of Python, and which we do not cover in this book. The `format()` method can be usefully called on any string containing so-called *replacement fields* which are surrounded by curly braces. The objects provided as arguments to `format()` are converted to strings and used to populate these fields. Here's an example:

```
>>> "The age of {0} is {1}".format('Jim', 32)
'The age of Jim is 32'
```

The field names, in this case 0 and 1, are matched up with the positional arguments to `format()`, and each argument is converted to a string behind the scenes.

A field name may be used more than once:

```
>>> "The age of {0} is {1}. {0}'s birthday is on {2}".format('Fred', 24,
'October 31')
```

However, if the field names are used exactly once and in the same order as the arguments, they can be omitted:

```
>>> "Reticulating spline {} of {}.".format(4, 23)
'Reticulating spline 4 of 23.'
```

If keyword arguments are supplied to `format()` then named fields can be used instead of ordinals:

```
>>> "Current position {latitude} {longitude}".format(latitude="60N",
                                                      longitude="5E")
'Current position 60N 5E'
```

It's possible to index into sequences using square brackets inside the replacement field:

```
>>> "Galactic position x={pos[0]}, y={pos[1]}, z={pos[2]}".\
format(pos=(65.2, 23.1, 82.2))
'Galactic position x=65.2, y=23.1, z=82.2'
```

We can even access object attributes. Here we pass the whole math module to `format()` using a keyword argument (Remember – modules are objects too!), then access two of its attributes from within the replacement fields:

```
>>> import math
>>> "Math constants: pi={m.pi}, e={m.e}".format(m=math)
'Math constants: pi=3.141592653589793 e=2.718281828459045'
```

Format strings also give us a lot of control over field alignment and floating-point formatting. Here's the same with the constants displayed to only three decimal places:

```
>>> "Math constants: pi={m.pi:.3f}, e={m.e:.3f}".format(m=math)
'Math constants: pi=3.142, e=2.718'
```

Other string methods

We recommend you spend some time familiarizing yourself with the other string methods. Remember, you can find out what they are using simply:

```
>>> help(str)
```

range – a collection of evenly spaced integers

Let's move on and look at range, which many developers wouldn't consider to be a collection, although we'll see that in Python 3 it most definitely is.

A range is a type of sequence used for representing an arithmetic progression of integers. Ranges are created by calls to the `range()` constructor, and there is no literal form. Most typically we supply only the stop value, as Python defaults to a starting value of zero:

```
>>> range(5)
range(0, 5)
```

Ranges are sometimes used to create consecutive integers for use as loop counters:

```
>>> for i in range(5):
...     print(i)
...
0
1
2
3
4
```

Note that the stop value supplied to `range()` is one past the end of the sequence, which is why the previous loop didn't print 5.

Starting value

We can also supply a starting value if we wish:

```
>>> range(5, 10)
range(5, 10)
```

Wrapping this in a call to the `list()` constructor is a handy way to force production of each item:

```
>>> list(range(5, 10))
[5, 6, 7, 8, 9]
```

This so-called half-open range convention — with the stop value not being included in the sequence — at first seems strange, but it actually makes a lot of sense if you're dealing with consecutive ranges because the end specified by one range is the start of the next one:

```
>>> list(range(10, 15))
[10, 11, 12, 13, 14]
>>> list(range(5, 10)) + list(range(10, 15))
[5, 6, 7, 8, 9, 10, 11, 12, 13, 14]
```

Step argument

Range also supports a step argument:

```
>>> list(range(0, 10, 2))
[0, 2, 4, 6, 8]
```

Note that in order to use the step argument, we must supply all three arguments. Range is curious in that it determines what its arguments mean by counting them. Providing only one argument means that the argument is the stop value. Two arguments are start and stop, and three arguments are start, stop and step. Python range() works this way so the first argument, start, can be made optional, something which isn't normally possible. Furthermore the range constructor doesn't support keyword arguments. You might almost describe it as unPythonic!

The arguably unPythonic constructor for range, where the interpretation of the arguments depends on whether one, two, or three are provided as shown in the following diagram:

Constructor	Arguments	Result
range(5)	stop	0, 1, 2, 3, 4
range(5, 10)	start, stop	5, 6, 7, 8, 9
range(10, 20, 2)	start, stop, step	10, 12, 14, 16, 18

Figure 5.4: UnPythonic constructor for range

Not using range: enumerate()

At this point we're going to show you another example of poorly styled code, except this time it's one you can, and should, avoid. Here's a poor way to print the elements in a list:

```
>>> s = [0, 1, 4, 6, 13]
>>> for i in range(len(s)):
...     print(s[i])
...
0
1
4
6
13
```

Although this works, it is most definitely unPythonic. Always prefer to use iteration over objects themselves:

```
>>> s = [0, 1, 4, 6, 13]
>>> for v in s:
...     print(v)
0
1
4
6
13
```

If you need a counter, you should use the built-in enumerate() function which returns an iterable series of pairs, each pair being a tuple. The first element of each pair is the index of the current item and the second element of each pair is the item itself:

```
>>> t = [6, 372, 8862, 148800, 2096886]
>>> for p in enumerate(t):
>>>     print(p)
(0, 6)
(1, 372)
(2, 8862)
(3, 148800)
(4, 2096886)
```

Even better, we can use tuple unpacking and avoid having to directly deal with the tuple:

```
>>> for i, v in enumerate(t):
...     print("i = {}, v = {}".format(i, v))
...
i = 0, v = 6
i = 1, v = 372
i = 2, v = 8862
i = 3, v = 148800
i = 4, v = 2096886
```

list in action

We've already covered lists a little, and we've been making good use of them. We know how to create lists using the literal syntax, add to them using the append() method, and get at and modify their contents using the square brackets indexing with positive, zero-based indexes.

Zero and positive integers index from the front of a list, so index four is the fifth element in the list:

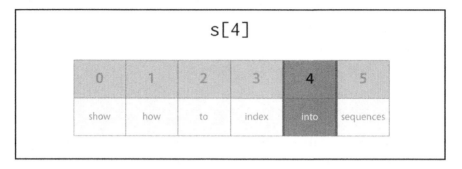

Figure 5.5: Zero and positive integers index

Now we'll take a deeper look.

Negative indexing for lists (and other sequences)

One very convenient feature of lists (and other Python sequences, for this applies to tuples too) is the ability to index from the end, rather than from the beginning. This is achieved by supplying *negative* indices. For example:

```
>>> r = [1, -4, 10, -16, 15]
>>> r[-1]
15
>>> r[-2]
-16
```

Negative integers are –1 based backwards from the end, so index –5 is the last but fourth element as shown in the following diagram:

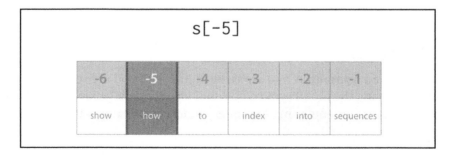

Figure 5.6: Reverse index

This is much more elegant than the clunky equivalent of computing a positive index, which you would otherwise need to use for retrieving that last element:

```
>>> r[len(r) - 1]
```

Note that indexing with -0 is the same as indexing with 0 and returns the first element in the list. Because there is no distinction between 0 and negative zero, negative indexing is essentially one-based rather than zero-based. This is good to keep in mind if you're calculating indices with even moderately complex logic: One-off errors can creep into negative indexing fairly easily.

Slicing lists

Slicing is a form of extended indexing which allows us to refer to portions of a list. To use it we pass the start and stop indices of a half-open range, separated by a colon, as the square-brackets index argument. Here's how:

```
>>> s = [3, 186, 4431, 74400, 1048443]
>>> s[1:3]
[186, 4431]
```

See how the second index is one beyond the end of the returned range. The slice [1:4] . Slicing extracts part of a list. The slice range is half-open, so the value at the **stop** index is not included:

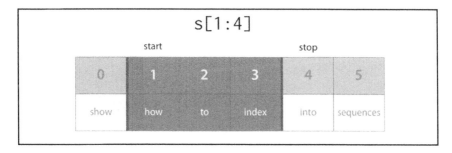

Figure 5.7: The half-open slice range

This facility can be combined with negative indices. For example, to take all elements except the first and last:

```
>>> s[1:-1]
[186, 4431, 74400]
```

The slice s[1:-1] is useful for excluding the first and last elements of a list as shown in the following image:

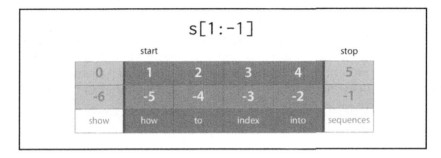

Figure 5.8: Excluding elements

Both the **start** and **stop** indices are optional. To slice all elements from the third to the end of the list:

```
>>> s[3:]
[74400, 1048443]
```

The slice s[3:] retains all the elements from the fourth, up to and including the last element, as shown in the following diagram

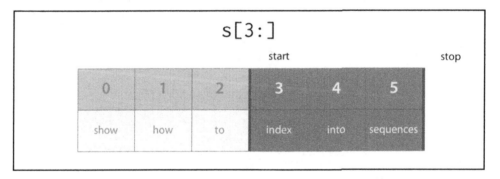

Figure 5.9: Slice-to-end

To slice all elements from the beginning up to, but not including, the third:

```
>>> s[:3]
[3, 186, 4431]
```

The slice `s[:3]` retains all elements from the beginning of the list up to, but not including, the fourth element as shown in the following diagram:

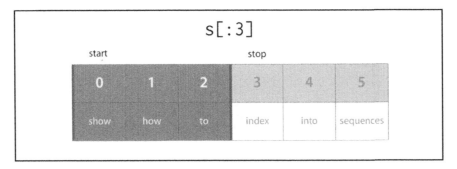

Figure 5.10: Silce from the beginning

Notice that these two lists are complementary, and together form the whole list, demonstrating the convenience of the half-open range convention.

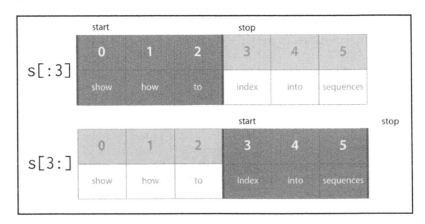

Figure 5.11: Complementary slices

Since both `start` and `stop` slice indices are optional, it's entirely possible to omit both and retrieve all of the elements:

```
>>> s[:]
[3, 186, 4431, 74400, 1048443]
```

This is a called a *full slice*, and it's an important technique in Python.

The slice `s[:]` is the full-slice and contains all of the elements from the list. It's an important idiom for copying lists:

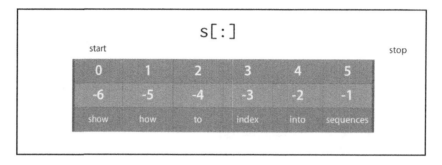

Figure 5.12: The full-slice

Copying lists

Indeed, the full slice is an important idiom for *copying* a list. Recall that assigning references never copies an object, but rather merely copies a reference to an object:

```
>>> t = s
>>> t is s
True
```

We deploy the full slice to perform a copy into a new list:

```
>>> r = s[:]
```

And confirm that the list obtained with the full slice has a distinct identity:

```
>>> r is s
False
```

Although it has an equivalent value:

```
>>> r == s
True
```

It's important to understand that although we have a new `list` object which can be independently modified, the elements within it are references to the same objects referred to by the original list. In the event that these objects are both mutable and modified (as opposed to replaced) the change will be seen in both lists.

We show this full-slice list copying idiom because you are likely to see it in the wild, and it's not immediately obvious what it does. You should be aware that there are other more readable ways of copying a list, such as the copy() method:

```
>>> u = s.copy()
>>> u is s
False
```

Or a simple call to the list constructor, passing the list to be copied:

```
>>> v = list(s)
```

Largely the choice between these techniques is a matter of taste. Our preference is for the third form using the list constructor, since it has the advantage of working with any iterable series as the source, not just lists.

Shallow copies

You must be aware, however, that all of these techniques perform a *shallow* copy. That is, they create a new list containing references to the same objects as the source list, but they don't copy the referred-to objects. To demonstrate this, we'll use nested lists, with the inner lists serving as mutable objects. Here's a list containing two elements, each of which is itself a list:

```
>>> a = [ [1, 2], [3, 4] ]
```

We copy this list using a full slice:

```
>>> b = a[:]
```

And convince ourselves that we do in fact have distinct lists:

```
>>> a is b
False
```

With equivalent values:

```
>>> a == b
True
```

Notice, however, that the references within these distinct lists refer not only to *equivalent* objects:

```
>>> a[0]
[1, 2]
>>> b[0]
[1, 2]
```

But, in fact, to the *same* object:

```
>>> a[0] is b[0]
True
```

Copies are shallow. When a list is copied the references to the containing objects (yellow diamonds) are copied, but the referred to objects (blue rectangles) are not, as shown in the following diagram:

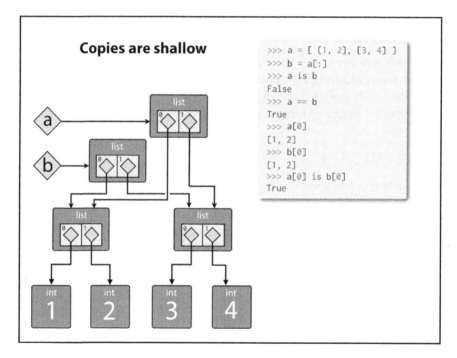

Figure 5.13: Copies are shallow.

This situation holds until we rebind the first element of a to a newly constructed list:

```
>>> a[0] = [8, 9]
```

Now the first elements of a and b refer to different lists:

```
>>> a[0]
[8, 9]
>>> b[0]
[1, 2]
```

The first elements of lists a and b are now uniquely owned, whereas the second elements are shared, as shown in the following diagram:

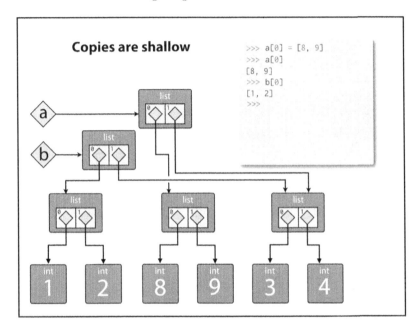

Figure 5.14: Unique and shared elements

The second elements of both a and b still refer to the same object. We'll demonstrate this by mutating that object through the a list:

```
>>> a[1].append(5)
>>> a[1]
[3, 4, 5]
```

We see the change reflected through the b list:

```
>>> b[1]
[3, 4, 5]
```

Modifying an object referred to by two lists, as shown in the following diagram:

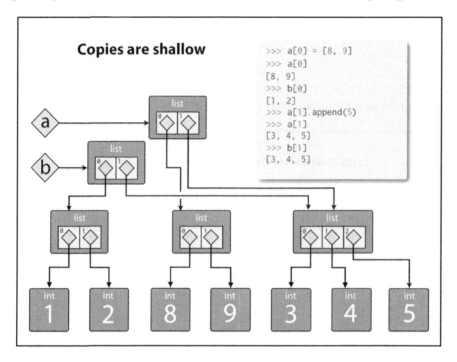

Figure 5.15:Mutating shared elements

For completeness, here is the final state of both the a and b lists:

```
>>> a
[[8, 9], [3, 4, 5]]
>>> b
[[1, 2], [3, 4, 5]]
```

The final state of list a.

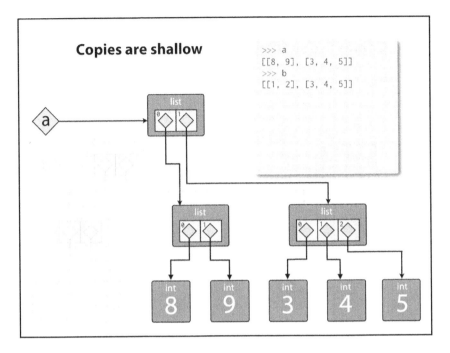

Figure 5.16: The final state of list a

The final state of list b:

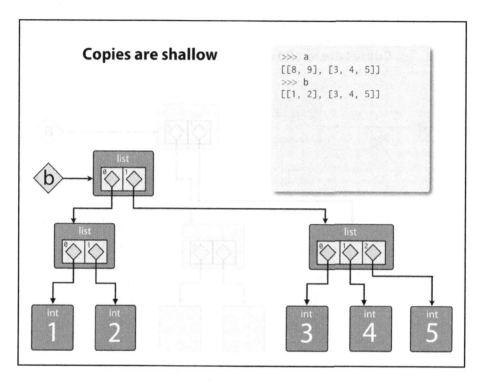

Figure 5.17: The final state of list b.

If you need to perform true deep copies of hierarchical data structures like this – which in our experience is a rarity – we recommend taking a look at the copy module in the Python Standard Library.

Repeating lists

As for strings and tuples, lists support repetition using the multiplication operator. It's simple enough to use:

```
>>> c = [21, 37]
>>> d = c * 4
>>> d
[21, 37, 21, 37, 21, 37, 21, 37]
```

Although it's rarely spotted in the wild in this form. It's most often useful for initializing a list of size known in advance to a constant value, such as zero:

```
>>> [0] * 9
[0, 0, 0, 0, 0, 0, 0, 0, 0]
```

Be aware, though, that in the case of mutable elements the same trap for the unwary lurks here, since repetition will repeat *the reference* to each element, without copying the value. Let's demonstrate using nested lists as our mutable elements again:

```
>>> s = [ [-1, +1] ] * 5
>>> s
[[-1, 1], [-1, 1], [-1, 1], [-1, 1], [-1, 1]]
```

Repetition is shallow, as illustrated in the following diagram:

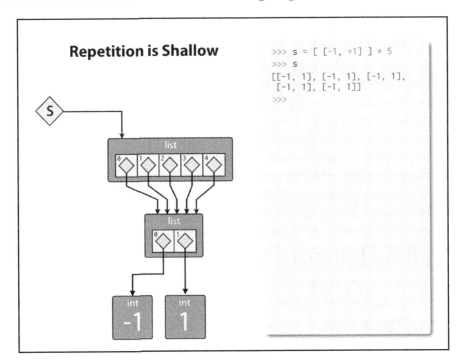

Figure 5.18: Repitition is shallow.

If we now modify the third element of the outer list:

```
>>> s[2].append(7)
```

We see the change through all five references which comprise the outer list elements:

```
>>> s
[[-1, 1, 7], [-1, 1, 7], [-1, 1, 7], [-1, 1, 7], [-1, 1, 7]]
```

Mutating the repeated contents of a list. Any change to the object is reflected in every index of the outer list:

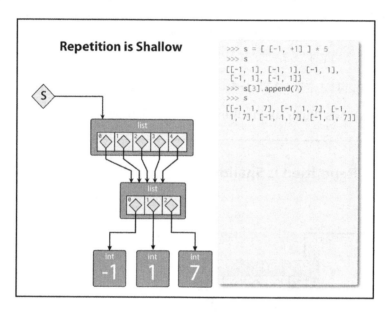

Figure 5.19: Repetition is mutation.

Finding list elements with index()

To find an element in a list, use the `index()` method passing the object you're searching for. The elements are compared for equivalence until the one you're looking for is found:

```
>>> w = "the quick brown fox jumps over the lazy dog".split()
>>> w
['the', 'quick', 'brown', 'fox', 'jumps', 'over', 'the', 'lazy', 'dog']
>>> i = w.index('fox')
>>> i
3
>>> w[i]
'fox'
```

If you search for a value that isn't present, you receive a `ValueError`:

```
>>> w.index('unicorn')
Traceback (most recent call last):
  File "<stdin>", line 1, in <module>
ValueError: 'unicorn' is not in list
```

We'll learn how to handle such errors gracefully in chapter 6, *Exceptions* .

Membership testing with count() and in

Another means of searching is to count() matching elements:

```
>>> w.count("the")
2
```

If you just want to test for membership, you can use the in operator:

```
>>> 37 in [1, 78, 9, 37, 34, 53]
True
```

A non-membership with not in:

```
>>> 78 not in [1, 78, 9, 37, 34, 53]
False
```

Removing list elements by index with del

Elements are removed using a keyword with which we have not yet become acquainted:
del. The del keyword takes a single parameter which is a reference to a list element and
removes it from the list, shortening the list in the process:

```
>>> u = "jackdaws love my big sphinx of quartz".split()
>>> u
['jackdaws', 'love', 'my', 'big', 'sphinx', 'of', 'quartz']
>>> del u[3]
>>> u
['jackdaws', 'love', 'my', 'sphinx', 'of', 'quartz']
```

Removing list elements by value with remove()

It's also possible to remove elements by value, rather than by position, using the `remove()` method:

```
>>> u.remove('jackdaws')
>>> u
['love', 'my', 'sphinx', 'of', 'quartz']
```

This is equivalent to the more verbose:

```
>>> del u[u.index('jackdaws')]
```

Attempting to `remove()` an item which is not present will also cause a `ValueError` to be raised:

```
>>> u.remove('pyramid')
Traceback (most recent call last):
  File "<stdin>", line 1, in <module>
ValueError: list.remove(x): x not in list
```

Inserting into a list

Items can be inserted into lists using the `insert()` method, which accepts the index of the new item and the new item itself:

```
>>> a = 'I accidentally the whole universe'.split()
>>> a
['I', 'accidentally', 'the', 'whole', 'universe']
>>> a.insert(2, "destroyed")
>>> a
['I', 'accidentally', 'destroyed', 'the', 'whole', 'universe']
>>> ' '.join(a)
'I accidentally destroyed the whole universe'
```

Concatenating lists

Concatenating lists using the addition operator results in a new list without modification of either of the operands:

```
>>> m = [2, 1, 3]
>>> n = [4, 7, 11]
>>> k = m + n
>>> k
[2, 1, 3, 4, 7, 11]
```

Whereas the augmented assignment operator += modifies the assignee in place:

```
>>> k += [18, 29, 47]
>>> k
[2, 1, 3, 4, 7, 11, 18, 29, 47]
```

A similar effect can also be achieved using the extend() method:

```
>>> k.extend([76, 129, 199])
>>> k
[2, 1, 3, 4, 7, 11, 18, 29, 47, 76, 123, 199]
```

Augmented assignment and the extend() method will work with any iterable series on the right-hand-side.

Rearranging list elements

Before we move on from lists, let's look at two operations which rearrange the elements in place: Reversing and sorting.

A list can be reversed in place simply by calling it's reverse() method:

```
>>> g = [1, 11, 21, 1211, 112111]
>>> g.reverse()
>>> g
[112111, 1211, 21, 11, 1]
```

A list can be sorted in place, using the sort() method:

```
>>> d = [5, 17, 41, 29, 71, 149, 3299, 7, 13, 67]
>>> d.sort()
>>> d
[5, 7, 13, 17, 29, 41, 67, 71, 149, 3299]
```

The `sort()` method accepts two optional arguments, key and reverse. The latter is self explanatory and when set to `True` gives a descending sort:

```
>>> d.sort(reverse=True)
>>> d
[3299, 149, 71, 67, 41, 29, 17, 13, 7, 5]
```

The `key` parameter is more interesting. It accepts any *callable* object which is then used to extract a *key* from each item. The items will then be sorted according to the relative ordering of these keys.

There are several types of callable objects in Python, although the only one we have encountered so far is the humble function. For example, the `len()` function is a callable object which is used to determine the length of a collection, such as a string.

Consider the following list of words:

```
>>> h = 'not perplexing do handwriting family where I illegibly know
doctors'.split()
>>> h
['not', 'perplexing', 'do', 'handwriting', 'family', 'where', 'I',
'illegibly', 'know', 'doctors']
>>> h.sort(key=len)
>>> h
['I', 'do', 'not', 'know', 'where', 'family', 'doctors', 'illegibly',
'perplexing', 'handwriting']
>>> ' '.join(h)
'I do not know where family doctors illegibly perplexing handwriting'
```

Out-of-place rearrangement

Sometimes an *in situ* sort or reversal is not what is required. For example, it may cause a function argument to be modified, giving the function confusing side effects. For out-of-place equivalents of the `reverse()` and `sort()` list methods you can use the `reversed()` and `sorted()` build-in functions which return a reverse iterator and a new sorted list respectively. For example:

```
>>> x = [4, 9, 2, 1]
>>> y = sorted(x)
>>> y
[1, 2, 4, 9]
>>> x
[4, 9, 2, 1]
```

We can also use the `reversed()` function:

```
>>> p = [9, 3, 1, 0]
>>> q = reversed(p)
>>> q
<list_reverseiterator object at 0x1007bf290>
>>> list(q)
[0, 1, 3, 9]
```

Notice how we used a `list` constructor to evaluate the result of `reversed()`. This is because `reversed()` returns an iterator, a topic which we'll cover in much more detail later.

These functions have the advantage that they'll work on any finite iterable source object.

Dictionaries

We'll now return to dictionaries, which lie at the heart of many Python programs, including the Python interpreter itself. We briefly looked at literal dictionaries previously, seeing how they are delimited with curly braces and contain comma-separated key value pairs, with each pair tied together by a colon:

```
>>> urls = {'Google': 'http://google.com',
...         'Twitter': 'http://twitter.com',
...         'Sixty North': 'http://sixty-north.com',
...         'Microsoft': 'http://microsoft.com' }
>>>
```

A dictionary of URLs. The order of dictionary keys is not preserved, refer to the following diagram:

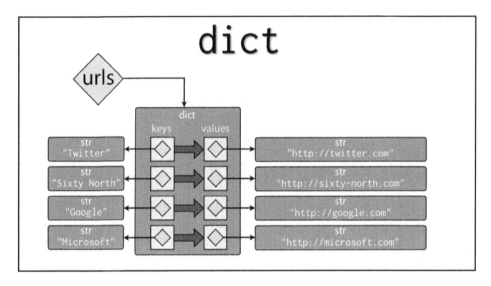

Figure 5.20: Dictionary

The values are accessible via the keys:

```
>>> urls['Twitter']
http://twitter.com
```

Since each key is associated with exactly one value, and lookup is through keys, the keys must be unique within any single dictionary. It's fine, however, to have duplicate values.

Internally, the dictionary maintains pairs of references to the key objects and the value objects. The key objects *must* be immutable, so strings, numbers and tuples are fine, but lists are not. The value objects can be mutable, and in practice often are. Our example URL map uses strings for both keys and values, which is fine.

You should never rely on the order of items in the dictionary – it's essentially random and may even vary between different runs of the same program.

As with the other collections, there's also a named constructor `dict()` which can convert other types to dictionaries. We can use the constructor to copy from an iterable series of key-value pairs stored in tuples, like this:

```
>>> names_and_ages = [ ('Alice', 32), ('Bob', 48), ('Charlie', 28),
                       ('Daniel', 33) ]
>>> d = dict(names_and_ages)
>>> d
{'Charlie': 28, 'Bob': 48, 'Alice': 32, 'Daniel': 33}
```

Recall that the items in a dictionary are not stored in any particular order, so the order of the pairs within the list is not preserved.

So long as the keys are legitimate Python identifiers it's even possible to create a dictionary directly from keyword arguments passed to `dict()`:

```
>>> phonetic = dict(a='alfa', b='bravo', c='charlie', d='delta', e='echo',
f='foxtrot')
>>> phonetic
{'a': 'alfa', 'c': 'charlie', 'b': 'bravo', 'e': 'echo', 'd': 'delta', 'f':
'foxtrot'}
```

Again, the order of the keyword arguments is not preserved.

Copying dictionaries

As with lists dictionary copying is shallow by default, copying only the references to the key and value objects, not the objects themselves. There are two means of copying a dictionary, of which we most commonly see the second. The first technique is to use the `copy()` method:

```
>>> d = dict(goldenrod=0xDAA520, indigo=0x4B0082, seashell=0xFFF5EE)
>>> e = d.copy()
>>> e
{'indigo': 4915330, 'goldenrod': 14329120, 'seashell': 16774638}
```

The second is simply to pass an existing dictionary to the `dict()` constructor:

```
>>> f = dict(e)
>>> f
{'indigo': 4915330, 'seashell': 16774638, 'goldenrod': 14329120}
```

Updating dictionaries

If you need to extend a dictionary with definitions from another dictionary you can use the `update()` method. This is called on the dictionary to be updated and is passed the contents of the dictionary which is to be merged in:

```
>>> g = dict(wheat=0xF5DEB3, khaki=0xF0E68C, crimson=0xDC143C)
>>> f.update(g)
>>> f
>>> {'crimson': 14423100, 'indigo': 4915330, 'goldenrod': 14329120,
    'wheat': 16113331, 'khaki': 15787660, 'seashell': 16774638}
```

If the argument to `update()` includes keys which are already present in the target dictionary, the values associated with these keys are replaced in the target by the corresponding values from the source:

```
>>> stocks = {'GOOG': 891, 'AAPL': 416, 'IBM': 194}
>>> stocks.update({'GOOG': 894, 'YHOO': 25})
>>> stocks
{'YHOO': 25, 'AAPL': 416, 'IBM': 194, 'GOOG': 894}
```

Iterating over dictionary keys

As we have seen in an earlier chapter, dictionaries are iterable and so can be used with `for`-loops. The dictionary yields only the *key* on each iteration, and it's up to us to retrieve the corresponding value by lookup using the square-brackets operator:

```
>>> colors = dict(aquamarine='#7FFFD4', burlywood='#DEB887',
...               chartreuse='#7FFF00', cornflower='#6495ED',
...               firebrick='#B22222', honeydew='#F0FFF0',
...               maroon='#B03060', sienna='#A0522D')
>>> for key in colors:
...     print("{key} => {value}".format(key=key, value=colors[key]))
...
firebrick => #B22222
maroon => #B03060
aquamarine => #7FFFD4
burlywood => #DEB887
honeydew => #F0FFF0
sienna => #A0522D
chartreuse => #7FFF00
cornflower => #6495ED
```

Notice that the keys are returned in an arbitrary order which is neither the order in which they were specified nor any other meaningful sort order.

Iterating over dictionary values

If we want to iterate over only the values, we can use the values() dictionary method. This returns an object which provides an iterable *view* onto the dictionary values without causing the values to be copied:

```
>>> for value in colors.values():
...     print(value)
...
#B22222
#B03060
#7FFFD4
#DEB887
#F0FFF0
#A0522D
#DEB887
#6495ED
```

There is no efficient or convenient way to retrieve the corresponding *key* from a value, so we only print the values

In the interests of symmetry, there is also a keys() method, although since the iterating over the dictionary object directly yields the keys, this is less commonly used:

```
>>> for key in colors.keys():
...     print(key)
...
firebrick
maroon
aquamarine
burlywood
honeydew
sienna
chartreuse
cornflower
```

Iterating over key-value pairs

Often though, we want to iterate over the keys and values in tandem. Each key-value pair in a dictionary is called an *item* and we can get hold of an iterable view of items using the items() dictionary method. When iterated the items() view yields each key-value pair as a tuple.

By using tuple unpacking in the for-statement we can get both key and value in one operation without the extra lookup:

```
>>> for key, value in colors.items():
...     print("{key} => {value}".format(key=key, value=value))
...
firebrick => #B22222
maroon => #B03060
aquamarine => #7FFFD4
burlywood => #DEB887
honeydew => #F0FFF0
sienna => #A0522D
chartreuse => #DEB887
cornflower => #6495ED
```

Membership testing for dictionary keys

The membership tests for dictionaries using the in and not in operators work on the keys:

```
>>> symbols = dict(
...     usd='\u0024', gbp='\u00a3', nzd='\u0024', krw='\u20a9',
...     eur='\u20ac', jpy='\u00a5',  nok='kr', hhg='Pu', ils='\u20aa')
>>> symbols
{'jpy': '¥', 'krw': '₩', 'eur': '€', 'ils': '₪', 'nzd': '$', 'nok': 'kr',
'gbp': '£', 'usd': '$', 'hhg': 'Pu'}
>>> 'nzd' in symbols
True
>>> 'mkd' not in symbols
True
```

Removing dictionary items

As for lists, to remove an entry from a dictionary, we use the `del` keyword:

```
>>> z = {'H': 1, 'Tc': 43, 'Xe': 54, 'Un': 137, 'Rf': 104, 'Fm': 100}
>>> del z['Un']
>>> z
{'H': 1, 'Fm': 100, 'Rf': 104, 'Xe': 54, 'Tc': 43}
```

Mutability of dictionaries

The keys in a dictionary should be immutable, although the values can be modified. Here's a dictionary which maps the element symbol to a list of mass numbers for different isotopes of that element:

```
>>> m = {'H': [1, 2, 3],
...      'He': [3, 4],
...      'Li': [6, 7],
...      'Be': [7, 9, 10],
...      'B': [10, 11],
...      'C': [11, 12, 13, 14]}
```

See how we split the dictionary literal over multiple lines. That's allowed because the curly braces for the dictionary literal are open.

Our string keys are immutable, which is a good thing for correct functioning of the dictionary. But there's no problem with modifying the dictionary values in the event that we discover some new isotopes:

```
>>> m['H'] += [4, 5, 6, 7]
>>> m
{'H': [1, 2, 3, 4, 5, 6, 7], 'Li': [6, 7], 'C': [11, 12, 13, 14],
 'B': [10, 11], 'He': [3, 4], 'Be': [7, 9, 10]}
```

Here, the augmented assignment operator is applied to the `list` object accessed through the `'H'` (for hydrogen) key; the dictionary is not being modified.

Of course, the dictionary itself is mutable; we know we can add new items:

```
>>> m['N'] = [13, 14, 15]
```

Pretty printing

With compound data structures such as our table of isotypes, it can be helpful to have them printed out in a much more readable form. We can do this with the Python Standard Library pretty-printing module called `pprint`, which contains a function called `pprint`:

```
>>> from pprint import pprint as pp
```

Note that if we didn't bind the `pprint` function to a different name `pp`, the function reference would overwrite the module reference, preventing further access to contents of the module:

```
>>> pp(m)
{
    'B': [10, 11],
    'Be': [7, 9, 10],
    'C': [11, 12, 13, 14],
    'H': [1, 2, 3, 4, 5, 6, 7],
    'He': [3, 4],
    'Li': [6, 7],
    'N': [13, 14, 15]
}
```

Gives us a much more comprehensible display.

Let's move on from dictionaries and look at a new built-in data structure, the set.

set – an unordered collection of unique elements

The set data type is an unordered collection of unique elements. The collection is mutable insofar as elements can be added and removed from the set, but each element must itself be immutable, very much like the keys of a dictionary.

Sets are unordered groups of distinct elements as illustrated in the following image:

Figure 5.21: Set

Sets have a literal form very similar to dictionaries, again delimited by curly braces, but each item is a single object, rather than a pair joined by a colon:

```
>>> p = {6, 28, 496, 8128, 33550336}
```

Note that like a dictionary, the set is unordered:

```
>>> p
{33550336, 8128, 28, 496, 6}
```

Of course, sets have type set:

```
>>> type(p)
<class 'set'>
```

The set constructor

Recall that somewhat confusingly, empty curly braces create an empty *dictionary*, rather than an empty set:

```
>>> d = {}
>>> type(d)
<class 'dict'>
```

To create an empty set we must resort to the `set()` constructor:

```
>>> e = set()
>>> e
set()
```

This is also the form Python echoes back to us for empty sets.

The `set()` constructor can create a set from any iterable series, such as a list:

```
>>> s = set([2, 4, 16, 64, 4096, 65536, 262144])
>>> s
{64, 4096, 2, 4, 65536, 16, 262144}
```

Duplicates in the input series are discarded. In fact, a common use of sets is to efficiently remove duplicate items from series of objects:

```
>>> t = [1, 4, 2, 1, 7, 9, 9]
>>> set(t)
{1, 2, 4, 9, 7}
```

Iterating over sets

Naturally, sets are iterable, although the order is arbitrary:

```
>>> for x in {1, 2, 4, 8, 16, 32}:
>>>     print(x)
32
1
2
4
8
16
```

Membership testing of sets

Membership is a fundamental operation for sets, and as with the other collection types is performed using the in and not in operators:

```
>>> q = { 2, 9, 6, 4 }
>>> 3 in q
False
>>> 3 not in q
True
```

Adding elements to sets

To add a single element to a set use the add() method:

```
>>> k = {81, 108}
>>> k
{81, 108}
>>> k.add(54)
>>> k
{81, 108, 54}
>>> k.add(12)
>>> k
{81, 108, 54, 12}
```

Adding an element that already exists has no effect:

```
>>> k.add(108)
```

Although neither does it produce an error. Multiple elements can be added in one go from any iterable series, including another set, using the update() method:

```
>>> k.update([37, 128, 97])
>>> k
{128, 81, 37, 54, 97, 12, 108}
```

Removing elements from sets

Two methods are provided for removing elements from sets. The first, remove(), requires that the element to be removed is present in the set, otherwise a KeyError is given:

```
>>> k.remove(97)
>>> k
{128, 81, 37, 54, 12, 108}
>>> k.remove(98)
Traceback (most recent call last):
  File "<stdin>", line 1, in <module>
KeyError: 98
```

The second method, discard(), is less fussy and simply has no effect if the element is not a member of the set:

```
>>> k.discard(98)
>>> k
{128, 81, 37, 54, 12, 108}
```

Copying sets

As with the other built-in collections, set sports a copy() method which performs a shallow copy of the set (copying references but not objects):

```
>>> j = k.copy()
>>> j
{128, 81, 37, 54, 108, 12}
```

As we have already shown, the set() constructor may be used:

```
>>> m = set(j)
>>> m
{128, 81, 37, 54, 108, 12}
```

Set algebra operations

Perhaps the most useful aspect of the set type is the group of powerful set algebra operations which are provided. These allow us to easily compute set unions, set differences, and set intersections, and to evaluate whether two sets have subset, superset, or disjoint relations.

To demonstrate these methods, we'll construct some sets of people according to various phenotypes:

```
>>> blue_eyes = {'Olivia', 'Harry', 'Lily', 'Jack', 'Amelia'}
>>> blond_hair = {'Harry', 'Jack', 'Amelia', 'Mia', 'Joshua'}
>>> smell_hcn = {'Harry', 'Amelia'}
>>> taste_ptc = {'Harry', 'Lily', 'Amelia', 'Lola'}
>>> o_blood = {'Mia', 'Joshua', 'Lily', 'Olivia'}
>>> b_blood = {'Amelia', 'Jack'}
>>> a_blood = {'Harry'}
>>> ab_blood = {'Joshua', 'Lola'}
```

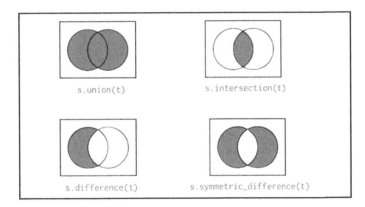

Figure 5.22: Set algebra operations

Union

To find all the people with blond hair, blue eyes or both, we can use the `union()` method:

```
>>> blue_eyes.union(blond_hair)
{'Olivia', 'Jack', 'Joshua', 'Harry', 'Mia', 'Amelia', 'Lily'}
```

Set union collects together all of the elements which are in either or both sets.

We can demonstrate that `union()` is a commutative operation (that is, we can swap the order of the operands) using the value equality operator to check for equivalence of the resulting sets:

```
>>> blue_eyes.union(blond_hair) == blond_hair.union(blue_eyes)
True
```

Intersection

To find all the people with blond hair *and* blue eyes, we can use the `intersection()` method:

```
>>> blue_eyes.intersection(blond_hair)
{'Amelia', 'Jack', 'Harry'}
```

Which collects together only the elements which are present in both sets. This is also commutative:

```
>>> blue_eyes.intersection(blond_hair) ==
blond_hair.intersection(blue_eyes)
True
```

Difference

To identify the people with blond hair who *don't* have blue eyes, we can use the `difference()` method:

```
>>> blond_hair.difference(blue_eyes)
{'Joshua', 'Mia'}
```

This finds all the elements which are in the first set which are not in the second set.

This is non-commutative because the people with blond hair who don't have blue eyes are not the same as the people who have blue eyes but don't have blond hair:

```
>>> blond_hair.difference(blue_eyes) == blue_eyes.difference(blond_hair)
False
```

Symmetric difference

However, if we want to determine which people have exclusively blond hair *or* blue eyes, but not both, we can use the `symmetric_difference()` method:

```
>>> blond_hair.symmetric_difference(blue_eyes)
{'Olivia', 'Joshua', 'Mia', 'Lily'}
```

This collects all the elements which are in the first set *or* the second set, but not both.

As you can tell from the name, `symmetric_difference()` is indeed commutative:

```
>>> blond_hair.symmetric_difference(blue_eyes) ==
blue_eyes.symmetric_difference(blond_hair)
True
```

Subset relationships

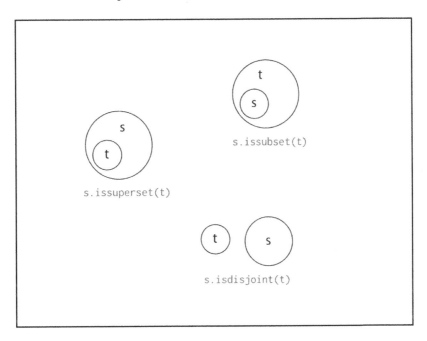

Figure 5.23: Set relationships

In addition, three predicate methods are provided which tell us about the relationships between sets. We can check whether one set is a subset of another using the `issubset()` method. For example, to check whether all of the people who can smell hydrogen cyanide also have blond hair:

```
>>> smell_hcn.issubset(blond_hair)
True
```

This checks that all the elements of the first set are also present in the second set.

To test whether all the people who can taste **phenylthiocarbamide** (**PTC**) can also smell hydrogen cyanide use the `issuperset()` method:

```
>>> taste_ptc.issuperset(smell_hcn)
True
```

This checks that all the elements of the second set are present in the first set.

A representation of PTC. It has the unusual property that it either tastes very bitter or is virtually tasteless, depending on the genetics of the taster:

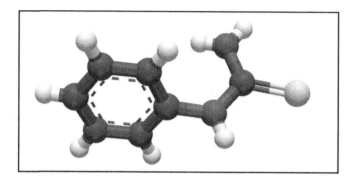

Figure 5.24: Representation of phenylthiocarbamide

To test that two sets have no members in common, use the `isdisjoint()` method. For example, your blood type is either A or O, never both:

```
>>> a_blood.isdisjoint(o_blood)
True
```

Collection protocols

In Python, a protocol is a group of operations or methods that a type must support if it is to implement that protocol. Protocols needn't be defined in the source code as separate interfaces or base classes as they would in a nominally typed language such as C# or Java. It's sufficient to simply have an object provide functioning implementations of those operations.

We can organize the different collections we have encountered in Python according to which protocols they support:

Protocol	Implementing collections
Container	`str`, `list`, `dict`, `range`, `tuple`, `set`, `bytes`
Sized	`str`, `list`, `dict`, `range`, `tuple`, `set`, `bytes`
Iterable	`str`, `list`, `dict`, `range`, `tuple`, `set`, `bytes`
Sequence	`str`, `list`, `tuple`, `range`, `bytes`
Mutable Sequence	`list`
Mutable Set	`set`
Mutable Mapping	`dict`

Support for a protocol demands specific behavior from a type.

Container protocol

The *container* protocol requires that membership testing using the in and not in operators be supported:

```
item in container
item not in container
```

Sized protocol

The *sized* protocol requires that the number of elements in a collection can be determined by calling `len(sized_collection)`

Iterable protocol

Iteration is such an important concept that we're devoting a whole chapter to it later in this book. In short, though, *iterables* provide a means for yielding elements one-by-one as they are requested.

One important property of *iterables* is that they can be used with `for`-loops:

```
for item in iterable:
    print(item)
```

Sequence protocol

The *sequence* protocol requires that items can be retrieved using square brackets with an integer index:

```
item = sequence[index]
```

The items can be searched for with `index()`:

```
i = sequence.index(item)
```

The items can be counted with `count()`:

```
num = sequence.count(item)
```

They can be a reversed copy of the sequence can be produced with `reversed()`:

```
r = reversed(sequence)
```

In addition, the *sequence* protocol requires that the object support the *iterable, sized,* and *containers.*

Other protocols

We won't cover the *mutable sequence, mutable mapping,* and *mutable set* here. Since we have only covered one representative type of each protocol, the generality afforded by the protocol concept doesn't gain us much at this juncture.

Summary

- Tuples are immutable sequence types
    - Literal syntax is optional parentheses around a comma-separated list.

- Notable syntax for single element tuples utilizing the trailing comma.

- Tuple unpacking - useful for multiple return values and swapping

- Strings

  - String concatenation is most efficiently performed with the `join()` method rather than the addition or augmented assignment operators.

  - The `partition()` method is a useful and elegant string parsing tool.

  - The `format()` method provided a powerful means of replacing placeholders with stringified values.

- Ranges

  - The `range` objects represent arithmetic progressions.

  - The `enumerate()` built-in function is often a superior alternative to `range()` for generating loop counters

- Lists

  - Lists support indexing from the end of the list with negative indices

  - Slice syntax allows us to copy all, or part, of a list.

  - The full slice is a common Python idiom for copying lists, although the `copy()` method and `list()` constructor are less obscure.

  - List (and other collection) copies in Python are shallow copies. References are copied, but the referenced objects are not.

- Dictionaries map from keys to values

  - Iteration and membership testing with dictionaries is done with respect to the keys.

  - The keys(), values() and items() methods provide views onto the different aspects of a dictionary, allowing convenient iteration.

- Sets store an unordered collection of unique elements.

  - Sets support powerful set-algebra operations and predicates.

  - The built in collections are can be organized according to which protocols they support, such as *iterable*, *sequence* and *mapping*.

In passing we have also discovered that:

- Underscore is commonly used for dummy or superfluous variables

- The pprint module supports pretty printing of compound data structures.

Back in Python 2 days range() was a function which returned a list. The Python 3 version of range is much more efficient, useful and powerful. This, of course, brings to mind the classic joke: The two hardest problems in programming are naming, cache coherence, and off-by-one errors. Arguably, it's poor design to have a module containing functions of the same name, because of this issue.

6
Exceptions

Exception handling is a mechanism for halting "normal" program flow and continuing at some surrounding context or code block.

The act of interrupting normal flow is called "raising" an exception. In some enclosing context the raised exception must be *handled*, which means control flow is transferred to an exception
handler. If an exception propagates up the call stack to the start of the program, then an unhandled exception will cause the program to terminate. An exception object, containing information about where and why an exceptional event occurred, is transported from the point at which the exception was raised to the exception handler so that the handler can interrogate the exception object and take appropriate action.

If you've used exceptions in other popular imperative languages like C++ or Java, then you've already got a good idea of how exceptions work in Python.

There have been long and tiresome debates over exactly what constitutes an "exceptional event", the core issue being that exceptionality is in reality a matter of degree (some things are more exceptional than others). This is problematic because programming languages impose a false
dichotomy by insisting that an event is either entirely exceptional or not at all exceptional.

The Python philosophy is at the liberal end of the spectrum when it comes to the use of exceptions. Exceptions are ubiquitous in Python, and it's crucial to understand how to handle them.

Exceptions and control flow

Since exceptions are a means of control flow, they can be clumsy to demonstrate at the REPL, so in this chapter we'll be using a Python module to contain our code. Let's start with a very simple module we can use for exploring these important concepts and behaviors. Place the this code in a module called `exceptional.py`:

```
"""A module for demonstrating exceptions."""

def convert(s):
    """Convert to an integer."""
    x = int(s)
    return x
```

Import the `convert()` function from this module into the Python REPL:

```
$ python3
Python 3.5.1 (v3.5.1:37a07cee5969, Dec  5 2015, 21:12:44)
[GCC 4.2.1 (Apple Inc. build 5666) (dot 3)] on darwin
Type "help", "copyright", "credits" or "license" for more information.
>>> from exceptional import convert
```

and call our function with a string to see that it has the desired effect:

```
>>> convert("33")
33
```

If we call our function with an object that can't be converted to an integer, we get a `traceback` from the `int()` call:

```
>>> convert("hedgehog")
Traceback (most recent call last):
  File "<stdin>", line 1, in <module>
  File "./exceptional.py", line 7, in convert
    x = int(s)
ValueError: invalid literal for int() with base 10: 'hedgehog'
```

What's happened here is that `int()` *raised* an exception because it couldn't sensibly perform the conversion. We didn't have a handler in place, so it was caught by the REPL and the stack trace was displayed. In other words, the exception went unhandled.

The `ValueError` referred to in the stack trace is the *type* of the `exception` object, and the error message "invalid literal for `int()` with base 10: 'hedgehog' is part of the payload of the exception object that has been retrieved and printed by the REPL.

Notice that the exception propagates across several levels in the call stack:

Call stack	Effect
`int()`	**Exception raised here**
`convert()`	Exception conceptually passes through here
REPL	Exception caught here

Handling exceptions

Let's make our `convert()` function more robust by handling the `ValueError` using a `try` ... `except` construct. Both the `try` and `except` keywords introduce new blocks. The `try` block contains code that could raise an exception and the `except` block contains the code which performs error handling in the event that an exception is raised. Modify the `convert()` function to look like this:

```
def convert(s):
    """Convert a string to an integer."""
    try:
        x = int(s)
    except ValueError:
        x = -1
    return x
```

We have decided that if a non-integer string is supplied, we'll return minus one. To reinforce your understanding of the control-flow here we'll also add a couple of print statements:

```
def convert(s):
    """Convert a string to an integer."""
    try:
        x = int(s)
        print("Conversion succeeded! x =", x)
    except ValueError:
        print("Conversion failed!")
        x = -1
    return x
```

Let's test this interactively after restarting the REPL:

```
>>> from exceptional import convert
>>> convert("34")
Conversion succeeded! x = 34
34
>>> convert("giraffe")
Conversion failed!
-1
```

Note how the `print()` in the `try` block after the point at which the exception was raised was *not* executed when we passed in `"giraffe"` as the function argument. Instead, execution was transferred directly to the first statement of the `except` block.

The `int()` constructor only accepts numbers or strings, so let's see what happens if we feed an object of another type into it, say a list:

```
>>> convert([4, 6, 5])
Traceback (most recent call last):
  File "<stdin>", line 1, in <module>
  File "./exceptional.py", line 8, in convert
    x = int(s)
TypeError: int() argument must be a string or a number, not 'list'
```

This time our handler didn't intercept the exception. If we look closely at the trace, we can see that this time we received a `TypeError` – a different type of exception.

Handling multiple exceptions

Each `try` block can have multiple corresponding `except` blocks which intercept exceptions of different types. Let's add a handler for `TypeError` too:

```
def convert(s):
    """Convert a string to an integer."""
    try:
        x = int(s)
        print("Conversion succeeded! x =", x)
    except ValueError:
        print("Conversion failed!")
        x = -1
    except TypeError:
        print("Conversion failed!")
        x = -1
    return x
```

Now if we re-run the same test in a fresh REPL we find that `TypeError` is handled too:

```
>>> from exceptional import convert
>>> convert([1, 3, 19])
Conversion failed!
-1
```

We've got some code duplication between our two exception handlers with that duplicated `print` statement and assignment. We'll move the assignment in front of the `try` block, which doesn't change the behavior of the program:

```
def convert(s):
    """Convert a string to an integer."""
    x = -1
    try:
        x = int(s)
        print("Conversion succeeded! x =", x)
    except ValueError:
        print("Conversion failed!")
    except TypeError:
        print("Conversion failed!")
    return x
```

Then we'll exploit the fact that both handlers do the same thing by collapsing them into one, using the ability of the except statement to accept a tuple of exception types:

```
def convert(s):
    """Convert a string to an integer."""
    x = -1
    try:
        x = int(s)
        print("Conversion succeeded! x =", x)
    except (ValueError, TypeError):
        print("Conversion failed!")
    return x
```

Now we see that everything still works as designed:

```
>>> from exceptional import convert
>>> convert(29)
Conversion succeeded! x = 29
29
>>> convert("elephant")
Conversion failed!
-1
>>> convert([4, 5, 1])
Conversion failed!
-1
```

Programmer errors

Now that we're confident with the control flow for exception behavior, we can remove the print statements:

```
def convert(s):
    """Convert a string to an integer."""
    x = -1
```

```
    try:
        x = int(s)
    except (ValueError, TypeError):
    return x
```

But now when we try to import our program:

```
>>> from exceptional import convert
Traceback (most recent call last):
  File "<stdin>", line 1, in <module>
  File "./exceptional.py", line 11
    return x
         ^
IndentationError: expected an indented block
```

we get yet another type of exception, an `IndentationError`, because our `except` block is now empty and empty blocks are not permitted in Python programs.

This is not an exception type that is *ever* useful to `catch` with an `except` block! Almost anything that goes wrong with a Python program results in an exception, but some exception types, such as `IndentationError`, `SyntaxError` and `NameError`, are the result of programmer errors which should be identified and corrected during development rather than handled at runtime. The fact that these things are exceptions is mostly useful if you're creating a Python development tool such as a Python IDE, embedding Python itself in a larger system to support application scripting, or designing a plugin system which dynamically loads code.

Empty blocks – the pass statement

With that said, we still have the problem of what to do with our empty `except` block. The solution arrives in the form of the `pass` keyword, which is a special statement that does precisely nothing! It's a no-op, and it's only purpose is to allow us to construct syntactically permissible blocks that are semantically empty:

```
def convert(s):
    """Convert a string to an integer."""
    x = -1
    try:
        x = int(s)
    except (ValueError, TypeError):
        pass
    return x
```

In this case though, it would be better to simplify further by using multiple `return` statements, doing away with the x variable completely:

```
def convert(s):
    """Convert a string to an integer."""
    try:
        return int(s)
    except (ValueError, TypeError):
        return -1
```

Exception objects

Sometimes, we'd like to get hold of the `exception` object – in this case an object of type `ValueError` or `TypeError` - and interrogate it for more details of what went wrong. We can get a named reference to the exception object by tacking an as clause onto the end of the `except` statement with a variable name that will be bound to the `exception` object:

```
def convert(s):
    """Convert a string to an integer."""
    try:
        return int(s)
    except (ValueError, TypeError) as e:
        return -1
```

We'll modify our function to print a message with exception details to the `stderr` stream before returning. To print to `stderr` we need to get a reference to the stream from the `sys` module, so at the top of our module we'll need to `import sys`. We can then pass `sys.stderr` as a keyword argument called file to `print()`:

```
import sys

def convert(s):
    """Convert a string to an integer."""
    try:
        return int(s)
    except (ValueError, TypeError) as e:
        print("Conversion error: {}".format(str(e)), file=sys.stderr)
        return -1
```

We take advantage of the fact that `exception` objects can be converted to strings using the `str()` constructor.

Let's see that at the REPL:

```
>>> from exceptional import convert
>>> convert("fail")
Conversion error: invalid literal for int() with base 10: 'fail'
-1
```

Imprudent return codes

Let's add a second function, `string_log()` to our module, which calls our `convert()` function and computes the natural log of the result:

```
from math import log

def string_log(s):
    v = convert(s)
    return log(v)
```

At this point we must confess that we've gone out of our way here to be deeply unPythonic by wrapping the perfectly good `int()` conversion, which raises exceptions on failure, in our `convert()` function which returns a good old-fashioned negative error code. Rest assured that this unforgivable Python heresy has been committed solely to demonstrate the greatest folly of error return codes: That they can be ignored by the caller, wreaking havoc amongst unsuspecting code later in the program. A slightly better program might test the value of v before proceeding to the log call.

Without such a check `log()` will of course fail when passed the negative error code value:

```
>>> from exceptional import string_log
>>> string_log("ouch!")
Conversion error: invalid literal for int() with base 10: 'ouch!'
Traceback (most recent call last):
  File "<stdin>", line 1, in <module>
  File "./exceptional.py", line 15, in string_log
    return log(v)
ValueError: math domain error
```

Naturally, the consequence of the `log()` failure is the raising of another exception, also a `ValueError`.

Much better, and altogether more Pythonic, to forget about error return codes completely and revert to raising an exception from `convert()`.

Re-raising exceptions

Instead of returning an unPythonic error code, we can simply emit our error message and re-raise the `exception` object we're currently handling. This can be done by replacing the `return -1` with a `raise` statement at the end of our exception handling block:

```
def convert(s):
    """Convert a string to an integer."""
    try:
        return int(s)
    except (ValueError, TypeError) as e:
        print("Conversion error: {}".format(str(e)), file=sys.stderr)
        raise
```

Without a parameter raise simply re-raises the exception that is currently being handled.

Testing in the REPL, we can see that the original exception type is re-raised whether it's a `ValueError` or a `TypeError`, and our `Conversion error` message is printed to `stderr` along the way:

```
>>> from exceptional import string_log
>>> string_log("25")
3.2188758248682006
>>> string_log("cat")
Conversion error: invalid literal for int() with base 10: 'cat'
Traceback (most recent call last):
  File "<stdin>", line 1, in <module>
  File "./exceptional.py", line 14, in string_log
    v = convert(s)
  File "./exceptional.py", line 6, in convert
    return int(s)
ValueError: invalid literal for int() with base 10: 'cat'
>>> string_log([5, 3, 1])
Conversion error: int() argument must be a string or a number, not 'list'
Traceback (most recent call last):
  File "<stdin>", line 1, in <module>
  File "./exceptional.py", line 14, in string_log
    v = convert(s)
  File "./exceptional.py", line 6, in convert
    return int(s)
TypeError: int() argument must be a string or a number, not 'list'
```

Exceptions are part of your function's API

Exceptions are an important aspect of the API of a function. Callers of a function need to know which exceptions to expect under various conditions so that they can ensure appropriate exception handlers are in place. We'll use square-root finding as an example, using a home-grown square-root function, courtesy of Heron of Alexandria (although he probably didn't use Python).

Callers of a function need to know which exceptions to expect:

CALLERS NEED TO KNOW WHICH EXCEPTIONS TO EXPECT, AND WHEN!

Figure 6.1: Callers need to know now

Place the following code in a file `roots.py`:

```python
def sqrt(x):
    """Compute square roots using the method of Heron of Alexandria.

    Args:
        x: The number for which the square root is to be computed.

    Returns:
        The square root of x.
    """
    guess = x
    i = 0
    while guess * guess != x and i < 20:
        guess = (guess + x / guess) / 2.0
        i += 1
    return guess

def main():
```

```
    print(sqrt(9))
    print(sqrt(2))

if __name__ == '__main__':
    main()
```

There's only one language feature in this program we haven't met before: The logical and operator which we use in this case to test that two conditions are `True` on each iteration of the loop. Python also includes a logical or operator which can be used to test whether either or both of its operands are `True`.

Running our program, we can see that Heron was really on to something:

```
$ python3 roots.py
3.0
1.41421356237
```

Exceptions raised by Python

Let's add a new line to the `main()` function which takes the square-root of `-1`:

```
def main():
    print(sqrt(9))
    print(sqrt(2))
    print(sqrt(-1))
```

If we run that, we get a new exception:

```
$ python3 sqrt.py
3.0
1.41421356237
Traceback (most recent call last):
  File "sqrt.py", line 14, in <module>
    print(sqrt(-1))
  File "sqrt.py", line 7, in sqrt
    guess = (guess + x / guess) / 2.0
ZeroDivisionError: float division
```

What has happened is that Python has intercepted a division by zero, which occurs on the second iteration of the loop, and raised an exception – a `ZeroDivisionError`.

Catching exceptions

Let's modify our code to catch the exception before it propagates up to the top of the call stack (thereby causing our program to stop) using the `try ... except` construct:

```
def main():
    print(sqrt(9))
    print(sqrt(2))
    try:
        print(sqrt(-1))
    except ZeroDivisionError:
        print("Cannot compute square root of a negative number.")

    print("Program execution continues normally here.")
```

Now when we run the script we see that we're handling the exception cleanly:

```
$ python sqrt.py
3.0
1.41421356237
Cannot compute square root of a negative number.
Program execution continues normally here.
```

We should be careful to avoid a beginners mistake of having too-tight scopes for exception handling blocks; we can easily use one `try ... except` block for all of our calls to `sqrt()`. We also add a third print statement to show how execution of the enclosed block is terminated:

```
def main():
    try:
        print(sqrt(9))
        print(sqrt(2))
        print(sqrt(-1))
        print("This is never printed.")
    except ZeroDivisionError:
        print("Cannot compute square root of a negative number.")

    print("Program execution continues normally here.")
```

Raising exceptions explicitly

This is an improvement on what we started with, but most likely users of a `sqrt()` function don't expect it to throw a `ZeroDivisionError`.

Python provides us with several standard exception types to signal common errors. If a function parameter is supplied with an illegal value, it is customary to raise a `ValueError`. We can do this by using the raise keyword with a newly created `exception` object which we can create by calling the `ValueError` constructor.

There are two ways in which we could deal with the division by zero. The first approach would be to wrap the root-finding `while`-loop in a `try ... except ZeroDivisionError` construct and then raise a new `ValueError` exception from inside the exception handler.

```python
def sqrt(x):
    """Compute square roots using the method of Heron of Alexandria.

    Args:
        x: The number for which the square root is to be computed.

    Returns:
        The square root of x.
    """
    guess = x
    i = 0
    try:
        while guess * guess != x and i < 20:
            guess = (guess + x / guess) / 2.0
            i += 1
    except ZeroDivisionError:
        raise ValueError()
    return guess
```

While it works, this would be wasteful; we would knowingly proceed with a non-trivial computation which will ultimately be pointless.

Figure 6.2: Wasteful

Guard clauses

We know this routine will always fail with negative numbers so we can detect this precondition early on and raise an exception at that point, a technique called a *guard clause*:

```python
def sqrt(x):
    """Compute square roots using the method of Heron of Alexandria.

    Args:
        x: The number for which the square root is to be computed.

    Returns:
        The square root of x.

    Raises:
        ValueError: If x is negative.
    """

    if x < 0:
        raise ValueError("Cannot compute square root of negative
                          number{}".format(x))

    guess = x
    i = 0
    while guess * guess != x and i < 20:
        guess = (guess + x / guess) / 2.0
        i += 1
    return guess
```

The test is a simple if-statement and a call to raise passing a newly minted exception object. The ValueError() constructor accepts an error message. See how we also modify the docstring to make it plain which exception type will be raised by sqrt() and under what circumstances.

But look what happens if we run the program – we're still getting a traceback and an ungraceful program exit:

```
$ python roots.py
3.0
1.41421356237
Traceback (most recent call last):
  File "sqrt.py", line 25, in <module>
    print(sqrt(-1))
  File "sqrt.py", line 12, in sqrt
    raise ValueError("Cannot compute square root of negative number\
                      {0}".format(x))
ValueError: Cannot compute square root of negative number -1
```

This happens because we forgot to modify our exception handler to catch `ValueError` rather than `ZeroDivisionError`. Let's modify our calling code to `catch` the right `exception` class and also assign the caught `exception` object to a named variable so we can interrogate it after it has been caught. In this case our interrogation is simply to print the `exception` object, which knows how to display itself as the message to `stderr`:

```python
import sys

def main():
    try:
        print(sqrt(9))
        print(sqrt(2))
        print(sqrt(-1))
        print("This is never printed.")
    except ValueError as e:
        print(e, file=sys.stderr)

    print("Program execution continues normally here.")
```

Running the program again, we can see that our exception is being gracefully handled:

```
$ python3 sqrt.py
3.0
1.41421356237
Cannot compute square root of negative number -1
Program execution continues normally here.
```

Exceptions, APIs, and protocols

Exceptions are part of a function's API, and more broadly are part of certain *protocols*. For example, objects which implement the sequence protocol should raise an `IndexError` exception for indices which are out of range.

The exceptions which are raised are as much a part of a function's specification as the arguments it accepts and must be documented appropriately.

There are a handful of common exception types in Python, and usually when you need to raise an exception in your own code, one of the built-in types is a good choice. Much more rarely, you'll need to define new exception types, but we don't cover that in this book. (See the next book in this series *The Python Journeyman* for how to do that.)

If you're deciding which exceptions your code should raise, you should look for similar cases in existing code. The more your code follows existing patterns, the easier it will be for people to integrate and understand. For example, suppose you were writing a key-value database.

It would be natural to use `KeyError` to indicate a request for a non-existent key because this is how dict works. Which is to say that "mapping" collections in Python follows certain protocols, and exceptions are part of those protocols.

Let's look at a few common exception types.

IndexError

An `IndexError` is raised when an integer index is out of range.

You can see this when you index past the end of a list:

```
>>> z = [1, 4, 2]
>>> z[4]
Traceback (most recent call last):
  File "<stdin>", line 1, in <module>
IndexError: list index out of range
```

ValueError

A `ValueError` is raised when an object is of the right type, but contains an inappropriate value.

We've seen this already when trying to construct an int from a non-numeric string:

```
>>> int("jim")
Traceback (most recent call last):
  File "<stdin>", line 1, in <module>
ValueError: invalid literal for int() with base 10: 'jim'
```

KeyError

A `KeyError` is raised when a look-up in a mapping fails.

You can see that here when we look up a non-existent key in a dict:

```
>>> codes = dict(gb=44, us=1, no=47, fr=33, es=34)
```

```
>>> codes['de']
Traceback (most recent call last):
  File "<stdin>", line 1, in <module>
    KeyError: 'de'
```

Choosing not to guard against TypeError

We tend not to protect against `TypeError`s in Python. To do so runs against the grain of dynamic typing in Python and limits the re-use potential of code we write.

For example, we could test whether the argument was an `str` using the built-in `isinstance()` function and raise a `TypeError` exception if it was not:

```
def convert(s):
    """Convert a string to an integer."""
    if not isinstance(s, str):
        raise TypeError("Argument must be a string".)

    try:
        return int(s)
    except (ValueError, TypeError) as e:
        print("Conversion error: {}".format(str(e)), file=sys.stderr)
        raise
```

But then we'd also want to allow arguments that are instances of `float` as well. It soon gets complicated if we want to check whether our function will work with types such as rational, complex, or any other kind of number, and in any case, who is to say that it does?!

Alternatively we could intercept `TypeError` inside our `sqrt()` function and re-raise it, but to what end?

Figure 6.3: Just let it fail

Usually in Python it's not worth adding type checking to your functions. If a function works with a particular type – even one you couldn't have known about when you designed the function – then that's all to the good. If not, execution will probably result in a `TypeError` anyway. Likewise, we tend not to *catch* `TypeErrors` with `except` blocks very frequently.

Pythonic style – EAFP versus LBYL

Now let's look at another tenet of Python philosophy and culture, the idea that "It's Easier to Ask for Forgiveness than for Permission".

There are only two approaches to dealing with a program operation that might fail. The first approach is to check that all the preconditions for a failure prone operation are met in advance of attempting the operation. The second approach is to blindly hope for the best, but be prepared to deal with the consequences if it doesn't work out.

In Python culture these two philosophies are known as **Look Before you Leap** (LBYL) and its **Easier to Ask for Forgiveness than for Permission (EAFP)** – which, incidentally, was coined by Rear Admiral Grace Hopper, inventor of the compiler.

Python is strongly in favor of EAFP because it puts primary logic for the "happy path" in its most readable form, with deviations from the normal flow handled separately, rather than interspersed with the main flow.

Let's consider an example – processing a file. The details of the processing aren't relevant. All we need to know is that the `process_file()` function will open a file and read some data from it.

First, the LBYL version:

```
import os

p = '/path/to/datafile.dat'

if os.path.exists(p):
    process_file(p)
else:
    print('No such file as {}'.format(p))
```

Before attempting to call `process_file()` we check that the file exists, and if it doesn't we avoid making the call and print a helpful message instead. There are several problems with this approach, some obvious and some insidious. One obvious problem is that we only perform an existence check. What if the file exists but contains garbage? What if the path refers to a directory instead of a file? According to LBYL we should add preemptive tests for those too.

A more subtle problem is that there is a race condition here. It's possible for the file to be deleted, for example by another process, *between* the existence check and the `process_file()` call ... a classic race condition. There's really no good way to deal with this – handling of errors from `process_file()` will be needed in any case!

Now consider the alternative, using the more Pythonic EAFP approach:

```
p = '/path/to/datafile.dat'

try:
    process_file(f)
except OSError as e:
    print('Could not process file because {}'.format(str(e)))
```

In this version we attempt the operation without checks in advance, but we have an exception handler in place to deal with any problems. We don't even need to know in a lot of detail exactly what might go wrong. Here we catch `OSError` which covers all manner of conditions such as file-not-found and using directories where files are expected.

EAFP is standard in Python, and following that philosophy is primarily facilitated by exceptions. Without exceptions, and being forced to use error codes instead, you are required to include error handling directly in the main flow of the logic. Since exceptions interrupt the main flow, they allow you to handle exceptional cases non-locally.

Exceptions coupled with EAFP are also superior because, unlike error codes, *exceptions cannot be easily ignored*. By default exceptions have a big effect, whereas error codes are silent by default. So the exception-/EAFP-based style makes it very difficult for problems to be silently ignored.

Clean-up actions

Sometimes you need to perform a clean-up action irrespective of whether an operation succeeds. In a later module we'll introduce context managers which are the modern solution to this common situation, but here we'll introduce the try ... finally construct, since creating a context manager can be overkill in simple cases. In any case, an understanding of try ... finally is useful for making your own context managers.

Consider this function, which uses various facilities of the standard library os module to change the current working directory, create a new directory at that location, and then restore the original working directory:

```
import os

def make_at(path, dir_name):
    original_path = os.getcwd()
    os.chdir(path)
    os.mkdir(dir_name)
    os.chdir(original_path)
```

At first sight this seems reasonable, but should the call to os.mkdir() fail for some reason the current working directory of the Python process won't be restored to it's original value, and the make_at() function will have had an unintended side-effect.

To fix this, we'd like the function to restore the original current working directory under all circumstances. We can achieve this with a try ... finally block. Code in the finally block is executed whether execution leaves the try block normally by reaching the end of the block, or exceptionally by an exception being raised.

This construct can be combined with except blocks, used below to add a simple failure logging facility:

```
import os
import sys

def make_at(path, dir_name):
  original_path = os.getcwd()
  try:
      os.chdir(path)
      os.mkdir(dir_name)
  except OSError as e:
      print(e, file=sys.stderr)
      raise
  finally:
      os.chdir(original_path)
```

Now, if `os.mkdir()` raises an `OSError`, the `OSError` handler will be run and the exception will be re-raised. But since the finally block is always run no matter how the `try`-block ends, we can be sure that the final directory change will take place in all circumstances.

Moment of zen

Moment of zen: Errors should never pass silently, unless explicitly silenced – Errors are like bells, And if we make them silent, They are of no use:

Figure 6.4: Moment of Zen

Platform-specific code

Detecting a single keypress from Python – such as the "Press any key to continue." functionality at the console – requires use of operating system specific modules. We can't use the built-in `input()` function, because that waits for the user to press *Enter* before giving us a string. To implement this on Windows we need to use functionality from the Windows-only `msvcrt` module, and on Linux and macOS we need to use functionality from the Unix-only `tty` and `termios` modules, in addition to the `sys` module.

This example is quite instructive as it demonstrates many Python language features including `import` and `def` as *statements*, as opposed to merely declarations:

```python
"""keypress - A module for detecting a single keypress."""

try:
    import msvcrt

    def getkey():
        """Wait for a keypress and return a single character
    string."""
        return msvcrt.getch()

except ImportError:

    import sys
    import tty
    import termios

    def getkey():
        """Wait for a keypress and return a single character
        string."""
        fd = sys.stdin.fileno()
        original_attributes = termios.tcgetattr(fd)
        try:
            tty.setraw(sys.stdin.fileno())
            ch = sys.stdin.read(1)
        finally:
            termios.tcsetattr(fd, termios.TCSADRAIN,
                              original_attributes)
        return ch

    # If either of the Unix-specific tty or termios modules are
    # not found, we allow the ImportError to propagate from here
```

Recall that top-level module code is executed on first import. Within the first `try`-block we attempt to `import msvcrt`, the Microsoft Visual C Runtime. If this succeeds, we then proceed to define a function `getkey()` which delegates to the `msvcrt.getch()` function. Even though we're inside a `try`-block at this point the function will be declared at the current scope, which is the module scope.

If, however, the `import` of `msvcrt` fails, because we're not running on Windows, an `ImportError` will be raised and execution will transfer to the `except`-block. This is a case of an error being silenced explicitly, because we're going to attempt an alternative course of action in the exception handler.

Within the `except`-block we import three modules needed for a `getkey()` implementation on Unix-like systems and then proceed to the alternative definition of `getkey()` which again binds the function implementation to a name in the module scope.

This Unix implementation of `getkey()` uses a `try ... finally` construct to restore various terminal attributes after the terminal has been put into raw mode for the purposes of reading a single character.

In the event that our program is running on a system that is neither Windows nor Unix-like, the `import tty` statement will raise a second `ImportError`. This time we make no attempt to intercept this exception; we allow it to propagate to our caller – which is whatever attempted to `import` this `keypress` module. We know how to signal this error, but not how to handle it, so we defer that decision to our caller. The error will not pass silently.

If the caller has more knowledge or alternative tactics available, it can in turn intercept this exception and take appropriate action, perhaps degrading to using Python's `input()` built-in function and giving a different message to the user.

Summary

- The raising of an exception interrupts normal program flow and transfers control to an exception handler.

- Exception handlers are defined using the `try ... except` construct.

- The `try` blocks define a context in which exceptions can be detected.

- Corresponding the `except` blocks define handlers for specific types of exceptions.

- Python uses exceptions pervasively and many built-in language features depend on them.

- The `except` blocks can capture an `exception` object, which is often of a standard type such as `ValueError`, `KeyError` or `IndexError`.

- Programmer errors such as `IndentationError` and `SyntaxError` should not normally be handled.

- Exceptional conditions can be signaled using the `raise` keyword which accepts a single parameter of an `exception` object.

- Raise without an argument within an `except` block re-raises the exception which is currently being processed.

- We tend not to routinely check for `TypeErrors`. To do so would negate the flexibility afforded to us by Python's dynamic type system.

- The `exception` objects can be converted to strings using the `str()` constructor for the purposes of printing message payloads.

- The exceptions thrown by a function form part of it's API and should be appropriately documented.

- When raising exceptions prefer to use the most appropriate built-in exception type.

- Clean-up and restorative actions can be performed using the `try ... finally` construct which may optionally be used in conjunction with `except` blocks.

Along the way we saw that:

- The output of the `print()` function can be redirected to `stderr` using the optional file argument.

- Python supports the logical operators and and or for combining boolean expressions.

- Return codes are too easily ignored.

- Platform specific actions can be implemented using an Easier to Ask Forgiveness than Permission approach facilitated by intercepting `ImportErrors` and providing alternative implementations.

7

Comprehensions, iterables, and generators

The abstract notion of a *sequence of objects* is ubiquitous in programming. It can be used to model such widely different concepts as simple strings, lists of complex objects, and indefinitely long sensor output streams. It probably won't surprise you to learn that Python includes some very powerful and elegant tools for working with sequences. In fact, Python's support for creating and manipulating sequences is one of the highlights of the language for many people.

In this chapter we'll look at three key tools that Python provides for working with sequences: Comprehensions, iterables, and generators. *Comprehensions* comprise a dedicated syntax for creating various types of sequences declaratively. *Iterables* and the *iteration protocols* form the core abstraction and API for sequences and iteration in Python; they allow you define new sequence types and exert fine-grained control over iteration.
Finally, *generators* allow us to define lazy sequences imperatively, a surprisingly powerful technique in many circumstances.

Let's jump right in to comprehensions.

Comprehensions

Comprehensions in Python are a concise syntax for describing lists, sets or dictionaries in a declarative or functional style. This short-hand is readable and expressive, meaning that comprehensions are very effective at communicating intent to human readers. Some comprehensions almost read like natural language, making them nicely self-documenting.

List comprehensions

As hinted at above, a *list comprehension* is a short-hand way of creating a list. It's an expression using a succinct syntax that describes *how list elements are defined*. Comprehensions are much easier to demonstrate than they are to explain, so let's bring up a Python REPL. First we'll create a list of words by splitting a string:

```
>>> words = "If there is hope it lies in the proles".split()
>>> words
['If', 'there', 'is', 'hope', 'it', 'lies', 'in', 'the', 'proles']
```

Now comes the list comprehension. The comprehension is enclosed in square brackets just like a literal list, but instead of literal elements it contains a fragment of declarative code which describes how to construct the elements of the list:

```
>>> [len(word) for word in words]
[2, 5, 2, 4, 2, 4, 2, 3, 6]
```

Here the new list is formed by binding the name word to each value in words in turn and then evaluating len(word) to create the corresponding value in the new list. In other words, this constructs a new list containing the lengths of the string in words; it's hard to imagine a much more effective way of expressing that new list!

List comprehension syntax

The general form for a list comprehension is:

```
[ expr(item) for item in iterable ]
```

That is, for each item in the iterable on the right we evaluate the expression expr(item) on the left (which is almost always, but not necessarily, in terms of the item). We use the result of that expression as the next element of the list we are constructing.

The comprehension above is the declarative equivalent of the following imperative code:

```
>>> lengths = []
>>> for word in words:
...     lengths.append(len(word))
...
>>> lengths
[2, 5, 2, 4, 2, 4, 2, 3, 6]
```

Elements of a list comprehension

Note that the `source` object over which we iterate in a list comprehension doesn't need to be a list itself. It can be any object with implements the iterable protocol, such as a tuple.

The expression part of the comprehension can be any Python expression. Here we find the number of decimal digits in each of the first 20 factorials using `range()` — which is an `iterable` object — to generate the source sequence:

```
>>> from math import factorial
>>> f = [len(str(factorial(x))) for x in range(20)]
>>> f
[1, 1, 1, 1, 2, 3, 3, 4, 5, 6, 7, 8, 9, 10, 11, 13, 14, 15, 16, 18]
```

Note also that the type of the object produced by list comprehensions is nothing more or less than a regular list:

```
>>> type(f)
<class 'list'>
```

It's important to keep this fact in mind as we look at other kinds of comprehensions and consider how to perform iteration over infinite sequences.

Set comprehensions

Sets support a similar comprehension syntax using, as you might expect, curly braces. Our previous "number of digits in factorials" result contained duplicates, but by building a set instead of a list we can eliminate them:

```
>>> s = {len(str(factorial(x))) for x in range(20)}
>>> s
{1, 2, 3, 4, 5, 6, 7, 8, 9, 10, 11, 13, 14, 15, 16, 18}
```

Like list comprehensions, set comprehension produce standard `set` objects:

```
>>> type(s)
<class 'set'>
```

Note that, since sets are unordered containers, the resulting set is not *necessarily* stored in a meaningful order.

Dictionary comprehensions

The third type of comprehension is the dictionary comprehension. Like the set comprehension syntax, the dictionary comprehension also uses curly braces. It is distinguished from the set comprehension by the fact that we now provide two colon-separated expressions — the first for the key and the second for the value — which will be evaluated in tandem for each new item in the resulting dictionary. Here's a dictionary we can play with:

```
>>> country_to_capital = { 'United Kingdom': 'London',
...                        'Brazil': 'Brasília',
...                        'Morocco': 'Rabat',
...                        'Sweden': 'Stockholm' }
```

One nice use for a dictionary comprehension is to invert a dictionary so we can perform efficient lookups in the opposite direction:

```
>>> capital_to_country = {capital: country for country, capital in
...                       country_to_capital.items()}
>>> from pprint import pprint as pp
>>> pp(capital_to_country)
{'Brasília': 'Brazil',
 'London': 'United Kingdom',
 'Rabat': 'Morocco',
 'Stockholm': 'Sweden'}
```

Note

The dictionary comprehensions do not operate directly on dictionary sources! If we want both keys and values from a source dictionary, then we should use the `items()` method coupled with tuple unpacking to access the keys and values separately.

Should your comprehension produce some identical keys, later keys will overwrite earlier keys. In this example we map the first letters of words to the words themselves, but only the last h-word is kept:

```
>>> words = ["hi", "hello", "foxtrot", "hotel"]
>>> { x[0]: x for x in words }
{'h': 'hotel', 'f': 'foxtrot'}
```

Comprehension complexity

Remember that there's no limit to the complexity of the expression you can use in any of the comprehensions. For the sake of your fellow programmers, though, you should avoid going overboard. Instead, extract complex expressions into separate functions to preserve readability. The following is close to the limit of being reasonable for a dictionary comprehension:

```
>>> import os
>>> import glob
>>> file_sizes = {os.path.realpath(p): os.stat(p).st_size for p in
                  glob.glob('*.py')}
>>> pp(file_sizes)
{'/Users/pyfund/examples/exceptional.py': 400,
 '/Users/pyfund/examples/keypress.py': 778,
 '/Users/pyfund/examples/scopes.py': 133,
 '/Users/pyfund/examples/words.py': 1185}
```

This uses the `glob` module to find all of the Python source files in a directory. It then creates a dictionary of paths to file sizes from those files.

Filtering comprehensions

All three types of collection comprehension support an optional filtering clause which allows us to choose which items of the source are evaluated by the expression on the left. The filtering clause is specified by adding `if <boolean expression>` after the sequence definition of the comprehension, If the boolean expression returns false for an item in the input sequence, then no value is evaluated for that item in the result.

To make this interesting, we'll first define a function that determines if its input is a prime number:

```
>>> from math import sqrt
>>> def is_prime(x):
...     if x < 2:
...         return False
...     for i in range(2, int(sqrt(x)) + 1):
...         if x % i == 0:
...             return False
...     return True
...
```

We can now use this in the filtering clause of a list comprehension to produce all primes less than `100`:

```
>>> [x for x in range(101) if is_prime(x)]
[2, 3, 5, 7, 11, 13, 17, 19, 23, 29, 31, 37, 41, 43, 47, 53, 59, 61, 67,
71, 73, 79, 83, 89, 97]
```

Combining filtering and transformation

We have a slightly odd-looking x for x construct here because we're not applying any transformation to the filtered values; the expression in terms of x is simply x itself. There's nothing to stop us, however, from combining a filtering predicate with a transforming expression. Here's a dictionary comprehension which maps numbers with exactly three divisors to a tuple of those divisors:

```
>>> prime_square_divisors = {x*x:(1, x, x*x) for x in range(101) if
                              is_prime(x)}
>>> pp(prime_square_divisors)
{4: (1, 2, 4),
 9: (1, 3, 9),
 25: (1, 5, 25),
 49: (1, 7, 49),
 121: (1, 11, 121),
 169: (1, 13, 169),
 289: (1, 17, 289),
 361: (1, 19, 361),
 529: (1, 23, 529),
 841: (1, 29, 841),
 961: (1, 31, 961),
 1369: (1, 37, 1369),
 1681: (1, 41, 1681),
 1849: (1, 43, 1849),
 2209: (1, 47, 2209),
 2809: (1, 53, 2809),
 3481: (1, 59, 3481),
 3721: (1, 61, 3721),
 4489: (1, 67, 4489),
 5041: (1, 71, 5041),
 5329: (1, 73, 5329),
 6241: (1, 79, 6241),
 6889: (1, 83, 6889),
 7921: (1, 89, 7921),
 9409: (1, 97, 9409)}
```

Moment of zen

Moment of zen: Code is written once but read over and over. Fewer is clearer:

Figure 7.1: Moment of Zen

Comprehensions are often more readable than the alternative. However it's possible to over-use comprehensions. Sometimes a long or complex comprehension may be *less* readable than the equivalent `for`-loop. There is no hard-and-fast rule about when one form should be preferred, but be conscientious when writing your code and try to choose the best form for your situation.

Above all your comprehensions should ideally be purely functional — that is they should have no side effects. If you need to create side effects, such as printing to the console during iteration, use another construct such as a `for`-loop instead.

Iteration protocols

Comprehensions and `for`-loops are the most frequently used language features for performing iteration. The both take items one by one from a source and do something with each in turn. However, both comprehensions and `for`-loops iterate over the whole sequence by default, whereas sometimes more fine-grained control is needed. In this section we'll see how you can exercise this kind of fine-grained control by investigating two important concepts on top of which a great deal of Python language behavior is constructed: `iterable` objects and `iterator` objects, both of which are reflected in standard Python protocols.

The *iterable protocol* defines an API that `iterable` objects must implement. That is, if you want to be able to iterate over an object using `for`-loops or comprehensions, that object must implement the iterable protocol. Built-in classes like list implement the iterable protocol. You can pass an object that implements the iterable protocol to the built-in `iter()` function to get an *iterator* for the `iterable` object.

Iterators, for their part, support the *iterator protocol*. This protocol requires that we can pass the `iterator` object to the built-in `next()` function to fetch the next value from the underlying collection.

An example of the iteration protocols

As usual, a demonstration at the Python REPL will help all of these concepts crystallize into something you can work with. We start with a list of the names of the seasons as our `iterable` object:

```
>>> iterable = ['Spring', 'Summer', 'Autumn', 'Winter']
```

We then ask our `iterable` object to give us an iterator using the `iter()` built-in:

```
>>> iterator = iter(iterable)
```

Next we request a value from the `iterator` object using the `next()` built-in:

```
>>> next(iterator)
'Spring'
```

Each call to `next()` moves the iterator through the sequence:

```
>>> next(iterator)
'Summer'
>>> next(iterator)
```

```
'Autumn'
>>> next(iterator)
'Winter'
```

But what happens when we reach the end?

```
>>> next(iterator)
Traceback (most recent call last):
  File "<stdin>", line 1, in <module>
StopIteration
```

In a spectacular display of liberalism, Python raises a StopIteration exception. Those of you coming from other programming languages with a more straight-laced approach to exceptions may find this mildly outrageous, but, really, what could be more exceptional than reaching the end of a collection? It only has one end after all!

This attempt at rationalizing the Python language design decision makes even more sense when one considers that the iterable series may be a potentially infinite stream of data. Reaching the end in that case really *would* be something to write home about, or indeed raise an exception for.

A more practical example of the iteration protocols

With for-loops and comprehensions at our fingertips, the utility of these lower level iteration protocols may not be obvious. To demonstrate a more concrete use, here's a little utility function which, when passed an iterable object, returns the first item from that series or, if the series is empty, raises a ValueError:

```
>>> def first(iterable):
...     iterator = iter(iterable)
...     try:
...         return next(iterator)
...     except StopIteration:
...         raise ValueError("iterable is empty")
...
```

This works as expected on any iterable object, in this case both a list and a set:

```
>>> first(["1st", "2nd", "3rd"])
'1st'
>>> first({"1st", "2nd", "3rd"})
'1st'
>>> first(set())
```

```
Traceback (most recent call last):
  File "./iterable.py", line 17, in first
    return next(iterator)
StopIteration

During handling of the above exception, another exception occurred:

Traceback (most recent call last):
  File "<stdin>", line 1, in <module>
  File "./iterable.py", line 19, in first
      raise ValueError("iterable is empty")
ValueError: iterable is empty
```

It's worth noting that the higher-level iteration constructs, such as `for`-loops and comprehensions, are built directly upon this lower-level iteration protocol.

Generator functions

Now we come on to *generator functions,* one of the most powerful and elegant features of the Python programming language. Python generators provide the means for describing iterable series with code in functions. These sequences are evaluated lazily, meaning they only compute the next value on demand. This important property allows them to model infinite sequences of values with no definite end, such as streams of data from a sensor or active log files. By carefully designing generator functions we can make generic stream processing elements which can be composed into sophisticated pipelines.

The yield keyword

Generators are defined by any Python function which uses the `yield` keyword at least once in its definition. They may also contain the `return` keyword with no arguments, and just like any other function, there is an implicit return at the end of the definition.

To understand what generators do, let's start with a simple example at the Python REPL. Let's define the generator, and then we'll examine how the generator works.

Generator functions are introduced by `def`, just as for a regular Python function:

```
>>> def gen123():
...     yield 1
...     yield 2
...     yield 3
...
```

Now let's call `gen123()` and assign its return value to `g`:

```
>>> g = gen123()
```

As you can see, `gen123()` is called just like any other Python function. But what has it returned?

```
>>> g
<generator object gen123 at 0x1006eb230>
```

Generators are iterators

The alphabet `g` is a `generator` object. Generators are, in fact, Python *iterators*, so we can use the iterator protocol to retrieve – or yield – successive values from the series:

```
>>> next(g)
1
>>> next(g)
2
>>> next(g)
3
```

Take note of what happens now that we've yielded the last value from our generator. Subsequent calls to `next()` raise a `StopIteration` exception, just like any other Python iterator:

```
>>> next(g)
Traceback (most recent call last):
  File "<stdin>", line 1, in <module>
StopIteration
```

Because generators are iterators, and because iterators must also be iterable, they can be used in all the usual Python constructs which expect `iterable` objects, such as `for`-loops:

```
>>> for v in gen123():
...     print(v)
...
1
2
3
```

Be aware that each call to the generator function returns a new `generator` object:

```
>>> h = gen123()
>>> i = gen123()
>>> h
```

```
<generator object gen123 at 0x1006eb2d0>
>>> i
<generator object gen123 at 0x1006eb280>
>>> h is i
False
```

Also note how each `generator` object can be advanced independently:

```
>>> next(h)
1
>>> next(h)
2
>>> next(i)
1
```

When is generator code executed?

Let's take a closer look at how — and crucially *when* — the code in the body of our generator function is executed. To do this, we'll create a slightly more complex generator that traces its execution with good old-fashioned print statements:

```
>>> def gen246():
...     print("About to yield 2")
...     yield 2
...     print("About to yield 4")
...     yield 4
...     print("About to yield 6")
...     yield 6
...     print("About to return")
...
>>> g = gen246()
```

At this point the `generator` object has been created and returned, but none of the code within the body of the generator function has yet been executed. Let's make an initial call to `next()`:

```
>>> next(g)
About to yield 2
2
```

See how, when we request the first value, the generator body runs up to and including the first `yield` statement. The code executes just far enough to literally yield the next value.

```
>>> next(g)
About to yield 4
4
```

When we request the next value from the generator, execution of the generator function *resumes* at the point it left off, and continues running until the next yield:

```
>>> next(g)
About to yield 6
6
```

After the final value has returned the next request causes the generator function to execute until it returns at the end of the function body, which in turn raises the expected `StopIteration` exception.

```
>>> next(g)
About to return
Traceback (most recent call last):
  File "<stdin>", line 1, in <module>
StopIteration
```

Now that we've seen how generator execution is initiated by calls to `next()` and interrupted by `yield` statements, we can progress to placing more complex code in our generator function body.

Maintaining explicit state in the generator function

Now we'll look at how our generator functions, which resume execution each time the next value is requested, can maintain state in local variables. In the process of doing so, our generators will be both more interesting and more useful. We'll be showing two generators which demonstrate lazy evaluation, and later we'll combine them into a generator pipeline.

The first stateful generator: take()

The first generator we'll look at is `take()` which retrieves a specified number of elements from the front of a sequence:

```
def take(count, iterable):
    """Take items from the front of an iterable.

    Args:
        count: The maximum number of items to retrieve.
        iterable: The source of the items.

    Yields:
        At most 'count' items from 'iterable'.
```

```
    """
    counter = 0
    for item in iterable:
        if counter == count:
            return
        counter += 1
        yield item
```

Note

That the function defines a generator because it contains at least one `yield` statement. This particular generator also contains a return statement to terminate the stream of yielded values. The generator simply uses a counter to keep track of how many elements have been yielded so far, returning when a request is made for any elements beyond that requested count.

Since generators are lazy, and only produce values on request, we'll drive execution with a `for`-loop in a `run_take()` function:

```
def run_take():
    items = [2, 4, 6, 8, 10]
    for item in take(3, items):
        print(item)
```

Here we create a source list named items which we pass to our generator function along with a count of 3. Internally, the `for`-loop will use the iterator protocol to retrieve values from the `take()` generator until it terminates.

The second stateful generator: distinct()

Now let's bring our second generator into the picture. This generator function, called `distinct()`, eliminates duplicate items by keeping track of which elements it's already seen in a set:

```
def distinct(iterable):
    """Return unique items by eliminating duplicates.

    Args:
        iterable: The source of the items.

    Yields:
        Unique elements in order from 'iterable'.
    """
    seen = set()
    for item in iterable:
```

```
        if item in seen:
            continue
        yield item
        seen.add(item)
```

In this generator we also make use of a control flow construct we have not previously seen: The `continue` keyword. The `continue` statement finishes the current iteration of the loop and begins the next iteration immediately. When executed in this case execution will be transferred back to the for statement, but as with `break` it can also be used with `while`-loops.

In this case, the continue is used to skip any values which have already been yielded. We can add a `run_distinct()` function to exercise `distinct()` as well:

```
def run_distinct():
    items = [5, 7, 7, 6, 5, 5]
    for item in distinct(items):
        print(item)
```

Understand these generators!

At this point you should spend some time exploring these two generators before moving on. Make sure you understand how they work and how control flows in and out of them as they maintain state. If you're using an IDE to run these example, you can use the debugger to follow control flow by putting breakpoints in the generators and in the code that uses them. You can accomplish the same by using Python's built-in pdb debugger (which we cover later) or even just by using old-fashioned print statements.

However you do it, make sure you're really comfortable with how these generators work before moving to the next sections.

Lazy generator pipelines

Now that you understand the generators individually, we'll arrange both of them into a lazy pipeline. We'll be using `take()` and `distinct()` together to fetch the first three unique items from a collection:

```
def run_pipeline():
    items = [3, 6, 6, 2, 1, 1]
    for item in take(3, distinct(items)):
        print(item)
```

Notice that the `distinct()` generator only does just enough work to satisfy the demands of the `take()` generator which is iterating over it

- It never gets as far as the last two items in the source list because they are not needed to produce the first three unique items. This lazy approach to computation is very powerful, but the complex control flows it produces can be difficult to debug. It's often useful during development to force evaluation of all of the generated values, and this is most easily achieved by inserting a call to the `list()` constructor:

```
take(3, list(distinct(items)))
```

This interspersed call to `list()` causes the `distinct()` generator to exhaustively process its source items before `take()` does its work. Sometimes when you're debugging lazily evaluated sequences, this can give you the insight you need to understand what's going on.

Laziness and the infinite

Generators are lazy, meaning that computation only happens just-in-time when the next result is requested. This interesting and useful property of generators means they can be used to model infinite sequences. Since values are only produced as requested by the caller, and since no data structure needs to be built to contain the elements of the sequence, generators can safely be used to produce never-ending (or just very large) sequences like:

- Sensor readings
- Mathematical sequences (Example: primes, factorials, and so on.)
- The contents of a multi-terabyte file

Generating the Lucas series

Allow us to present a generator function for the Lucas series:

```
def lucas():
    yield 2
    a = 2
    b = 1
    while True:
        yield b
        a, b = b, a + b
```

The Lucas series starts with 2, 1, and each value after that is the sum of the two preceding values. So the first few value of the sequence are:

```
2, 1, 3, 4, 7, 11
```

The first yield produces the value 2. The function then initializes a and b which hold the "previous two values" needed as the function proceeds. Then the function enters an infinite while-loop where:

1. It yields the value of b
2. a and b are updated to hold the new "previous two" values using a neat application of tuple unpacking

Now that we have a generator, it can be used like any other iterable object. For instance, to print the Lucas numbers you could use a loop like this:

```
>>> for x in lucas():
...     print(x)
...
2
1
3
4
7
11
18
29
47
76
123
199
```

Of course, since the Lucas sequence is infinite this will run forever, printing out values until your computer runs out of memory. Use *Ctrl+C* to terminate the loop.

Generator expressions

Generator expressions are a cross between comprehensions and generator functions. They use a similar syntax as comprehensions, but they result in the creation of a generator object which produces the specified sequence lazily. The syntax for generator expressions is very similar to list comprehensions:

```
( expr(item) for item in iterable )
```

It is delimited by parentheses instead of the brackets used for list comprehensions.

Generator expressions are useful for situations where you want the lazy evaluation of generators with the declarative concision of comprehensions. For example, this generator expression yields a list of the first one-million square numbers:

```
>>> million_squares = (x*x for x in range(1, 1000001))
```

At this point, none of the squares have been created; we've just captured the specification of the sequence into a `generator` object:

```
>>> million_squares
<generator object <genexpr> at 0x1007a12d0>
```

We can force evaluation of the generator by using it to create a (long!) list:

```
>>> list(million_squares)
. . .
999982000081, 999984000064, 999986000049, 999988000036, 999990000025,
999992000016, 999994000009, 999996000004, 999998000001, 1000000000000]
```

This list obviously consumes a significant chunk of memory - in this case about 40 MB for the `list` object and the `integer` objects contained therein.

Generator objects only run once

Notice that a generator object is just an iterator and, once run exhaustively in this way, will yield no more items. Repeating the previous statement returns an empty list:

```
>>> list(million_squares)
[]
```

Generators are single use objects. Each time we call a generator *function* we create a new `generator` object. To recreate a generator from a generator expression we must execute the expression itself once more.

Iteration without memory

Let's raise the stakes by computing the sum of the first *ten* million squares using the built-in `sum()` function which accepts an iterable series of numbers. If we were to use a list comprehension we could expect this to consume around 400 MB of memory. Using, a generator expression memory usage will be insignificant:

```
>>> sum(x*x for x in range(1, 10000001))
333333383333335000000
```

This produces a result in a second or so and uses almost no memory.

Optional parentheses

Looking carefully, you see that in this case we didn't supply separate enclosing parentheses for the generator expression in addition to those needed for the `sum()` function call. This elegant ability to have the parentheses used for the function call also serve for the generator expression aids readability. You can include the second set of parentheses if you wish.

Using an if-clause in generator expressions

As with comprehensions, you can include an `if`-clause at the end of the generator expression. Reusing our admittedly inefficient `is_prime()` predicate, we can determine the sum of those integers from the first thousand which are prime like this:

```
>>> sum(x for x in range(1001) if is_prime(x))
76127
```

Note that is is not the same thing as computing the sum of the first `1000` primes, which is a more awkward question because we don't know in advance how many integers we need to test before we clock up a thousand primes.

Batteries included iteration tools

So far we've covered the many ways Python offers for creating `iterable` objects. Comprehensions, generators, and any object that follows the iterable or iterator protocols can be used for iteration, so it should be clear that iteration is a central feature of Python.

Python provides a number of built-in functions for performing common iterator operations. These functions form the core of a sort of *vocabulary* for working with iterators, and they can be combined to produce powerful statements in very concise, readable code. We've met some of these functions already, including `enumerate()` for producing integer indices and `sum()` for computing summation of numbers.

Introducing itertools

In addition to the built-in functions, the `itertools` module contains a wealth of useful functions and generators for processing iterable streams of data.

We'll start demonstrating these functions by solving the first thousand primes problem using built-in `sum()` with two generator functions from `itertools`: `islice()` and `count()`.

Earlier we made our own `take()` generator function for lazily retrieving the start of the sequence. We needn't have bothered, however, because `islice()` allows us to perform lazy slicing similar to the built-in list slicing functionality. To get the first 1000 primes we need to do something like:

```
from itertools import islice, count

islice(all_primes, 1000)
```

But how to generate `all_primes`? Previously, we've been using `range()` to create the raw sequences of integers to feed into our primality test, but ranges must always be finite, that is, bounded at both ends. What we'd like is an open ended version of `range()`, and that is exactly what `itertools.count()` provides. Using `count()` and `islice()`, our first thousand primes expression can be written out as:

```
>>> thousand_primes = islice((x for x in count() if is_prime(x)), 1000)
```

This returns a special `islice` object which is iterable. We can convert it to a list using the `list` constructor.

```
>>> thousand_primes
<itertools.islice object at 0x1006bae10>
>>> list(thousand_primes)
[2, 3, 5, 7, 11, 13 ... ,7877, 7879, 7883, 7901, 7907, 7919]
```

Answering our question about the sum of the first thousand primes is now easy, remembering to recreate the generators:

```
>>> sum(islice((x for x in count() if is_prime(x)), 1000))
3682913
```

Sequences of booleans

Two other very useful built-ins which facilitate elegant programs are `any()` and `all()`. They're equivalent to the logical operators and and or but for iterable series of bool values:

```
>>> any([False, False, True])
True
>>> all([False, False, True])
False
```

Here we'll use `any()` together with a generator expression to answer the question of whether there are any prime numbers in the range 1328 to 1360 inclusive:

```
>>> any(is_prime(x) for x in range(1328, 1361))
False
```

For a completely different type of problem we can check that all of these city names are proper nouns with initial upper-case letters:

```
>>> all(name == name.title() for name in ['London','Paris','Tokyo'])
True
```

Merging sequences with zip

The last built-in we'll look at is `zip()`, which, as its name suggests, gives us a way to synchronise iterations over two iterable series. For example, let's zip together two columns of temperature data, one from Sunday and one from Monday:

```
>>> sunday = [12, 14, 15, 15, 17, 21, 22, 22, 23, 22, 20, 18]
>>> monday = [13, 14, 14, 14, 16, 20, 21, 22, 22, 21, 19, 17]
>>> for item in zip(sunday, monday):
...     print(item)
...
(12, 13)
(14, 14)
(15, 14)
(15, 14)
(17, 16)
```

```
(21, 20)
(22, 21)
(22, 22)
(23, 22)
(22, 21)
(20, 19)
(18, 17)
```

We can see that `zip()` yields tuples when iterated. This in turn means we can use it with tuple unpacking in the `for`-loop to calculate the average temperature for each hour on these days:

```
>>> for sun, mon in zip(sunday, monday):
...         print("average =", (sun + mon) / 2)
...
average = 12.5
average = 14.0
average = 14.5
average = 14.5
average = 16.5
average = 20.5
average = 21.5
average = 22.0
average = 22.5
average = 21.5
average = 19.5
average = 17.5
```

More than two sequences with zip()

In fact, `zip()` can accept any number of iterable arguments. Let's add a third time-series and use other built-ins to calculate statistics for corresponding times:

```
>>> tuesday = [2, 2, 3, 7, 9, 10, 11, 12, 10, 9, 8, 8]
>>> for temps in zip(sunday, monday, tuesday):
...         print("min = {:4.1f}, max={:4.1f}, average={:4.1f}".format(
...             min(temps), max(temps), sum(temps) / len(temps)))
...
min =  2.0, max=13.0, average= 9.0
min =  2.0, max=14.0, average=10.0
min =  3.0, max=15.0, average=10.7
min =  7.0, max=15.0, average=12.0
min =  9.0, max=17.0, average=14.0
min = 10.0, max=21.0, average=17.0
min = 11.0, max=22.0, average=18.0
min = 12.0, max=22.0, average=18.7
```

```
min = 10.0, max=23.0, average=18.3
min =  9.0, max=22.0, average=17.3
min =  8.0, max=20.0, average=15.7
min =  8.0, max=18.0, average=14.3
```

Note how we've used string formatting features to control the numeric column width to four characters.

Lazily concatenating sequences with chain()

Perhaps, though, we'd like one long temperature series for Sunday, Monday and Tuesday. Rather than creating a new list by eagerly combining the three lists of temperatures, we can *lazily* concatenate iterables using `itertools.chain()`:

```
>>> from itertools import chain
>>> temperatures = chain(sunday, monday, tuesday)
```

The `temperatures` variable is an `iterable` object that first yields the values from `sunday`, followed by those from `monday`, and finally those from `tuesday`. Since it's lazy, though, it never creates a single list that contains all of the elements; in fact, it never creates an intermediate list of any sort!

We can now check that all of those temperatures are above freezing point, without the memory impact of data duplication:

```
>>> all(t > 0 for t in temperatures)
True
```

Pulling it all together

Before we summarize, let's pull a few pieces of what we have made together and leave your computer computing the Lucas primes:

```
>>> for x in (p for p in lucas() if is_prime(p)):
...     print(x)
...
2
3
7
11
29
47
199
```

```
521
2207
3571
9349
3010349
54018521
370248451
6643838879
119218851371
5600748293801
688846502588399
32361122672259149
```

When you've seen enough of these, we recommend you spend some time exploring the `itertools` module. The more you familiarize yourself with Python's existing support for `iterables`, the more elegant and concise your own code will become.

Summary

- Comprehensions are a concise syntax for describing lists, sets and dictionaries.

- Comprehensions operate on a `iterable` source object and apply an optional predicate filter and a mandatory expression, both of which are usually in terms of the current item.

- The `iterables` objects are objects over which we can iterate item-by-item.

- We retrieve an iterator from an `iterable` object using the built-in `iter()` function.

- Iterators produce items one-by-one from the underlying `iterable` series each time they are passed to the built-in `next()` function.

- Iterators raise a `StopIteration` exception when the collection is exhausted.

Generators

- Generator functions allow us to describe sequences using imperative code.

- Generator functions contain at least one use of the `yield` keyword.

- Generators are iterators. When the iterator is advanced with `next()` the generator starts or resumes execution up to and including the next yield.

- Each call to a generator function creates a new `generator` object.

- Generators can maintain explicit state in local variables between iterations.

- Generators are lazy and so can model infinite series of data.

- Generator expressions have a similar syntactic form to list comprehensions and allow for a more declarative and concise way of creating `generator` objects.

Iteration tools

Python includes a rich set of tools for dealing with iterable series, both in the form of built-in functions such as `sum()`, `any()` and `zip()` as well as in the `itertools` module.

1. We have covered the `iterable` protocol in detail in this chapter.

2. Well, they can, but recall that iterating over a dictionary yields only the keys!

3. We often just use the term *generator* to refer to generator functions, though sometimes it may be necessary to distinguish generator *functions* from generator *expressions*, which we cover later.

4. The authors are sworn by sacred oath never to use either Fibonacci or Quicksort implementations in demonstrations or exercises.

5. This has nothing whatsoever to do with the order in which you should watch the episodes of Star Wars. If that's what you're looking for, might we suggest `Machete Order`.

8

Defining new types with classes

You can get a long way in Python using the built in scalar and collections types. For many problems the built in types, together with those available in the Python Standard Library, are completely sufficient. Sometimes though, they aren't quite what's required, and the ability to create custom types is where classes come in.

As we've seen, all objects in Python have a type, and when we report that type using the `type()` built-in function the result is couched in terms of the *class* of that type:

```
>>> type(5)
<class 'int'>
>>> type("python")
<class 'str'>
>>> type([1, 2, 3])
<class 'list'>
>>> type(x*x for x in [2, 4, 6])
<class 'generator'>
```

A class is used to define the structure and behaviour of one or more objects, each of which we refer to as an *instance* of the class. By and large, objects in Python have a fixed type from the time they are created – or *instantiated* – to the time they are destroyed. It may be helpful to think of a class as a sort of template or cookie-cutter used to construct new objects. The class of an object controls its initialization and which attributes and methods are available through that object. For example, on
a string object the methods we can use on that object, such as `split()`, are defined in the `str` class.

Classes are an important piece of machinery for **Object-Oriented Programming (OOP)** in Python, and although it's true that OOP can be useful for making complex problems more tractable, it often has the effect of making the solution to simple problems unnecessarily complex. A great thing about Python is that it's highly object-oriented without forcing you to deal with classes until you really need them. This sets the language starkly apart from Java and C#.

Defining classes

Class definitions are introduced by the class keyword followed by the class name. By convention, new class names in Python use camel case – sometimes known as Pascal case – with an initial capital letter for each and every component word, without separating underscores. Since classes are a bit awkward to define at the REPL, we'll be using a Python module file to hold the class definitions
we use in this chapter.

Let's start with the very simplest class, to which we'll progressively add features. In our example we'll model a passenger aircraft flight between two airports by putting this code into `airtravel.py`:

```
"""Model for aircraft flights."""


class Flight:
    pass
```

The class statement introduces a new block, so we indent on the next line. Empty blocks aren't allowed, so the simplest possible class needs at least a do-nothing pass statement to be syntactically admissible.

Just as with def for defining functions, class is a *statement* that can occur anywhere in a program and which binds a class definition to a class name. When the top-level code in the `airtravel` module is executed, the class will be defined.

We can now import our new class into the REPL and try it out.

```
>>> from airtravel import Flight
```

The thing we've just imported is the class object. Everything is an object in Python, and classes are no exception.

```
>>> Flight
<class 'airtravel.Flight'>
```

To use this class to mint a new object, we must call its constructor, which is done by *calling* the class, as we would a function. The constructor returns a new object, which here we assign to a name f:

```
>>> f = Flight()
```

If we use the type() function to request the type of f, we get airtravel.Flight:

```
>>> type(f)
<class 'airtravel.Flight'>
```

The type of f literally *is* the class.

Instance methods

Let's make our class a little more interesting, by adding a so-called *instance method* which returns the flight number. Methods are just functions defined within the class block, and instance methods are functions which can be called on objects which are instances of our class, such as f. Instance methods must accept a reference to the instance on which the method was called as the first formal argument, and by convention this argument is always called self.

We have no way of configuring the flight number value yet, so we'll just return a constant string:

```
class Flight:

    def number(self):
        return "SN060"
```

And from a fresh REPL:

```
>>> from airtravel import Flight
>>> f = Flight()
>>> f.number()
SN060
```

Notice that when we call the method, we do not provide the instance f for the actual argument self in the argument list. That's because the standard method invocation form with the dot, like this:

```
>>> f.number()
SN060
```

Is simply syntactic sugar for:

```
>>> Flight.number(f)
SN060
```

If you try the latter, you'll find that it works as expected, although you'll almost never see this form used for real.

Instance initializers

This class isn't very useful, because it can only represent one particular flight. We need to make the flight number configurable at the point a Flight is created. To do that we need to write an `initializer` method.

If provided, the `initializer` method is called as part of the process of creating a new object when we call the constructor. The `initializer` method must be called __init__ () delimited by the double underscores used for Python runtime machinery. Like all other instance methods, the first argument to __init__ () must be self.

In this case, we also pass a second formal argument to __init__ () which is the flight number:

```
class Flight:

    def __init__(self, number):
        self._number = number

    def number(self):
        return self._number
```

The `initializer` should not return anything – it simply modifies the object referred to by self.

If you're coming from a Java, C#, or C++ background it's tempting to think of __init__ () as being the constructor. This isn't quite accurate; in Python the the purpose of __init__ () is to *configure* an object that already exists by the time __init__ () is called. The self argument is, however, analogous to this in Java, C#, or C++. In Python the actual constructor is provided by the Python runtime system and one of the things it does is check for the existence of an instance initializer and call it when present.

Within the initializer we assign to an *attribute* of the newly created instance called _number . Assigning to an object attribute that doesn't yet exist is sufficient to bring it into existence.

Just as we don't need to declare variables until we create them, neither do we need to declare object attributes before we create them. We `choose` _number with a leading underscore for two reasons. First, because it avoids a name clash with the method of the same name. Methods are functions, functions are objects, and these functions are bound to attributes of the object, so we already have an attribute called number and we don't want to replace it. Second, there is a widely followed convention that the implementation details of objects which are not intended for consumption or manipulation by clients of the object should be prefixed with an underscore.

We also modify our `number()` method to access the _number attribute and return it.

Any actual arguments passed to the flight constructor will be forwarded to the initializer, so to create and configure our `Flight` object we can now do this:

```
>>> from airtravel import Flight
>>> f = Flight("SN060")
>>> f.number()
SN060
```

We can also directly access the implementation details:

```
>>> f._number
SN060
```

Although this is not recommended for production code, it's very handy for debugging and early testing.

A lack of access modifiers

If you're coming from a bondage and discipline language like Java or C# with `public`, `private` and `protected` access modifiers, Python's "everything is public" approach can seem excessively open-minded.

The prevailing culture among Pythonistas is that "We"re all consenting adults here". In practice, the leading underscore convention has proven sufficient protection even in large and complex Python systems we have worked with. People know not to use these attributes directly, and in fact they tend not to. Like so many doctrines, lack of access modifiers is a much bigger problem in theory than in practice.

Validation and invariants

It's good practice for the initializer of an object to establish so-called *class invariants*. The invariants are truths about objects of that class that should endure for the lifetime of the object. One such invariant for flights is that the flight number always begins with an upper case two-letter airline code followed by a three or four digit route number.

In Python, we establish class invariants in the __init__() method and raise exceptions if they can't be attained:

```python
class Flight:

    def __init__(self, number):
        if not number[:2].isalpha():
            raise ValueError("No airline code in '{}'".format(number))

        if not number[:2].isupper():
            raise ValueError("Invalid airline
                             code'{}'".format(number))

        if not (number[2:].isdigit() and int(number[2:]) <= 9999):
            raise ValueError("Invalid route
                             number'{}'".format(number))

        self._number = number

    def number(self):
        return self._number
```

We use string slicing and various methods of the string class to perform validation. For the first time in this book we also see the logical negation operator not.

Ad hoc testing in the REPL is a very effective technique during development:

```python
>>> from airtravel import Flight
>>> f = Flight("SN060")
>>> f = Flight("060")
Traceback (most recent call last):
  File "<stdin>", line 1, in <module>
  File "./airtravel.py", line 8, in __init__
    raise ValueError("No airline code in '{};".format(number))
    ValueError: No airline code in '060'
>>> f = Flight("sn060")
Traceback (most recent call last):
  File "<stdin>", line 1, in <module>
  File "./airtravel.py", line 11, in __init__
    raise ValueError("Invalid airline code '{}'".format(number))
```

```
    ValueError: Invalid airline code 'sn060'
>>> f = Flight("snabcd")
Traceback (most recent call last):
  File "<stdin>", line 1, in <module>
  File "./airtravel.py", line 11, in __init__
    raise ValueError("Invalid airline code '{}'".format(number))
    ValueError: Invalid airline code 'snabcd'
>>> f = Flight("SN12345")
Traceback (most recent call last):
  File "<stdin>", line 1, in <module>
  File "./airtravel.py", line 11, in __init__
    raise ValueError("Invalid airline code '{}'".format(number))
    ValueError: Invalid airline code 'sn12345'
```

Now that we're sure of having a valid flight number, we'll add a second method to return just the airline code. Once the class `invariants` have been established, most query methods can be very simple:

```
def airline(self):
    return self._number[:2]
```

Adding a second class

One of the things we'd like to do with our flight is accept seat bookings. To do that we need to know the seating layout, and for that we need to know the type of aircraft. Let's make a second class to model different kinds of aircraft:

```
class Aircraft:

    def __init__(self, registration, model, num_rows,
                 num_seats_per_row):
        self._registration = registration
        self._model = model
        self._num_rows = num_rows
        self._num_seats_per_row = num_seats_per_row

    def registration(self):
        return self._registration

    def model(self):
        return self._model
```

The `initializer` creates four attributes for the aircraft: registration number, a model name, the number of rows of seats, and the number of seats per row. In a production code scenario we could validate these arguments to ensure, for example, that the number of rows is not negative.

This is straightforward enough, but for the seating plan we'd like something a little more in line with our booking system. Rows in aircraft are numbered from one, and the seats within each row are designated with letters from an alphabet which omits **I** to avoid confusion with **1**:

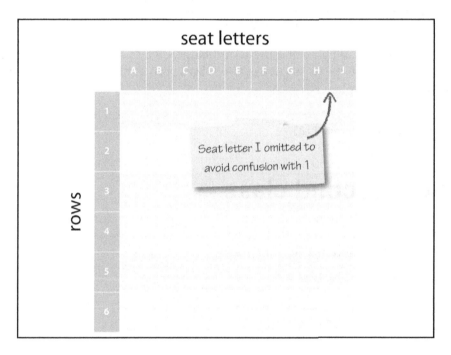

Figure 8.1: Aircraft seating plan.

We'll add a `seating_plan()` method which returns the allowed rows and seats as a 2-tuple containing a `range` object and a string of seat letters:

```
def seating_plan(self):
    return (range(1, self._num_rows + 1),
            "ABCDEFGHJK"[:self._num_seats_per_row])
```

It's worth pausing for a second to make sure you understand how this function works. The call to the `range()` constructor produces a range object which can be used as an iterable series of row numbers, up to the number of rows in the plane. The string and its `slice` method return a string with one character per seat. These two objects – the range and the string – are bundled up into a tuple.

Let's construct a plane with a seating plan:

```
>>> from airtravel import *
>>> a = Aircraft("G-EUPT", "Airbus A319", num_rows=22,
                 num_seats_per_row=6)
>>> a.registration()
'G-EUPT'
>>> a.model()
'Airbus A319'
>>> a.seating_plan()
(range(1, 23), 'ABCDEF')
```

See how we used keyword arguments for the rows and seats for documentary purposes. Recall the ranges are half-open, so `23` is correctly one-beyond-the-end of the range.

Collaborating classes

The Law of Demeter is an object-oriented design principle that says you should never call methods on objects you receive from other calls. Or, put another way: Only talk to your immediate friends.

Figure 8.2: The Law of Demeter

We'll now modify our Flight class to accept an aircraft object when it is constructed, and we'll follow the Law of Demeter by adding a method to report the aircraft model. This method will delegate to Aircraft on behalf of the client rather than allowing the client to "reach through" the Flight and interrogate the Aircraft object directly:

```python
class Flight:
    """A flight with a particular passenger aircraft."""

    def __init__(self, number, aircraft):
        if not number[:2].isalpha():
            raise ValueError("No airline code in '{}'".format(number))

        if not number[:2].isupper():
            raise ValueError("Invalid airline code'{}'".format(number))

        if not (number[2:].isdigit() and int(number[2:]) <= 9999):
            raise ValueError("Invalid route number'{}'".format(number))

        self._number = number
        self._aircraft = aircraft

    def number(self):
        return self._number

    def airline(self):
        return self._number[:2]

    def aircraft_model(self):
        return self._aircraft.model()
```

We've also added a docstring to the class. These work just like function and module docstrings, and must be the first non-comment line within the body of the class.

We can now construct a flight with a specific aircraft:

```python
>>> from airtravel import *
>>> f = Flight("BA758", Aircraft("G-EUPT", "Airbus A319", num_rows=22,
...                              num_seats_per_row=6))
>>> f.aircraft_model()
'Airbus A319'
```

Notice that we construct the `Aircraft` object and directly pass it to the `Flight` constructor without needing an intermediate named reference for it.

Moment of zen

Figure 8.3: Complex is better than complicated

The `aircraft_model()` method is an example of 'complex is better than complicated':

```
def aircraft_model(self):
    return self._aircraft.model()
```

The Flight class is more *complex* – it contains additional code to drill down through the aircraft reference to find the model. However, all clients of Flight can now be less *complicated*; none of them need to know about the Aircraft class, dramatically simplifying the system.

Booking seats

Now we can proceed with implementing a simple booking system. For each flight we simply need to keep track of who is sitting in each seat. We'll represent the seat allocations using a list of dictionaries. The list will contain one entry for each seat row, and each entry will be a dictionary mapping from seat-letter to occupant name. If a seat is unoccupied, the corresponding dictionary value will contain None.

We initialize the seating plan in Flight.__init__() using this fragment:

```
rows, seats = self._aircraft.seating_plan()
self._seating = [None] + [{letter: None for letter in seats} for _ in rows]
```

In the first line we retrieve the seating plan for the aircraft and use tuple unpacking to put the row and seat identifiers into local variables rows and seats. In the second line we create a list for the seat allocations. Rather than continually deal with the fact that row indexes are one-based whereas Python lists use zero-based indexes, we choose to waste one entry at the beginning of the list. This first wasted entry is the single element list containing None. To this single element list we concatenate another list containing one entry for each real row in the aircraft. This list is constructed by a list comprehension which iterates over the rows object, which is the range of row numbers retrieved from the _aircraft on the previous line:

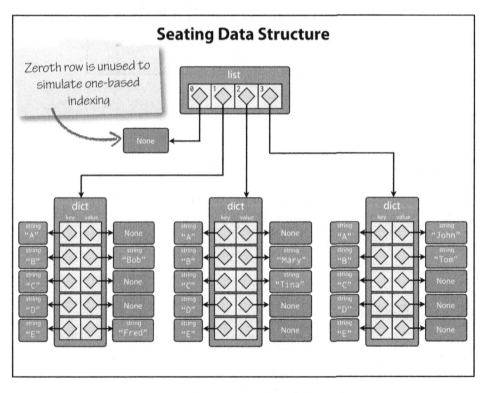

Figure 8.4: The object graph for the seating-plan data structure

We're not actually interested in the row number, since we know it will match up with the list index in the final list, so we discard it by using the dummy underscore variable.

The item expression part of the list comprehension is itself a comprehension; specifically a dictionary comprehension! This iterates over each row letter, and creates a mapping from the single character string to None to indicate an empty seat.

We use a list comprehension, rather than list replication with the multiplication operator, because we want a distinct dictionary object to be created for each row; remember, repetition is shallow.

Here's the code after we put it into the initializer:

```
def __init__(self, number, aircraft):
    if not number[:2].isalpha():
        raise ValueError("No airline code in '{}'".format(number))

    if not number[:2].isupper():
        raise ValueError("Invalid airline code '{}'".format(number))

    if not (number[2:].isdigit() and int(number[2:]) <= 9999):
        raise ValueError("Invalid route number '{}'".format(number))

    self._number = number
    self._aircraft = aircraft

    rows, seats = self._aircraft.seating_plan()
    self._seating = [None] + [{letter: None for letter in seats} for _
                             in rows]
```

Before we go further, let's test our code in the REPL:

```
>>> from airtravel import *
>>> f = Flight("BA758", Aircraft("G-EUPT", "Airbus A319", num_rows=22,
...                              num_seats_per_row=6))
>>>
```

Thanks to the fact that everything is "public" we can access implementation details during development. It's clear enough that we're deliberately defying convention here during development, since the leading underscore reminds us what's public and what's private:

```
>>> f._seating
[None, {'F': None, 'D': None, 'E': None, 'B': None, 'C': None,
       'A': None},
{'F': None, 'D': None, 'E': None, 'B': None, 'C': None, 'A': None}, {'F':
None,'D': None, 'E': None, 'B': None, 'C': None, 'A': None},
{'F': None, 'D': None,'E': None, 'B': None, 'C': None, 'A': None}, {'F':
```

```
None, 'D': None, 'E': None,'B': None, 'C': None, 'A': None},
{'F': None, 'D': None, 'E': None, 'B': None,'C': None, 'A': None}, {'F':
None, 'D': None, 'E': None, 'B': None, 'C': None,'A': None}, {'F': None,
'D': None, 'E': None, 'B': None, 'C': None, 'A': None},
{'F': None, 'D': None, 'E': None, 'B': None, 'C': None, 'A': None}, {'F':
None,'D': None, 'E': None, 'B': None, 'C': None, 'A': None}, {'F': None,
'D': None,'E': None, 'B': None, 'C': None, 'A': None}, {'F': None, 'D':
None, 'E': None,'B': None, 'C': None, 'A': None}, {'F': None, 'D': None,
'E': None, 'B': None,'C': None, 'A': None}, {'F': None, 'D': None, 'E':
None, 'B': None, 'C': None,'A': None}, {'F': None, 'D': None, 'E': None,
'B': None, 'C': None, 'A': None},
{'F': None, 'D': None, 'E': None, 'B': None, 'C': None, 'A': None}, {'F':
None,'D': None, 'E': None, 'B': None, 'C': None, 'A': None}, {'F': None,
'D': None,'E': None, 'B': None, 'C': None, 'A': None}, {'F': None, 'D':
None, 'E': None,'B': None, 'C': None, 'A': None}, {'F': None, 'D': None,
'E': None, 'B': None,'C': None, 'A': None}, {'F': None, 'D': None, 'E':
None, 'B': None, 'C': None,'A': None}, {'F': None, 'D': None, 'E': None,
'B': None, 'C': None, 'A': None}]
```

Tha's accurate, but not particularly beautiful. Let's try again with pretty-print:

```
>>> from pprint import pprint as pp
>>> pp(f._seating)
[None,
 {'A': None, 'B': None, 'C': None, 'D': None, 'E': None, 'F': None},
 {'A': None, 'B': None, 'C': None, 'D': None, 'E': None, 'F': None},
 {'A': None, 'B': None, 'C': None, 'D': None, 'E': None, 'F': None},
 {'A': None, 'B': None, 'C': None, 'D': None, 'E': None, 'F': None},
 {'A': None, 'B': None, 'C': None, 'D': None, 'E': None, 'F': None},
 {'A': None, 'B': None, 'C': None, 'D': None, 'E': None, 'F': None},
 {'A': None, 'B': None, 'C': None, 'D': None, 'E': None, 'F': None},
 {'A': None, 'B': None, 'C': None, 'D': None, 'E': None, 'F': None},
 {'A': None, 'B': None, 'C': None, 'D': None, 'E': None, 'F': None},
 {'A': None, 'B': None, 'C': None, 'D': None, 'E': None, 'F': None},
 {'A': None, 'B': None, 'C': None, 'D': None, 'E': None, 'F': None},
 {'A': None, 'B': None, 'C': None, 'D': None, 'E': None, 'F': None},
 {'A': None, 'B': None, 'C': None, 'D': None, 'E': None, 'F': None},
 {'A': None, 'B': None, 'C': None, 'D': None, 'E': None, 'F': None},
 {'A': None, 'B': None, 'C': None, 'D': None, 'E': None, 'F': None},
 {'A': None, 'B': None, 'C': None, 'D': None, 'E': None, 'F': None},
 {'A': None, 'B': None, 'C': None, 'D': None, 'E': None, 'F': None},
 {'A': None, 'B': None, 'C': None, 'D': None, 'E': None, 'F': None},
 {'A': None, 'B': None, 'C': None, 'D': None, 'E': None, 'F': None},
 {'A': None, 'B': None, 'C': None, 'D': None, 'E': None, 'F': None}]
```

Perfect!

Allocating seats to passengers

Now we'll add behavior to Flight to allocate seats to passengers. To keep this simple, a passenger will simply be a string name:

```
class Flight:

    # ...

    def allocate_seat(seat, passenger):
        """Allocate a seat to a passenger.

        Args:
            seat: A seat designator such as '12C' or '21F'.
            passenger: The passenger name.

        Raises:
            ValueError: If the seat is unavailable.
        """
        rows, seat_letters = self._aircraft.seating_plan()

        letter = seat[-1]
        if letter not in seat_letters:
            raise ValueError("Invalid seat letter {}".format(letter))

        row_text = seat[:-1]
        try:
            row = int(row_text)
        except ValueError:
            raise ValueError("Invalid seat row {}".format(row_text))

        if row not in rows:
            raise ValueError("Invalid row number {}".format(row))

        if self._seating[row][letter] is not None:
            raise ValueError("Seat {} already occupied".format(seat))

        self._seating[row][letter] = passenger
```

Most of this code is validation of the seat designator and it contains some interesting snippets:

- Line 6: Methods are functions, so deserve docstrings too.

- Line 17: We get the seat letter by using negative indexing into the seat string.

- Line 18: We test that the seat letter is valid by checking for membership of `seat_letters` using the in membership testing operator.

- Line 21: We extract the row number using string slicing to take all but the last character.

- Line 23: We try to convert the row number substring to an integer using the `int()` constructor. If this fails, we catch the `ValueError` and in the handler raise a *new* `ValueError` with a more appropriate message payload.

- Line 27: We conveniently validate the row number by using the in operator against the `rows` object which is a range. We can do this because `range()` objects support the *container* protocol.

- Line 30: We check that the requested seat is unoccupied using an identity test with None. If it's occupied we raise a `ValueError`.

- Line 33: If we get this far, everything is is good shape, and we can assign the seat.

This code also contains a bug, which we'll discover soon enough!

Trying our seat allocator at the REPL:

```
>>> from airtravel import *
>>> f = Flight("BA758", Aircraft("G-EUPT", "Airbus A319",
...            num_rows=22, num_seats_per_row=6))
>>> f.allocate_seat('12A', 'Guido van Rossum')
Traceback (most recent call last):
  File "<stdin>", line 1, in <module>
  TypeError: allocate_seat() takes 2 positional arguments but 3 were
             given
```

Oh dear! Early on in your object-oriented Python career you're likely to see `TypeError` messages like this quite often. The problem has occurred because we forgot to include the self argument in the definition of the `allocate_seat()` method:

```
def allocate_seat(self, seat, passenger):
    # ...
```

Once we fix that, we can try again:

```
>>> from airtravel import *
>>> from pprint import pprint as pp
>>> f = Flight("BA758", Aircraft("G-EUPT", "Airbus A319",
```

```
...                                    num_rows=22, num_seats_per_row=6))
>>> f.allocate_seat('12A', 'Guido van Rossum')
>>> f.allocate_seat('12A', 'Rasmus Lerdorf')
Traceback (most recent call last):
  File "<stdin>", line 1, in <module>
  File "./airtravel.py", line 57, in allocate_seat
      raise ValueError("Seat {} already occupied".format(seat))
      ValueError: Seat 12A already occupied
>>> f.allocate_seat('15F', 'Bjarne Stroustrup')
>>> f.allocate_seat('15E', 'Anders Hejlsberg')
>>> f.allocate_seat('E27', 'Yukihiro Matsumoto')
Traceback (most recent call last):
  File "<stdin>", line 1, in <module>
  File "./airtravel.py", line 45, in allocate_seat
      raise ValueError("Invalid seat letter {}".format(letter))
      ValueError: Invalid seat letter 7
>>> f.allocate_seat('1C', 'John McCarthy')
>>> f.allocate_seat('1D', 'Richard Hickey')
>>> f.allocate_seat('DD', 'Larry Wall')
Traceback (most recent call last):
  File "./airtravel.py", line 49, in allocate_seat
  row = int(row_text)
  ValueError: invalid literal for int() with base 10: 'D'

During handling of the above exception, another exception occurred:

Traceback (most recent call last):
  File "<stdin>", line 1, in <module>
  File "./airtravel.py", line 51, in allocate_seat
      raise ValueError("Invalid seat row {}".format(row_text))
      ValueError: Invalid seat row D

>>> pp(f._seating)
[None,
  {'A': None,
  'B': None,
  'C': 'John McCarthy',
  'D': 'Richard Hickey',
  'E': None,
  'F': None},
  {'A': None, 'B': None, 'C': None, 'D': None, 'E': None, 'F': None},
  {'A': None, 'B': None, 'C': None, 'D': None, 'E': None, 'F': None},
  {'A': None, 'B': None, 'C': None, 'D': None, 'E': None, 'F': None},
  {'A': None, 'B': None, 'C': None, 'D': None, 'E': None, 'F': None},
  {'A': None, 'B': None, 'C': None, 'D': None, 'E': None, 'F': None},
  {'A': None, 'B': None, 'C': None, 'D': None, 'E': None, 'F': None},
  {'A': None, 'B': None, 'C': None, 'D': None, 'E': None, 'F': None},
  {'A': None, 'B': None, 'C': None, 'D': None, 'E': None, 'F': None},
```

```
  {'A': None, 'B': None, 'C': None, 'D': None, 'E': None, 'F': None},
  {'A': None, 'B': None, 'C': None, 'D': None, 'E': None, 'F': None},
  {'A': 'Guido van Rossum','B': None,'C': None,'D': None,'E': None,
   'F': None},
  {'A': None, 'B': None, 'C': None, 'D': None, 'E': None, 'F': None},
  {'A': None, 'B': None, 'C': None, 'D': None, 'E': None, 'F': None},
  {'A': None,'B': None,'C': None,'D': None,'E': 'Anders Hejlsberg',
   'F': 'Bjarne Stroustrup'},
  {'A': None, 'B': None, 'C': None, 'D': None, 'E': None, 'F': None},
  {'A': None, 'B': None, 'C': None, 'D': None, 'E': None, 'F': None},
  {'A': None, 'B': None, 'C': None, 'D': None, 'E': None, 'F': None},
  {'A': None, 'B': None, 'C': None, 'D': None, 'E': None, 'F': None},
  {'A': None, 'B': None, 'C': None, 'D': None, 'E': None, 'F': None},
  {'A': None, 'B': None, 'C': None, 'D': None, 'E': None, 'F': None},
  {'A': None, 'B': None, 'C': None, 'D': None, 'E': None, 'F': None}]
```

The Dutchman is quite lonely there in row 12, so we'd like to move him back to row 15 with the Danes. To do so, we'll need a `relocate_passenger()` method.

Naming methods for implementation details

First we'll perform a small refactoring and extract the seat designator parsing and validation logic into it's own method, `_parse_seat()`. We use a leading underscore here because this method is an implementation detail:

```python
class Flight:

    # ...

    def _parse_seat(self, seat):
        """Parse a seat designator into a valid row and letter.

        Args:
            seat: A seat designator such as 12F

        Returns:
            A tuple containing an integer,string for row and seat.
        """
        row_numbers, seat_letters = self._aircraft.seating_plan()

        letter = seat[-1]
        if letter not in seat_letters:
            raise ValueError("Invalid seat letter {}".format(letter))

        row_text = seat[:-1]
```

```
        try:
            row = int(row_text)
        except ValueError:
            raise ValueError("Invalid seat row {}".format(row_text))

        if row not in row_numbers:
            raise ValueError("Invalid row number {}".format(row))

        return row, letter
```

The new `_parse_seat()` method returns a tuple with an integer row number and a seat letter string. This has made `allocate_seat()` much simpler:

```
def allocate_seat(self, seat, passenger):
    """Allocate a seat to a passenger.

    Args:
        seat: A seat designator such as '12C' or '21F'.
        passenger: The passenger name.

    Raises:
        ValueError: If the seat is unavailable.
    """
    row, letter = self._parse_seat(seat)

    if self._seating[row][letter] is not None:
        raise ValueError("Seat {} already occupied".format(seat))

    self._seating[row][letter] = passenger
```

Notice how the call to `_parse_seat()` also requires explicit qualification with the self prefix.

Implementing relocate_passenger()

Now we've laid the groundwork for our `relocate_passenger()` method:

```
class Flight:

    # ...

    def relocate_passenger(self, from_seat, to_seat):
        """Relocate a passenger to a different seat.

        Args:
            from_seat: The existing seat designator for the
```

```
                    passenger to be moved.

              to_seat: The new seat designator.
          """
          from_row, from_letter = self._parse_seat(from_seat)
          if self._seating[from_row][from_letter] is None:
              raise ValueError(
                  "No passenger to relocate in seat {}".format(from_seat))

          to_row, to_letter = self._parse_seat(to_seat)
          if self._seating[to_row][to_letter] is not None:
              raise ValueError(
                  "Seat {} already occupied".format(to_seat))

          self._seating[to_row][to_letter] = self._seating[from_row]
          [from_letter]
          self._seating[from_row][from_letter] = None
```

This parses and validates the `from_seat` and `to_seat` arguments and then moves the passenger to the new location.

It's also getting tiresome recreating the `Flight` object each time, so we'll add a *module* level convenience function for that too:

```
def make_flight():
    f = Flight("BA758", Aircraft("G-EUPT", "Airbus A319",
              num_rows=22, num_seats_per_row=6))
    f.allocate_seat('12A', 'Guido van Rossum')
    f.allocate_seat('15F', 'Bjarne Stroustrup')
    f.allocate_seat('15E', 'Anders Hejlsberg')
    f.allocate_seat('1C', 'John McCarthy')
    f.allocate_seat('1D', 'Richard Hickey')
    return f
```

In Python it's quite normal to mix related functions and classes in the same module. Now, from the REPL:

```
>>> from airtravel import make_flight
>>> f = make_flight()
>>> f
<airtravel.Flight object at 0x1007a6690>
```

You may find it remarkable that we have access to the `Flight` class when we have only imported a single function, `make_flight`. This is quite normal and it's a powerful aspect of Python's dynamic type system that facilitates this very loose coupling between code.

Let's get on and move Guido back to row 15 with his fellow Europeans:

```
>>> f.relocate_passenger('12A', '15D')
>>> from pprint import pprint as pp
>>> pp(f._seating)
[None,
  {'A': None,'B': None, 'C': 'John McCarthy', 'D': 'Richard Hickey',
   'E': None, 'F': None},
  {'A': None, 'B': None, 'C': None, 'D': None, 'E': None, 'F': None},
  {'A': None, 'B': None, 'C': None, 'D': None, 'E': None, 'F': None},
  {'A': None, 'B': None, 'C': None, 'D': None, 'E': None, 'F': None},
  {'A': None, 'B': None, 'C': None, 'D': None, 'E': None, 'F': None},
  {'A': None, 'B': None, 'C': None, 'D': None, 'E': None, 'F': None},
  {'A': None, 'B': None, 'C': None, 'D': None, 'E': None, 'F': None},
  {'A': None, 'B': None, 'C': None, 'D': None, 'E': None, 'F': None},
  {'A': None, 'B': None, 'C': None, 'D': None, 'E': None, 'F': None},
  {'A': None, 'B': None, 'C': None, 'D': None, 'E': None, 'F': None},
  {'A': None, 'B': None, 'C': None, 'D': None, 'E': None, 'F': None},
  {'A': None, 'B': None, 'C': None, 'D': None, 'E': None, 'F': None},
  {'A': None, 'B': None, 'C': None, 'D': None, 'E': None, 'F': None},
  {'A': None,'B': None,'C': None,'D': 'Guido van Rossum',
   'E': 'Anders Hejlsberg','F': 'Bjarne Stroustrup'},
  {'A': None, 'B': None, 'C': None, 'D': None, 'E': None, 'F': None},
  {'A': None, 'B': None, 'C': None, 'D': None, 'E': None, 'F': None},
  {'A': None, 'B': None, 'C': None, 'D': None, 'E': None, 'F': None},
  {'A': None, 'B': None, 'C': None, 'D': None, 'E': None, 'F': None},
  {'A': None, 'B': None, 'C': None, 'D': None, 'E': None, 'F': None},
  {'A': None, 'B': None, 'C': None, 'D': None, 'E': None, 'F': None},
  {'A': None, 'B': None, 'C': None, 'D': None, 'E': None, 'F': None}]
```

Counting available seats

It's important during booking to know how many seats are available. To this end we'll write
a num_available_seats() method. This uses two nested generator expressions. The
outer expression filters for all rows which are not None to exclude our dummy first row.
The value of each item in the outer expression is the sum of the number of None values in
each row. This inner expression iterates over values of the dictionary and adds 1 for each
None found:

```
def num_available_seats(self):
    return sum( sum(1 for s in row.values() if s is None)
        for row in self._seating
            if row is not None )
```

Notice how we have split the outer expression over three lines to improve readability.

```
>>> from airtravel import make_flight
```

```
>>> f = make_flight()
>>> f.num_available_seats()
127
```

A quick check shows that our new calculation is correct:

```
>>> 6 * 22 - 5
127
```

Sometimes the only object you need is a function

Now we'll show how it's quite possible to write nice object-oriented code without needing classes. We have a requirement to produce boarding cards for our passengers in alphabetical order. However, we realize that the `Flight` class is probably not a good home for details of printing boarding passes. We could go ahead and create a `BoardingCardPrinter` class, although that is probably overkill. Remember that functions are objects too and are perfectly sufficient for many cases. Don't feel compelled to make classes without good reason.

Rather than have a card printer query all the passenger details from the flight, we'll follow the object-oriented design principle of "Tell! Don't Ask." and have the Flight *tell* a simple card printing function what to do.

First the card printer, which is just a module level function:

```
def console_card_printer(passenger, seat, flight_number, aircraft):
    output = "| Name: {0}"          \
             "  Flight: {1}"         \
             "  Seat: {2}"           \
             "  Aircraft: {3}" \
             " |".format(passenger, flight_number, seat, aircraft)
    banner = '+' + '-' * (len(output) - 2) + '+'
    border = '|' + ' ' * (len(output) - 2) + '|'
    lines = [banner, border, output, border, banner]
    card = '\n'.join(lines)
    print(card)
    print()
```

A Python feature we're introducing here is the use of line continuation backslash characters, \, which allow us to split long statements over several lines. This is used here, together with implicit string concatenation of adjacent strings, to produce one long string with no line breaks.

We measure the length of this output line, build some banners and borders around it and, concatenate the lines together using the `join()` method called on a newline separator. The whole card is then printed, followed by a blank line. The card printer doesn't know anything about `Flights` or `Aircraft` – it's very loosely coupled. You can probably easily envisage an HTML card printer that has the same interface.

Making Flight create boarding cards

To the `Flight` class we add a new method `make_boarding_cards()` which accepts a `card_printer`:

```
class Flight:

    # ...

    def make_boarding_cards(self, card_printer):
        for passenger, seat in sorted(self._passenger_seats()):
            card_printer(passenger, seat, self.number(),
            self.aircraft_model())
```

This tells the `card_printer` to print each passenger, having sorted a list of passenger-seat tuples obtained from a `_passenger_seats()` implementation detail method (note the leading underscore). This method is in fact a generator function which searches all seats for occupants, yielding the passenger and the seat number as they are found:

```
def _passenger_seats(self):
    """An iterable series of passenger seating allocations."""
    row_numbers, seat_letters = self._aircraft.seating_plan()
    for row in row_numbers:
        for letter in seat_letters:
            passenger = self._seating[row][letter]
            if passenger is not None:
                yield (passenger, "{}{}".format(row, letter))
```

Now if we run this on the REPL, we can see that the new boarding card printing system works:

```
>>> from airtravel import console_card_printer, make_flight
>>> f = make_flight()
>>> f.make_boarding_cards(console_card_printer)
+----------------------------------------------------------------+
|                                                                |
|Name: Anders Hejlsberg Flight: BA758   Seat: 15E   Aircraft:Airbus A319 |
|                                                                |
+----------------------------------------------------------------+
```

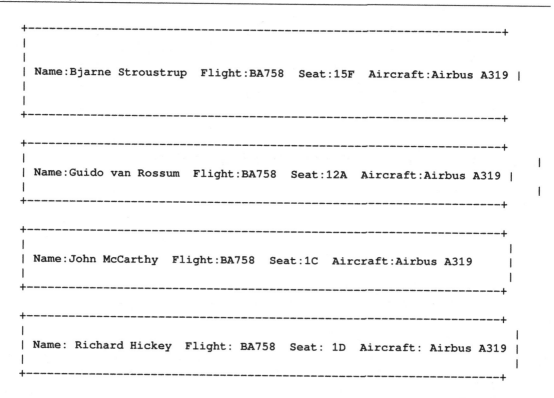

```
+----------------------------------------------------------------------+
|                                                                      |
|                                                                      |
|  Name:Bjarne Stroustrup  Flight:BA758  Seat:15F  Aircraft:Airbus A319 |
|                                                                      |
|                                                                      |
+----------------------------------------------------------------------+


+----------------------------------------------------------------------+
|                                                                      |
|  Name:Guido van Rossum  Flight:BA758  Seat:12A  Aircraft:Airbus A319 |
|                                                                      |
+----------------------------------------------------------------------+


+----------------------------------------------------------------------+
|                                                                      |
|  Name:John McCarthy  Flight:BA758  Seat:1C  Aircraft:Airbus A319     |
|                                                                      |
+----------------------------------------------------------------------+


+----------------------------------------------------------------------+
|                                                                      |
|  Name: Richard Hickey  Flight: BA758  Seat: 1D  Aircraft: Airbus A319 |
|                                                                      |
+----------------------------------------------------------------------+
```

Polymorphism and duck-typing

Polymorphism is a programming language feature which allows us to use objects of different types through a uniform interface. The concept of polymorphism applies to both functions and more complex objects. We've just seen an example of polymorphism with the card printing example. The `make_boarding_card()` method didn't need to know about an actual – or as we say "concrete" – card printing type, only the abstract details of its interface. This interface is essentially just the order of it's arguments. Replacing our `console_card_printer` with a `putative html_card_printer` would exercise polymorphism.

Polymorphism in Python is achieved through duck typing. Duck typing is in turn named after the "duck test", attributed to James Whitcomb Riley, the American poet:

Figure 8.5: James Whitcomb Riley

When I see a bird that walks like a duck and swims like a duck and quacks like a duck, I call that bird a duck.

Duck typing, where an object's fitness for a particular use is only determined at runtime, is the cornerstone of Python's object system. This is different from many statically typed languages where a compiler determines if an object can be used. In particular, it means that an object's suitability is not based on inheritance hierarchies, base classes, or anything except the attributes an object has *at the time of use.*

This is in stark contrast to languages such as Java which depend on what is called *nominal sub-typing* through inheritance from base classes and interfaces. We'll talk more about inheritance in the context of Python shortly.

Refactoring Aircraft

Let's return to our Aircraft class:

```
class Aircraft:

    def __init__(self, registration, model, num_rows,
                 num_seats_per_row):
        self._registration = registration
        self._model = model
        self._num_rows = num_rows
        self._num_seats_per_row = num_seats_per_row

    def registration(self):
        return self._registration

    def model(self):
        return self._model

    def seating_plan(self):
        return (range(1, self._num_rows + 1),
```

```
                    "ABCDEFGHJK"[:self._num_seats_per_row])
```

The design of this class is somewhat flawed, in that objects instantiated using it depend on being supplied with a seating configuration that matches the aircraft model. For the purposes of this exercise we can assume that the seating arrangement is fixed per aircraft model.

Better, and simpler, perhaps to get rid of the Aircraft class entirely and make separate classes for each specific model of aircraft with a fixed seating configuration. Here's an Airbus A319:

```
class AirbusA319:

    def __init__(self, registration):
        self._registration = registration

    def registration(self):
        return self._registration

    def model(self):
        return "Airbus A319"

    def seating_plan(self):
        return range(1, 23), "ABCDEF"
```

And here's a Boeing 777:

```
class Boeing777:

    def __init__(self, registration):
        self._registration = registration

    def registration(self):
        return self._registration

    def model(self):
        return "Boeing 777"

    def seating_plan(self):
        # For simplicity's sake, we ignore complex
        # seating arrangement for first-class
        return range(1, 56), "ABCDEGHJK"
```

These two aircraft classes have no explicit relationship to each other, or to our original Aircraft class, beyond having identical interfaces (with the exception of the initializer, which now takes fewer arguments). As such we can use these new types in place of each other.

Let's change our `make_flight()` method to `make_flights()` so we can use them:

```
def make_flights():
    f = Flight("BA758", AirbusA319("G-EUPT"))
    f.allocate_seat('12A', 'Guido van Rossum')
    f.allocate_seat('15F', 'Bjarne Stroustrup')
    f.allocate_seat('15E', 'Anders Hejlsberg')
    f.allocate_seat('1C', 'John McCarthy')
    f.allocate_seat('1D', 'Richard Hickey')

    g = Flight("AF72", Boeing777("F-GSPS"))
    g.allocate_seat('55K', 'Larry Wall')
    g.allocate_seat('33G', 'Yukihiro Matsumoto')
    g.allocate_seat('4B', 'Brian Kernighan')
    g.allocate_seat('4A', 'Dennis Ritchie')

    return f, g
```

The different types of aircraft both work fine when used with `Flight` because they both quack like ducks. Or fly like planes. Or something:

```
>>> from airtravel import *
>>> f, g = make_flights()
>>> f.aircraft_model()
'Airbus A319'
>>> g.aircraft_model()
'Boeing 777'
>>> f.num_available_seats()
127
>>> g.num_available_seats()
491
>>> g.relocate_passenger('55K', '13G')
>>> g.make_boarding_cards(console_card_printer)
+----------------------------------------------------------------------+    |
|                                                                      |    |
|                                                                      |
| Name:Brian Kernighan  Flight:AF72  Seat:4B  Aircraft:Boeing 777    | |
|                                                                      |
|                                                                      |
|                                                                      |
+----------------------------------------------------------------------+

+----------------------------------------------------------------------+
|                                                                      |
| Name:Dennis Ritchie  Flight:AF72  Seat:4A  Aircraft:Boeing 777    |
|                                                                      |
+----------------------------------------------------------------------+
```

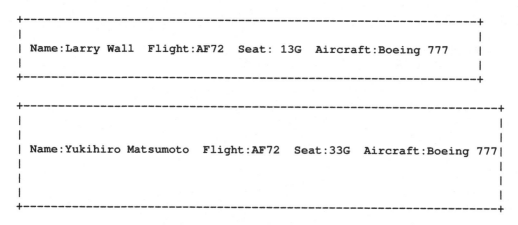

```
+-----------------------------------------------------------+
|                                                           |
|  Name:Larry Wall   Flight:AF72   Seat: 13G   Aircraft:Boeing 777  |
|                                                           |
+-----------------------------------------------------------+


+--------------------------------------------------------------+
|                                                              |
|                                                              |
|  Name:Yukihiro Matsumoto   Flight:AF72   Seat:33G   Aircraft:Boeing 777|
|                                                              |
|                                                              |
|                                                              |
+--------------------------------------------------------------+
```

Duck typing and polymorphism is very important in Python. In fact it's the basis for the collection protocols we discussed such as *iterator*, *iterable* and *sequence*.

Inheritance and implementation sharing

Inheritance is a

mechanism

  whereby one class can be derived from a base-class allowing us to make behavior more specific in the subclass. In nominally typed languages such as Java, class-based inheritance is the means by which run-time polymorphism is achieved. Not so in Python, as we have just demonstrated. The fact that no Python method calls or attribute lookups are bound to actual objects until the point at which they are called – known as late-binding – means we can attempt polymorphism with any object and it will succeed if the object fits.

Although inheritance in Python can be used to facilitate polymorphism – after all, derived classes will have the same interfaces as base classes – inheritance in Python is most useful for sharing implementation between classes.

A base class for aircraft

As usual, this will make much more sense with an example. We would like our aircraft classes AirbusA319 and Boeing777 to provide a way of returning the total number of seats. We'll add a method called num_seats() to both classes to do this:

```
def num_seats(self):
```

```
        rows, row_seats = self.seating_plan()
        return len(rows) * len(row_seats)
```

The implementation can be identical in both classes, since it can be calculated from the seating plan.

Unfortunately, we now have duplicate code across two classes, and as we add more aircraft types the code duplication will worsen.

The solution is to extract the common elements of AirbusA319 and Boeing777 into a base class from which both aircraft types will derive. Let's recreate the class Aircraft, this time with the goal of using it as a base class:

```
class Aircraft:

    def num_seats(self):
        rows, row_seats = self.seating_plan()
        return len(rows) * len(row_seats)
```

The Aircraft class contains just the method we want to inherit into the derived classes. This class isn't usable on its own because it depends on a method called seating_plan() which isn't available at this level. Any attempt to use it standalone will fail:

```
>>> from airtravel import *
>>> base = Aircraft()
>>> base.num_seats()
Traceback (most recent call last):
  File "<stdin>", line 1, in <module>
  File "./airtravel.py", line 125, in num_seats
    rows, row_seats = self.seating_plan()
AttributeError: 'Aircraft' object has no attribute 'seating_plan'
```

The class is *abstract* in so far as it is never useful to instantiate it alone.

Inheriting from Aircraft

Now for the derived classes. We specify inheritance in Python using parentheses containing the base class name immediately after the class name in the class statement.

Here's the Airbus class:

```
class AirbusA319(Aircraft):

    def __init__(self, registration):
        self._registration = registration
```

```
    def registration(self):
        return self._registration

    def model(self):
        return "Airbus A319"

    def seating_plan(self):
        return range(1, 23), "ABCDEF"
```

And this is the Boeing class:

```
class Boeing777(Aircraft):

    def __init__(self, registration):
        self._registration = registration

    def registration(self):
        return self._registration

    def model(self):
        return "Boeing 777"

    def seating_plan(self):
        # For simplicity's sake, we ignore complex
        # seating arrangement for first-class
        return range(1, 56), "ABCDEGHJK"
```

Let's exercise them at the REPL:

```
>>> from airtravel import *
>>> a = AirbusA319("G-EZBT")
>>> a.num_seats()
132
>>> b = Boeing777("N717AN")
>>> b.num_seats()
495
```

We can see that both subtype aircraft inherited the `num_seats()` method, which now works as expected because the call to `seating_plan()` is successfully resolved on the self object at runtime.

Hoisting common functionality into a base class

Now we have the base Aircraft class we can refactor by hoisting into it other common functionality. For example, both the initializer and `registration()` methods are identical between the two subtypes:

```
class Aircraft:

    def __init__(self, registration):
        self._registration = registration

    def registration(self):
        return self._registration

    def num_seats(self):
        rows, row_seats = self.seating_plan()
        return len(rows) * len(row_seats)


class AirbusA319(Aircraft):

    def model(self):
        return "Airbus A319"

    def seating_plan(self):
        return range(1, 23), "ABCDEF"


class Boeing777(Aircraft):

    def model(self):
        return "Boeing 777"

    def seating_plan(self):
        # For simplicities sake, we ignore complex
        # seating arrangement for first-class
        return range(1, 56), "ABCDEGHJK"
```

These derived classes only contain the specifics for that aircraft type. All general functionality is shared from the base class by inheritance.

Thanks to duck-typing, inheritance is less used on Python than in other languages. This is generally seen as a good thing because inheritance is a very tight coupling between classes.

Summary

- All types in Python have a class.

- Classes define the structure and behavior of an object.

- The class of an object is determined when the object is created and is almost always fixed for the lifetime of the object.

- Classes are the key support for Object-Oriented Programming in Python.

- Classes are defined using the class keyword followed by the class name, which is in CamelCase.

- Instances of a class are created by calling the class as if it were a function.

- Instance methods are functions defined inside the class which should accept an object instance called self as the first parameter.

- Methods are called using the `instance.method()` syntax which is syntactic sugar for passing the instance as the formal self argument to the method.

- An optional special initializer method called __init__() can be provided which is used to configure the self object at creation time.

- The constructor calls the __init__() method if one is present.

- The __init__() method is *not* the constructor. The object has been already constructed by the time the initializer is called. The initializer configures the newly created object before it it returned to the caller of the constructor.

- Arguments passed to the constructor are forwarded to the initializer.

- Instance attributes are brought into existence simply by assigning to them.

- Attributes and methods which are implementation details are by convention prefixed with an underscore. There are no `public`, `protected` or `private` access modifiers in Python.

- Access to implementation details from outside the class can be very useful during development, testing and debugging.

- Class invariants should be established in the initializer. If the invariants can't be established raise exceptions to signal failure.

- Methods can have docstrings, just like regular functions.

- Classes can have docstrings.

- Even within an object method calls must be qualified with self.

- You can have as many classes and functions in a module as you wish. Related classes and global functions are usually grouped together this way.

- Polymorphism in Python is achieved through duck typing where attributes and methods are only resolved at point of use - a behaviour called late-binding.

- Polymorphism in Python does not require shared base classes or named interfaces.

- Class inheritance in Python is primarily useful for sharing implementation rather than being necessary for polymorphism.

- All methods are inherited, including special methods like the `initialiser` method.

Along the way we found that:

- Strings support slicing, because they implement the *sequence* protocol.

- Following the Law of Demeter can reduce coupling.

- We can nest comprehensions.

- It can sometimes be useful to discard the current item in a comprehension using a dummy reference, conventionally the underscore.

- When dealing with one-based collections it's often easier just to waste the zeroth list entry.

- Don't feel compelled to use classes when a simple function will suffice. Functions are also objects.

- Complex comprehensions or generator expressions can be split over multiple lines to aid readability.

- Statements can be split over multiple lines using the backslash line continuation character. Use this feature sparingly and only when it improves readability.

- Object-oriented design where one object *tells* another information can be more loosely coupled than those where one object queries another. "Tell! Don't ask."

1. In fact, it is possible to change the class of an object at runtime, although this is an advanced topic, and the technique is only rarely used.

2. It's generally unhelpful to think about the *destruction* of objects in Python. Better to think of objects becoming unreachable.

3. The *formal* arguments of a function are the arguments listed in the function *definition*.

4. The *actual* arguments of a function are the arguments listed in a function *call*.

9

Files and Resource Management

Reading and writing files is a key part of what many real-world programs do. The notion of a *file*, however, is somewhat abstract. In some cases a file might mean collection of bytes on a hard disk; in others cases it might mean, for example, an HTTP resource on a remote system. These two entities share some behavior. For example, you can read a sequence of bytes from each. At the same time, they're not identical. You can, for example, generally write bytes back to a local file while you can't do that with HTTP resources.

In this chapter we'll look at Python's basic support for working with files. Since dealing with local files is both common and important, we'll focus primarily on working with them. Be aware, though, that Python and its ecosystem of libraries provides similar *file-like* APIs for many other kinds of entities, including URI-based resources, databases, and many other sources of data. This use of a common API is very convenient and makes it easy to write code that can work against a wide range of data sources without change.

Also in this chapter we'll look at *context managers*, one of Python's primary means for managing resources. Context managers allow you to write code that is robust and predictable in the face of exceptions, ensuring that resources such as files are properly closed and accounted for when errors occur.

Files

To open a local file in Python we call the built-in open() function. This takes a number of arguments, but the most commonly used are:

- file: the path to the file. *This is required.*
- mode: read, write, append and binary or text. This is optional, but we recommend always specifying it for clarity. Explicit is better than implicit.
- encoding: If the file contains encoded text data, which encoding to use. It's often a good idea to specify this. If you don't specify it, Python will choose a default encoding for you.

Binary and text modes

At the filesytem level, of course, files contain only a series of bytes. Python, however, distinguishes between files opened in binary and text modes, even when the underlying operating system doesn't. When you open a file in binary mode, you are instructing Python to use the data in the file without any decoding; binary mode file reflects the raw data in the file.

A file opened in text mode, on the other hand, treats its contents as if it contains text strings of the str type. When you get data from a text mode file, Python first decodes the raw bytes using either a platform-dependent encoding or, if provided, the encoding argument to open().

By default, text mode files also engage support for Python's *universal newlines*. This causes translation between a single portable newline character in our program strings ('\n') and a platform dependent newline representation in the raw bytes stored in the file system (for example carriage-return-newline ('\r\n') on Windows).

The important of encoding

Getting the encoding right is *crucial* for correctly interpreting the contents of a text file, so we want to labor the point a bit. Python can't reliably determine the encoding of a text file, so it doesn't try. Yet without knowing the encoding of a file, Python can't properly manipulate the data in the file. That's why it's critical that you tell Python which encoding to use.

If you don't specify an encoding Python will use the default from
`sys.getdefaultencoding()`. In our case, the default encoding is 'utf-8':

```
>>> import sys
>>> sys.getdefaultencoding()
'utf-8'
```

Always remember, though, that there's no guarantee that the default encoding on your
system is the same as the default encoding on another system with which you wish to
exchange files. It's better for all concerned to make a conscious decision about the text-to-
bytes encoding by specifying it in your calls to `open()`. You can get a list of supported text
encodings in the `Python documentation`.

Opening a file for writing

Let's start working with files by opening a file in *write* mode. We'll be explicit about using
the UTF-8 encoding, because we have no way of knowing what your default encoding is.
We'll also use keyword arguments to make things clearer still:

```
>>> f = open('wasteland.txt', mode='wt', encoding='utf-8')
```

The first argument is the filename. The mode argument is a string containing letters with
different meanings. In this case `w` means *write* and `t` means *text*.

All mode strings should consist of one of `read`, `write` or `append` mode. This table lists the
mode codes along with their meanings in the following format Code: Meaning :

- **r**: Open file for reading. The stream is positioned at the beginning of the file. This
  is the default.
- **r+**: Open for reading and writing. The stream is positioned at thebeginning of the
  file.
- **w**: Truncate file to zero length or create file for writing. The stream is positioned
  at the beginning of the file.
- **w+**: Open for reading and writing. The file is created if it does not exist, otherwise
  it is truncated. The stream is positioned at the beginning of the file.
- **a**: Open for writing. The file is created if it does not exist. The stream is positioned
  at the end of the file. Subsequent writes to the file will always end up at the then
  current end of file, irrespective of any intervening seeks or similar.

- **a+**: Open for reading and writing. The file is created if it does not exist. The stream is positioned at the end of the file. Subsequent writes to the file will always end up at the then current end of file, irrespective of any intervening seeks or similar.

One of the preceding should be combined with a selector from the next table for specifying *text* or *binary* mode in the following format Code: Meaning :

- **t**: File contents interpreted as encoded text strings. The bytes in the file will be encoded and decoded according the to the specified text encoding, and universal newline translation will be in effect (unless explicitly disabled). All methods which write and read data from the file accept and return `str` objects. *This is the default*.
- **b**: File contents are treated as raw bytes. All methods which write and read data from the file accept and return bytes objects.

Examples of typical mode strings might be `wb` for write binary or at for append text. Although both parts of the mode code support defaults, we recommend being explicit for the sake of readability.

The exact type of the object returned by `open()` depends on how the file was opened. This is dynamic typing in action! For most purposes, however, the actual type returned by `open()` is unimportant. It is sufficient to know that the returned object is a *file-like object*, and as such we can expect it to support certain attributes and methods.

Writing to files

We've shown previously how we can request `help()` for modules and methods and types, but in fact we can request help on instances too. This makes sense when you remember that *everything* is an object.

```
>>> help(f)
. . .
 |  write(self, text, /)
 |      Write string to stream.
 |      Returns the number of characters written (which is always
 |      equal to the length of the string).
. . .
```

Browsing through the help, we can see that `f` supports a method `write()`. Quit the help with q and continue at the REPL.

Now let's write some text to our file using the `write()` method:

```
>>> f.write('What are the roots that clutch, ')
32
```

The call to `write()` returns the number of codepoints or characters written to the file. Let's add a few more lines:

```
>>> f.write('what branches grow\n')
19
>>> f.write('Out of this stony rubbish? ')
27
```

You'll notice that we're explicitly including newlines in the text we write to the file. It's the callers responsibility to provide newline characters where they are needed; Python does not provide a `writeline()` method.

Closing files

When we've finished writing, we should remember to close the file by calling the `close()` method:

```
>>> f.close()
```

Note that it's only after we close the file that we can be certain that the data we've written becomes visible to external processes. Closing files is important!

Also remember that you can no longer read from or write to a file after closing it. Attempts to do so will result in an exception.

The file outside of Python

If you now exit the REPL, and look in your filesystem you can see that you have indeed created a file. On Unix use the ls command:

```
$ ls -l
-rw-r--r--  1 rjs  staff    78 12 Jul 11:21 wasteland.txt
```

You should see the `wasteland.txt` file with 78 bytes.

On Windows use `dir`:

```
> dir
  Volume is drive C has no label.
  Volume Serial Number is 36C2-FF83

  Directory of c:\Users\pyfund

12/07/2013  20:54                    79 wasteland.txt
                 1 File(s)              79 bytes
                 0 Dir(s)   190,353,698,816 bytes free
```

In this case you should see `wasteland.txt` with `79 bytes` because Python's universal newline behavior for files has translated the line ending to your platform's native endings.

The number returned by the `write()` method is the number of codepoints (or characters) in the string passed to `write()`, *not* the number of `bytes` written to the file after encoding and universal newline translation. In general, when working with text files, you cannot sum the quantities returned by `write()` to determine the length of the file in bytes.

Reading files

To read the file back we use `open()` again, but this time we pass 'rt', for *read-text*, as the mode:

```
>>> g = open('wasteland.txt', mode='rt', encoding='utf-8')
```

If we know how many bytes to read, or if we want to read the whole file, we can use `read()`. Looking back through our REPL we can see that the first write was 32 characters long, so let's read that back with a call to the `read()` method:

```
>>> g.read(32)
'What are the roots that clutch, '
```

In text mode, the `read()` method accepts the number of *characters* to read from the file, not the number of bytes. The call returns the text and advances the file pointer to the end of what was read. Because we opened the file in text mode, the return type is `str`.

To read *all* the remaining data in the file we can call `read()` without an argument:

```
>>> g.read()
'what branches grow\nOut of this stony rubbish? '
```

This gives us parts of two lines in one string — note the newline character in the middle.

At the end of the file, further calls to `read()` return an empty string:

```
>>> g.read()
''
```

Normally when we have finished reading a file we would `close()` it. For the purposes of this exercise, though, we'll keep the file open and use `seek()` with an argument of zero to move the file pointer back to the start of the file:

```
>>> g.seek(0)
0
```

The return value of `seek()` is the new file pointer position.

Readline line by line

Using `read()` for text is quite awkward, and thankfully Python provides better tools for reading text files line by line. The first of these is `readline()` function:

```
>>> g.readline()
'What are the roots that clutch, what branches grow\n'
>>> g.readline()
'Out of this stony rubbish? '
```

Each call to `readline()` returns a single line of text. The returned lines are terminated by a single newline character, if there is one present in the file. The last line here does not terminate with a newline because there is no newline sequence at the end of the file. You shouldn't *rely* on the string returned by `readline()` being terminated by a newline. And remember that the universal newline support will have translated whatever the platform native newline sequence into '\n'.

Once we reach the end of the file further calls to `readline()` return an empty string:

```
>>> g.readline()
''
```

Reading multiple lines at once

Let's rewind our file pointer again and read our file in a different way:

```
>>> g.seek(0)
```

Sometimes when we know we want to read every line in the file — and if we're sure we have enough memory to do so — we can read all lines from the file into a list with the `readlines()` method:

```
>>> g.readlines()
['What are the roots that clutch, what branches grow\n',
 'Out of this stony rubbish? ']
```

This is particularly useful if parsing the file involves hopping backwards and forwards between lines; it's much easier to do this with a list of lines than with a file stream of characters.

This time, we'll close the file before moving on:

```
>>> g.close()
```

Appending to files

Sometimes we would like to append to an existing file, and we can do that by using the mode `'a'`. In with this mode, the file is opened for writing and the file pointer is moved to the end of any existing data. In this example we combine `'a'` with `'t'` to be explicit about using text mode:

```
>>> h = open('wasteland.txt', mode='at', encoding='utf-8')
```

Although there is no `writeline()` method in Python, there is a `writelines()` method which writes an iterable series of strings to the stream. If you want line endings on your strings *you must provide them yourself.* This may seem odd at first, but it preserves symmetry with `readlines()` whilst also giving us the flexibility for using `writelines()` to write any iterable series of strings to a file:

```
>>> h.writelines(
... ['Son of man,\n',
... 'You cannot say, or guess, ',
... 'for you know only,\n',
... 'A heap of broken images, ',
... 'where the sun beats\n'])
>>> h.close()
```

Notice that only three lines are completed here — we say *completed* because the file we're appending to did not itself end with a newline.

File objects as iterators

The culmination of these increasingly sophisticated text file reading tools is the fact that file objects support the *iterator* protocol. When you iterate over a file, each iteration yields the next line in the file. This means that they can be used in `for`-loops and any other place where an iterator can be used. At this point, we'll take the opportunity to create a Python module file `files.py`:

```
import sys

def main(filename):
    f = open(filename, mode='rt', encoding='utf-8')
    for line in f:
        print(line)
    f.close()

if __name__ == '__main__':
    main(sys.argv[1])
```

We can call this directly from the system command line, passing the name of our text file:

```
$ python3 files.py wasteland.txt
What are the roots that clutch, what branches grow

Out of this stony rubbish? Son of man,

You cannot say, or guess, for you know only

A heap of broken images, where the sun beats
```

You'll notice that there are empty lines between each line of the poem. This occurs because each line in the file is terminated by a new line, and then `print()` adds its own. To fix that, we could use the `strip()` method to remove the whitespace from the end of each line prior to printing. Instead we'll use the `write()` method of the `stdout` stream. This is *exactly* the same `write()` method we used to write to the file earlier — and can be used because the `stdout` stream is itself a file-like object. We get hold of a reference to the `stdout` stream from the `sys` module:

```
import sys

def main(filename):
    f = open(filename, mode='rt', encoding='utf-8')
    for line in f:
        sys.stdout.write(line)
    f.close()
```

```
if __name__ == '__main__':
    main(sys.argv[1])
```

If we re-run our program we get:

```
$ python3 files.py wasteland.txt
What are the roots that clutch, what branches grow
Out of this stony rubbish? Son of man,
You cannot say, or guess, for you know only
A heap of broken images, where the sun beats
```

Now, alas, it's time to move on from one of the most important poems of the twentieth century and get to grips with something *almost* as exciting, context managers.

Context Managers

For the next set of examples we're going to need a data file containing some numbers. Using the code in recaman.py below, we'll write a sequence of numbers called Recaman's sequence to a text file, with one number per line:

```
import sys
from itertools import count, islice

def sequence():
    """Generate Recaman's sequence."""
    seen = set()
    a = 0
    for n in count(1):
        yield a
        seen.add(a)
        c = a - n
        if c < 0 or c in seen:
            c = a + n
        a = c

def write_sequence(filename, num):
    """Write Recaman's sequence to a text file."""
    f = open(filename, mode='wt', encoding='utf-8')
    f.writelines("{0}\n".format(r)
                 for r in islice(sequence(), num + 1))
    f.close()

if __name__ == '__main__':
    write_sequence(filename=sys.argv[1],
                   num=int(sys.argv[2]))
```

Recaman's sequence itself isn't important to this exercise; we just needed a way of generating numeric data. As such, we won't be explaining the `sequence()` generator. Feel free to experiment though.

The module contains a generator for yielding the Recaman numbers and a function which writes the start of the sequence to file using the `writelines()` method. A generator expression is used to convert each number to a string and add a `newline`. `itertools.islice()` is used to truncate the otherwise infinite sequence.

We'll write the first 1000 Recaman numbers to a file by executing the module, passing the filename and series length as command line arguments:

```
$ python3 recaman.py recaman.dat 1000
```

Now let's make a complementary module `series.py` which reads this data file back in:

```python
"""Read and print an integer series."""

import sys

def read_series(filename):
    f = open(filename, mode='rt', encoding='utf-8')
    series = []
    for line in f:
        a = int(line.strip())
        series.append(a)
    f.close()
    return series

def main(filename):
    series = read_series(filename)
    print(series)

if __name__ == '__main__':
    main(sys.argv[1])
```

We simply read one line at a time from the open file, strip the newline with a call to the `strip()` string method, and convert it to an integer. If we run it from the command line, everything should work as expected:

```
$ python3 series.py recaman.dat
[0, 1, 3, 6, 2, 7, 13,
 ...
,3683, 2688, 3684, 2687, 3685, 2686, 3686]
```

Now let's deliberately create an exceptional situation. Open `recaman.dat` in a text editor and replace one of the numbers with something that isn't an stringified integer:

```
0
1
3
6
2
7
13
oops!
12
21
```

Save the file, and re-run `series.py`:

```
$ python3 series.py recaman.dat
Traceback (most recent call last):
  File "series.py", line 19, in <module>
    main(sys.argv[1])
  File "series.py", line 15, in main
    series = read_series(filename)
  File "series.py", line 9, in read_series
    a = int(line.strip())
ValueError: invalid literal for int() with base 10: 'oops!'
```

The `int()` constructor raises a `ValueError` when passed our new, invalid line. The exception is unhandled, and so the program terminates with stack trace.

Managing resources with finally

One problem here is that our `f.close()` call was never executed.

To fix that, we can insert a `try ... finally` block:

```
def read_series(filename):
    try:
        f = open(filename, mode='rt', encoding='utf-8')
        series = []
        for line in f:
            a = int(line.strip())
            series.append(a)
    finally:
        f.close()
    return series
```

Now the file will always be closed, even in the presence of exceptions. Making this change opens up the opportunity for another refactoring: we can replace the `for`-loop with a list comprehension and `return` this list directly:

```
def read_series(filename):
    try:
        f = open(filename, mode='rt', encoding='utf-8')
        return [ int(line.strip()) for line in f ]
    finally:
        f.close()
```

Even in this situation `close()` will still be called; the `finally` block is called no matter how the `try` block is exited.

The with-blocks

Up to now our examples have all followed a pattern: `open()` a file, work with the file, `close()` the file. The `close()` is important because it informs the underlying operating system that you're done working with the file. If you don't close a file when you're done with it, it's possible to lose data. There may be pending writes buffered up which might not get written completely. Furthermore, if you're opening lots of files, your system may run out of resources. Since we always want to pair every `open()` with a `close()`, we would like a mechanism that enforces the relationship even if we forget.

This need for resource clean up is common enough that Python implements a specific control flow structure called `with`-blocks to support it. The `with`-blocks can be used with any object that supports the *context-manager* protocol, which includes the file-objects returned by `open()`. Exploiting the fact the the file object is a context manager, our `read_series()` function can become simply:

```
def read_series(filename):
    with open(filename, mode='rt', encoding='utf-8') as f:
        return [int(line.strip()) for line in f]
```

We no longer need to call `close()` explicitly because the with construct will call it for us when execution exits the block, no matter how we exit the block.

Now we can go back and modify our Recaman series writing program to use a `with`-block, too, again removing the need for the explicit `close()`:

```
def write_sequence(filename, num):
    """Write Recaman's sequence to a text file."""
    with open(filename, mode='wt', encoding='utf-8') as f:
```

```
f.writelines("{0}\n".format(r)
              for r in islice(sequence(), num + 1))
```

Moment of zen

Figure 9.1: Beautiful is better than ugly

The with-block syntax looks like this:

```
with EXPR as VAR:
    BLOCK
```

This is so-called *syntactic sugar* for a much more complex arrangement of try...except and try...finally blocks:

```
mgr = (EXPR)
exit = type(mgr).__exit__   # Not calling it yet
value = type(mgr).__enter__(mgr)
exc = True
try:
```

```
try:
    VAR = value   # Only if "as VAR" is present
    BLOCK
except:
    # The exceptional case is handled here
    exc = False
    if not exit(mgr, *sys.exc_info()):
        raise
    # The exception is swallowed if exit() returns true
finally:
    # The normal and non-local-goto cases are handled here
    if exc:
        exit(mgr, None, None, None)
```

Which do you prefer?

Few of us would want our code to look this convoluted, but this is how it would need to look without the with statement. Sugar may not be good for your health, but it can be very healthy for your code!

Binary files

So far we've looked at text files, where we deal with the file contents as Unicode strings. There are many cases, however, where files contain data that is not encoded text. In these situations we need to be able to work with the exact bytes that are present in the file, without any intermediate encoding or decoding. This is what *binary mode* is for.

The BMP file format

To demonstrate handling of binary files, we need an interesting binary data format. BMP is an image file format that contains Device Independent Bitmaps. It's simple enough that we can make a BMP file writer from scratch. Place the following code in a module called bmp.py:

```
# bmp.py

"""A module for dealing with BMP bitmap image files."""

def write_grayscale(filename, pixels):
    """Creates and writes a grayscale BMP file.

    Args:
        filename: The name of the BMP file to me created.
```

```
        pixels: A rectangular image stored as a sequence of rows.
                Each row must be an iterable series of integers in the
                range 0-255.

    Raises:
        OSError: If the file couldn't be written.
    """
    height = len(pixels)
    width = len(pixels[0])

    with open(filename, 'wb') as bmp:
        # BMP Header
        bmp.write(b'BM')

        # The next four bytes hold the filesize as a 32-bit
        # little-endian integer. Zero placeholder for now.
        size_bookmark = bmp.tell()
        bmp.write(b'\x00\x00\x00\x00')

        # Two unused 16-bit integers - should be zero
        bmp.write(b'\x00\x00')
        bmp.write(b'\x00\x00')

        # The next four bytes hold the integer offset
        # to the pixel data. Zero placeholder for now.
        pixel_offset_bookmark = bmp.tell()
        bmp.write(b'\x00\x00\x00\x00')

        # Image Header
        bmp.write(b'\x28\x00\x00\x00')      # Image header size in bytes -
                                            40 decimal
        bmp.write(_int32_to_bytes(width))    # Image width in pixels
        bmp.write(_int32_to_bytes(height))   # Image height in pixels
                                             # Rest of header is
                                             essentially fixed
        bmp.write(b'\x01\x00')              # Number of image planes
        bmp.write(b'\x08\x00')              # Bits per pixel 8 for
                                           grayscale
        bmp.write(b'\x00\x00\x00\x00')     # No compression
        bmp.write(b'\x00\x00\x00\x00')     # Zero for uncompressed images
        bmp.write(b'\x00\x00\x00\x00')     # Unused pixels per meter
        bmp.write(b'\x00\x00\x00\x00')     # Unused pixels per meter
        bmp.write(b'\x00\x00\x00\x00')     # Use whole color table
        bmp.write(b'\x00\x00\x00\x00')     # All colors are important

# Color palette - a linear grayscale
        for c in range(256):
            bmp.write(bytes((c, c, c, 0)))  # Blue, Green, Red, Zero
```

```
# Pixel data
pixel_data_bookmark = bmp.tell()
for row in reversed(pixels):  # BMP files are bottom to top
    row_data = bytes(row)
    bmp.write(row_data)
    padding = b'\x00' * ((4 - (len(row) % 4)) % 4)
    # Pad row to multiple of four bytes
    bmp.write(padding)

# End of file
eof_bookmark = bmp.tell()

# Fill in file size placeholder
bmp.seek(size_bookmark)
bmp.write(_int32_to_bytes(eof_bookmark))

# Fill in pixel offset placeholder
bmp.seek(pixel_offset_bookmark)
bmp.write(_int32_to_bytes(pixel_data_bookmark))
```

This may look complex, but as you'll see it's relatively straightforward.

For simplicity's sake, we have decided to deal only with 8-bit grayscale images. These have the nice property that they are one byte per pixel. The `write_grayscale()` function accepts two arguments: The filename and a collection of pixel values. As the docstring points out, this collection should be a sequence of sequences of integers. For example, a list of lists of `int` objects will do just fine. Furthermore:

- Each `int` must be a pixel value from 0 to 255
- Each inner list is a row of pixels from left to right
- The outer list is a list of pixel rows, from top to bottom.

The first thing we do is figure out the size of the image by counting the number of rows (line 19) to give the height and the number of items in the zeroth row to get the width (line 20). We assume, but don't check, that all rows have the same length (in production code that's a check we would want to make).

Next , we `open()` (line 22) the file for *write in binary* mode using the `wb` mode string. We don't specify an encoding - that makes no sense for raw binary files.

Inside the with-block we start writing what is called the 'BMP Header' which begins the BMP format.

The header must start with a so-called "magic" byte sequence b'BM' to identify it as a BMP file. We use the `write()` method (line 24), and, because the file was opened in binary mode, we must pass a bytes object.

The next four bytes should hold a 32-bit integer containing the file size, a value that we don't yet know. We could have computed it in advance, but instead we'll take a different approach: we'll write a placeholder value then return to this point later to fill in the details. To be able to come back to this point we use the `tell()` method of the file object (line 28); this gives us the file poiner's offset from the beginning of the file. We'll store this offset in a variable which will act as a sort of bookmark. We write four zero-bytes as the placeholder (line 29), using escaping syntax to specify the zeros.

The next two pairs of bytes are unused, so we just write zero bytes to them too (lines 32 and 33).

The next four bytes are for another 32-bit integer which should contain the offset in bytes from the beginning of the file to the start of the pixel data. We don't know that value yet either, so we'll store another bookmark using `tell()` (line 37) and write another four byte placeholder (line 38); we'll return here shortly when we know more.

The next section is called the `Image Header`. The first thing we have to do is write the length of the image header as a 32-bit integer (line 41). In our case the header will always be 40 bytes long. We just hardwire that in hexadecimal. Notice that the BMP format is `little-endian` - the least significant `byte` is written first.

The next four bytes are the image width as a `little-endian` 32-bit integer. We call a module scope implementation detail function here called `_int32_to_bytes()` which converts an int object into a `bytes` object containing exactly four bytes (line 42). We then use the same function again to deal with the `Image height` (line 43).

The remainder of the header is essentially fixed for 8-bit grayscale images and the details aren't important here, except to note that the whole header does in fact total 40 bytes (line 45).

Each pixel in an 8-bit BMP image is an index into a color table with 256 entries. Each entry is a four-byte BGR color. For grayscale images we need to write 256 4-byte gray values on a linear scale (line 54). This snippet is fertile ground for experimentation, and an natural enhancement to this function would be to be able to supply this palette separately as an optional function argument.

At last, we're ready to write the pixel data, but before we do we make a note of the current file pointer offset using tell() (line 59) as this was one of the locations we need to go back and fill in later.

Writing the pixel data itself is straightforward enough. We use the reversed() built-in function (line 60) to flip the order of the rows; BMP images are written bottom to top. For each row we simply pass the iterable series of integers to the bytes() constructor (line 61). If any of the integers are out of the range 0–255, the constructor will raise a ValueError.

Each row of pixel data in a BMP file must be a multiple of four bytes long, irrespective of image width. To do this (line 63), we take the row length modulus four, to give a number between zero and three inclusive, which is the the number of bytes over the *previous* four-byte boundary the end of our row falls. To get the number of padding bytes required to take us up to the *next* four byte boundary we subtract this modulus value from four to give a value of 4 to 1 inclusive. However, we never want to pad with four bytes, only with one, two or three, so we must take modulus four again, to convert the four byte padding to zero byte padding.

This value is used with the repetition operator applied to a single zero-byte to produce a bytes object containing zero, one, two or three bytes. We write this to the file, to terminate each row (line 65).

After the pixel data we are at the end of the file. We undertook to record this offset value earlier, so we record the current position using tell() (line 68) into an end-of-file bookmark variable.

Now we can return and fulfill our promises by replacing the placeholder offsets we recorded with the real thing. First, the file length. To do this we seek() (line 71) back to the size_bookmark we remembered back near the beginning of the file and write() (line 72) the size stored in eof_bookmark as a little-endian 32-bit integer using our _int32_to_bytes() function.

Finally, we seek() (line 75) to the pixel data offset placeholder bookmarked by pixel_offset_bookmark and write the 32-bit integer stored in pixel_data_bookmark (line 76).

As we exit the with-block we can rest assured that the context manager will close the file and commit any buffered writes to the file system.

Bitwise operators

Dealing with binary files often requires pulling apart or assembling data at the byte level. This is exactly what our _int32_to_bytes() function is doing. We'll take a quick look at it because it shows some features of Python we haven't seen before:

```python
def _int32_to_bytes(i):
    """Convert an integer to four bytes in little-endian format."""
    return bytes((i & 0xff,
                  i >> 8 & 0xff,
                  i >> 16 & 0xff,
                  i >> 24 & 0xff))
```

The function uses the >> (*bitwise-shift*) and & (*bitwise-and*) operators to extract individual bytes from the integer value. Note that bitwise-and uses the ampersand symbol to distinguish it from *logical-and* which is the spelled out word "and". The >> operator shifts the binary representation of the integer right by the specified number of bits. The routine shifts the integer argument one, two, and three bytes to the right before extracting the least significant byte with & after each shift. The four resulting integers are used to construct a tuple which is then passed to the bytes() constructor to produce a four byte sequence.

Writing a BMP file

In order to generate a BMP image file, we're going to need some pixel data. We've included a simple module fractal.py which produces pixel values for the iconic Mandelbrot set fractal.

We're not going to explain the fractal generation code in detail, still less the math behind it. But the code is simple enough, and it doesn't rely on any Python features we haven't encountered previously:

```python
# fractal.py

"""Computing Mandelbrot sets."""

import math

def mandel(real, imag):
    """The logarithm of number of iterations needed to
    determine whether a complex point is in the
    Mandelbrot set.

    Args:
        real: The real coordinate
        imag: The imaginary coordinate
```

```
Returns:
    An integer in the range 1-255.
"""
x = 0
y = 0
for i in range(1, 257):
    if x*x + y*y > 4.0:
        break
    xt = real + x*x - y*y
    y = imag + 2.0 * x * y
    x = xt
return int(math.log(i) * 256 / math.log(256)) - 1


def mandelbrot(size_x, size_y):
    """Make an Mandelbrot set image.

    Args:
        size_x: Image width
        size_y: Image height

    Returns:
        A list of lists of integers in the range 0-255.
    """
    return [ [mandel((3.5 * x / size_x) - 2.5,
                     (2.0 * y / size_y) - 1.0)
             for x in range(size_x) ]
           for y in range(size_y) ]
```

The key takeaway is that the `mandelbrot()` function uses nested list comprehensions to produce a list of lists of integers in the range 0–255. This list of lists represents an image of the fractal. The integer value for each point is produced by the `mandel()` function.

Generating fractal images

Let's fire up a REPL and use the fractal and bmp modules together. First we use the `mandelbrot()` function to product an image of 448 by 256 pixels. You'll get best results using images with an aspect ratio of 7:4:

```
>>> import fractal
>>> pixels = fractal.mandelbrot(448, 256)
```

This call to `mandelbrot()` may take a second or so — our fractal generator is simple rather than efficient!

We can take a look at the returned data structure:

```
>>> pixels
```

```
[[31, 31, 31, 31, 31, 31, 31, 31, 31, 31, 31, 31, 31, 31, 31, 31, 31,
  31,31, 31, 31, 31, 31, 31, 31, 31, 31, 31, 31, 31, 31, 31, 31,
  31, 31,
  ...
  49, 49, 49, 49, 49, 49, 49, 49, 49, 49, 49, 49, 49, 49, 49, 49, 49,
  49]]
```

It's a list of lists of integers, just as we were promised. Let's write those pixel values to a BMP file:

```
>>> import bmp
>>> bmp.write_grayscale("mandel.bmp", pixels)
```

Find the file and open it in an image viewer, for example by opening it in your web browser.

Picture of grayscale Mandelbrot set:

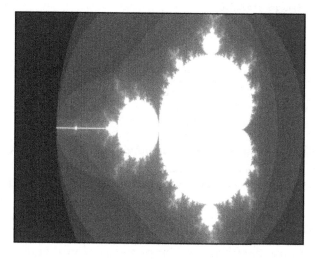

Figure 9.2: Grayscale Mandelbrot

Reading binary files

Now that we're producing beautiful Mandelbrot images, we should see about reading those BMPs back with Python. We're not going to write a full-blown BMP reader, although that would be an interesting exercise. We'll just make a simple function to determine the image dimension in pixels from a BMP file. We'll add the code into bmp.py:

```
def dimensions(filename):
```

```
"""Determine the dimensions in pixels of a BMP image.

    Args:
        filename: The filename of a BMP file.

    Returns:
        A tuple containing two integers with the width
        and height in pixels.

    Raises:
        ValueError: If the file was not a BMP file.
        OSError: If there was a problem reading the file.
    """

    with open(filename, 'rb') as f:
        magic = f.read(2)
        if magic != b'BM':
            raise ValueError("{} is not a BMP file".format(filename))

        f.seek(18)
        width_bytes = f.read(4)
        height_bytes = f.read(4)

        return (_bytes_to_int32(width_bytes),
                _bytes_to_int32(height_bytes))
```

Of course, we use a `with`-statement to manage the file, so we don't have to worry about it being properly closed. Inside the `with`-block we perform a simple validation check by looking for the two first magic bytes that we expect in a BMP file. If they're not present, we raise a `ValueError` which will, of course, cause the context manager to close the file.

Looking back at our BMP writer, we can determine that the image dimensions are stored exactly 18 bytes from the beginning of the file. We `seek()` to that location and use the `read()` method to read two chunks of four bytes each for the two 32-bit integers which represent the dimensions. Because we opened the file in binary mode, `read()` returns a `bytes` object. We pass each of these two bytes objects to another implementation detail function called `_bytes_to_int32()` which assembles them back into an integer. The two integers, representing image width and height, are returned as a tuple.

The `_bytes_to_int32()` function uses `<<` (*bitwise left-shift*) and `|` (*bitwise-or*), together with indexing of the `bytes` object, to reassemble the integer. Note that indexing into a `bytes` object returns an integer:

```
def _bytes_to_int32(b):
    """Convert a bytes object containing four bytes into an integer."""
    return b[0] | (b[1] << 8) | (b[2] << 16) | (b[3] << 24)
```

If we use our new reader code, we can see that it does indeed read the correct values:

```
>>> bmp.dimensions("mandel.bmp")
(448, 256)
```

File-like objects

There is a notion in Python of "file-like objects". This isn't as formal as a specific protocol, but, thanks to the polymorphism afforded by duck-typing, it works well in practice.

The reason it's not closely specified is that different types of data streams and devices have many different capabilities, expectations, and behaviors. So in fact defining a set of protocols to model them would be quite complex, and it wouldn't actually gain us much in practice, other than a smug sense of theoretical achievement. This is where the EAFP philosophy comes into its own: If you want to perform `seek()` on a file-like object without knowing in advance that it supports random access, go ahead and try (literally!). Just be prepared to fail if the `seek()` method doesn't exist, or if it *does* exist but doesn't behave as you expect.

You might say "If it looks like a file and reads like a file, then it is a file".

You've already seen file-like objects!

We've actually seen file-like objects in action already; the objects returned to us when we open files in text and binary mode are actually of different types, although both with definite file-like behavior. There are other types in the Python standard library which implement file-like behavior, and in fact we saw one of them in action back at the beginning of the book, when we used `urlopen()` to retrieve data from a URL on the Internet.

Using file-like objects

Let's exploit this polymorphism across file-like objects by writing a function to count the number of words per line in a file and return that information as a list:

```
>>> def words_per_line(flo):
...     return [len(line.split()) for line in flo.readlines()]
```

Now we'll open a regular text file containing the fragment of T.S. Eliot's masterpiece we created earlier, and pass it to our new function:

```
>>> with open("wasteland.txt", mode='rt', encoding='utf-8') as real_file:
...     wpl = words_per_line(real_file)
...
>>> wpl
[9, 8, 9, 9]
```

The actual type of `real_file` is:

```
>>> type(real_file)
<class '_io.TextIOWrapper'>
```

But you shouldn't normally concern yourself with this specific type; is an internal Python implementation detail. You're just care that it behaves "like a file".

We'll now do the same using a file-like object representing a web resource referred to by a URL:

```
>>> from urllib.request import urlopen
>>> with urlopen("http://sixty-north.com/c/t.txt") as web_file:
...     wpl = words_per_line(web_file)
...
>>> wpl
[6, 6, 6, 6, 6, 6, 6, 6, 6, 6, 5, 5, 7, 8, 14, 12, 8]
```

The type of `web_file` is quite different from what we just saw:

```
>>> type(web_file)
<class 'http.client.HTTPResponse'>
```

However, since they are both file-like objects, our function can work with both.

There's nothing magical about file-like objects; it's just a convenient and fairly informal description for a set of expectations we can place on an object which are exploited through duck-typing.

Other resources

The `with`-statement construct can be used with any type of object which implements the context manager protocol. We're not going to show you how to implement a context-manager is this book – for that you'll need to refer to *The Python Journeyman* – but we will show you a simple way to make your own classes usable in a with statement. Put this code into a the module `fridge.py`:

```
# fridge.py

"""Demonstrate raiding a refrigerator."""

class RefrigeratorRaider:
    """Raid a refrigerator."""

    def open(self):
        print("Open fridge door.")

    def take(self, food):
        print("Finding {}...".format(food))
        if food == 'deep fried pizza':
            raise RuntimeError("Health warning!")
        print("Taking {}".format(food))

    def close(self):
        print("Close fridge door.")

    def raid(food):
        r = RefrigeratorRaider()
        r.open()
        r.take(food)
        r.close()
```

We'll import `raid()` into the REPL and go on the rampage:

```
>>> from fridge import raid
>>> raid("bacon")
Open fridge door.
Finding bacon...
Taking bacon
Close fridge door.
```

Importantly, we remembered to close the door, so the food will be preserved until our next raid. Let's try another raid for something slightly less healthy:

```
>>> raid("deep fried pizza")
Open fridge door.
Finding deep fried pizza...
Traceback (most recent call last):
  File "<stdin>", line 1, in <module>
  File "./fridge.py", line 23, in raid
    r.take(food)
  File "./fridge.py", line 14, in take
    raise RuntimeError("Health warning!")
RuntimeError: Health warning!
```

This time, we were interrupted by the health warning and didn't get around to closing the door. We can fix that by using a function called `closing()` in the Python Standard Library `contextlib` module. After importing the function we wrap our `RefrigeratorRaider` constructor call in a call to `closing()`. This wraps our object in a context manager that always calls the `close()` method on the wrapped object before exiting. We use this
object to initialise a `with`-block:

```
"""Demonstrate raiding a refrigerator."""

from contextlib import closing

class RefrigeratorRaider:
    """Raid a refrigerator."""

    def open(self):
        print("Open fridge door.")

    def take(self, food):
        print("Finding {}...".format(food))
        if food == 'deep fried pizza':
            raise RuntimeError("Health warning!")
        print("Taking {}".format(food))

    def close(self):
        print("Close fridge door.")

    def raid(food):
        with closing(RefrigeratorRaider()) as r:
        r.open()
        r.take(food)
        r.close()
```

Now when we execute a raid:

```
>>> raid("spam")
Open fridge door.
Finding spam...
Taking spam
Close fridge door.
Close fridge door.
```

We see that our explicit call to `close()` is unnecessary, so let's fix that up:

```
def raid(food):
    with closing(RefrigeratorRaider()) as r:
        r.open()
        r.take(food)
```

A more sophisticated implementation would check that the door was already closed and ignore other requests.

So does it work? Let's try eating some deep fried pizza once more:

```
>>> raid("deep fried pizza")
Open fridge door.
Finding deep fried pizza...
Close fridge door.
Traceback (most recent call last):
  File "<stdin>", line 1, in <module>
  File "./fridge.py", line 23, in raid
    r.take(food)
  File "./fridge.py", line 14, in take
    raise RuntimeError("Health warning!")
RuntimeError: Health warning!
```

This time, even though the health warning was triggered, the door was still closed for us by the context manager.

Summary

- Files are opened using the built-in `open()` function which accepts a file mode to control read/write/append behaviour and whether the file is to be treated as raw binary or encoded text data.
- For text data you should specify a text encoding.
- Text files deal with string objects and perform universal newline translation and string encoding.

- Binary files deal with bytes objects with no newline translation or encoding.
- When writing files, it's your responsibility to provide newline characters for line breaks.
- Files should always be closed after use.
- Files provide various line-oriented methods for reading, and are also iterators which yield line by line.
- Files are context managers and the `with`-statement can be used with context managers to ensure that clean up operations, such as closing files, are performed.
- The notion of file-like objects is loosely defined, but very useful in practice. Exercise EAFP to make the most of them.
- Context managers aren't restricted to file-like objects. We can use tools in the `contextlib` standard library module, such as the `closing()` wrapper to create our own context managers.

Along the we way found that:

- The `help()` function can be used on instance objects, not just types.
- Python supports bitwise operators `&`, `|`, `<<` and `>>`.

1. Nor any language, for that matter.

2. You can get the full details of the `with`-statements syntactic equivalence in PEP 343.

3. You can learn all about the BMP format here.

4. Like, for example, *sequence* protocol is for tuple-like-objects.

5. Easier to **A**sk **F**orgiveness **T**han **P**ermission.

10
Unit testing with the Python standard library

When we build programs of even minor complexity, there are countless ways for defects to creep into our code. This can happen when we initially write the code, but we're just as likely to introduce defects when we make modifications to it. To help get a handle on defects and keep our code quality high, it's often very useful to have a set of tests that you can run that will tell if you if the code is acting as you expect.

To help make such tests, the Python standard library includes the `unittest module`. Despite
what its name suggests, this module helps with more than just unit testing. It is, in fact, a flexible framework for automating tests of all sorts, from acceptance tests to integration tests to unit tests. Its key feature, like many testing frameworks in many languages, is that it helps you make *automated* and *repeatable* tests. With tests like these, you can cheaply and easily verify the behavior of your code at any time.

Test cases

The `unittest` module is built around a handful of key concepts, at the center of which is the notion of a *test case*. A test case — embodied in the `unittest.TestCase class` — groups together a set of related test methods, and it is the basic unit of test organization in the unittest framework. The individual test methods, as we'll see later, are implemented as methods on a `unittest.TestCase` subclass.

Fixtures

The next important concept is that of *fixtures*. Fixtures are pieces of code which run before and/or after every test method. Fixtures serve two main purposes:

1. *Set-up* fixtures ensure that the test environment is in an expected state before a test is run.
2. *Tear-down* fixtures clean up the environment after a test has been run, generally by freeing up resources.

For example, a set-up fixture might create a specific entry in a database prior to running a test. Similarly, a tear-down fixture might remove database entries created by a test. Fixtures are not required for tests, but they are very common, and they are often critical for making tests repeatable.

Assertions

The final key concept is that of *assertions*. Assertions are specific checks inside test methods which ultimately determine whether a test passes or fails. Among other things, assertions can:

- Make simple boolean checks
- Perform object equality tests
- Verify that the proper exceptions are thrown

If an assertion fails, then a test method fails, so assertions represent the lowest level of testing you can perform. You can find a `full list of assertions in the unittest documentation`.

Unit testing example: text analysis

With those concepts in mind, let's see how we can actually use the unittest module in practice. For this example, we'll use *test-driven development* to write a simple text-analysis function. This function will take a file name as its only parameter. It will then read that file and calculate:

- The number of lines in the file
- The number of characters in the file

TDD is an iterative development process, so rather than work at the REPL we'll put the code for our tests in a file named `text_analyzer.py`. To start with, we'll create our first test with just enough supporting code to actually run it:

```
# text_analyzer.py

import unittest

class TextAnalysisTests(unittest.TestCase):
    """Tests for the ``analyze_text()`` function."""

    def test_function_runs(self):
        """Basic smoke test: does the function run."""
        analyze_text()

if __name__ == '__main__':
    unittest.main()
```

Ths first thing we do is import the `unittest` module. We then create our test case by defining a class – `TextAnalysisTests` – which derives from `unittest.TestCase`. This is how you create test cases with the `unittest` framework.

To define individual test methods in a test case, you simple create methods on your `TestCase` subclasses that start with `test_`. The unittest framework automatically discovers methods like this at execution time, so you don't need to explicitly register your test methods.

In this case we define the simplest possible test: We check whether the `analyze_text()` function runs at all! Our test doesn't make any explicit checks, but rather it relies on the fact that a test method will fail if it throws any exceptions. In this case, our test will fail if `analyze_text()` isn't defined.

Finally, we define the idiomatic "main" block which calls `unittest.main()` when this module is executed. The `unittest.main()` function will search for all `TestCase` subclasses in a module and execute all of their test methods.

Running the initial tests

Since we're using test-driven design, we expect our tests to fail at first. And indeed our test fails spectacularly for the simple reason that we haven't yet defined `analyze_text()`:

```
$ python text_analyzer.py
E
======================================================================
ERROR: test_function_runs (__main__.TextAnalysisTests)
----------------------------------------------------------------------
Traceback (most recent call last):
  File "text_analyzer.py", line 5, in test_function_runs
    analyze_text()
NameError: global name 'analyze_text' is not defined


----------------------------------------------------------------------
Ran 1 test in 0.001s

FAILED (errors=1)
```

As you can see, `unittest.main()` produces a simple report telling us how many tests were run and how many failed. It also shows us *how* the tests failed, in this case showing us that we got a NameError when we tried to run the non-existent function `analyze_text()`.

Making the test pass

Let's fix our failing test by defining `analyze_text()`. Remember that in test-driven development we only write enough code to satisfy our tests, so all we do right now is create an empty function. For simplicity's sake we'll put this function in `text_analyzer.py`, though normally your test code and implementation code will be in different modules:

```
# text_analyzer.py

def analyze_text():
    """Calculate the number of lines and characters in a file.
    """
    pass
```

Put this function at module scope. Running the test again, we find that they now pass:

```
% python text_analyzer.py
.
----------------------------------------------------------------------
Ran 1 test in 0.001s

OK
```

We've completed a single TDD cycle, but of course our code doesn't really do anything yet. We'll iteratively improve our tests and implementation to arrive at a real solution.

Using fixtures to create temporary files

The next thing want to do is be able to pass a filename to `analyze_text()` so that it knows what to process. Of course, for `analyze_text()` to work this filename should refer to a file that actually exists! To make sure that a file exists for our tests, we're going to define some fixtures.

The first fixture we can define is the method `TestCase.setUp()`. If defined, this method is run before each `test` method in the `TestCase`. In this case, we'll use `setUp()` to create a file for us and remember the filename as a member of the `TestCase`:

```
# text_analyzer.py

class TextAnalysisTests(unittest.TestCase):
    . . .
    def setUp(self):
        "Fixture that creates a file for the text methods to use."
        self.filename = 'text_analysis_test_file.txt'
        with open(self.filename, 'w') as f:
            f.write('Now we are engaged in a great civil war,\n'
                    'testing whether that nation,\n'
                    'or any nation so conceived and so dedicated,\n'
                    'can long endure.')
```

The second fixture available to us is `TestCase.tearDown()`. The `tearDown()` method is run after each test method in the `TestCase`, and in this case we're going to use it to delete the file we created in `setUp()`:

```
# text_analyzer.py

import os
. . .
class TextAnalysisTests(unittest.TestCase):
    . . .
    def tearDown(self):
        "Fixture that deletes the files used by the test methods."
        try:
            os.remove(self.filename)
        except OSError:
            pass
```

Note that since we're using the os module in `tearDown()` we need to import it at the top of the file.

Also notice how `tearDown()` swallows any exceptions thrown by `os.remove()`. We do this because `tearDown()` can't actually be certain that the file exists, so it simply tries to remove the file and assumes that any exception can safely be ignored.

Using the new fixtures

With our two fixtures in place, we now have a file that is created before each test method and which is deleted after each test method. This means that each test method is starting in a stable, known state. This is critical to making reproducible tests. Let's pass this filename to `analyze_text()` by modifying our existing test:

```
# text_analyzer.py

class TextAnalysisTests(unittest.TestCase):
    . . .
    def test_function_runs(self):
        "Basic smoke test: does the function run."
        analyze_text(self.filename)
```

Remember that our `setUp()` stored the filename on `self.filename`. Since the self argument passed to the fixtures is the same instance as that passed to the test methods, our test can access the filename using that attribute.

Of course, when we run our test we see that this test fails because `analyze_text()` doesn't accept any arguments yet:

```
% python text_analyzer.py
E
======================================================================
ERROR: test_function_runs (__main__.TextAnalysisTests)
----------------------------------------------------------------------
Traceback (most recent call last):
  File "text_analyzer.py", line 25, in test_function_runs
    analyze_text(self.filename)
TypeError: analyze_text() takes no arguments (1 given)


----------------------------------------------------------------------
Ran 1 test in 0.003s

FAILED (errors=1)
```

We can fix this by simply adding a parameter to `analyze_text()`:

```
# text_analyzer.py

def analyze_text(filename):
    pass
```

And if we run our tests again, we see that we're once again passing:

```
% python text_analyzer.py
.
----------------------------------------------------------------------
Ran 1 test in 0.003s

OK
```

We still don't have an implementation that does anything useful, but you can start to see how the tests drive the implementation.

Using assertions to test behavior

Now that we're satisfied that `analyze_text()` exists and accepts the right number of arguments, let's see if we can make it do real work. The first thing we want is for the function to return the number of lines in the file, so let's define that test:

```
# text_analyzer.py

class TextAnalysisTests(unittest.TestCase):
    . . .
    def test_line_count(self):
        "Check that the line count is correct."
        self.assertEqual(analyze_text(self.filename), 4)
```

Here we see our first example of an assertion. The `TestCase` class has many assertion methods, and in this case we used `assertEqual()` to check that the number of lines counted by our function is equal to four. If the value returned by `analyze_text()` is not equal to four, this assertion will cause the test method to fail. And if we run our new test, we see that this is precisely what happens:

```
% python text_analyzer.py
.F
======================================================================
FAIL: test_line_count (__main__.TextAnalysisTests)
----------------------------------------------------------------------
Traceback (most recent call last):
  File "text_analyzer.py", line 28, in test_line_count
    self.assertEqual(analyze_text(self.filename), 4)
AssertionError: None != 4


----------------------------------------------------------------------
Ran 2 tests in 0.003s

FAILED (failures=1)
```

Here we see that we're now running two tests, that one of them passes, and that the new one fails with an `AssertionError`.

Counting lines

Let's break from the TDD rules and move a bit faster now. First we'll update the function to return the number of lines in the file:

```python
# text_analyzer.py

def analyze_text(filename):
    """Calculate the number of lines and characters in a file.

    Args:
      filename: The name of the file to analyze.

    Raises:
      IOError: If ``filename`` does not exist or can't be read.

    Returns: The number of lines in the file.
    """
    with open(filename, 'r') as f:
        return sum(1 for _ in f)
```

This change indeed gives us the results we want:

```
% python text_analyzer.py
..
----------------------------------------------------------------------
Ran 2 tests in 0.003s

OK
```

Counting characters

So let's add a test for the other feature we want, which is to count the number of characters in the file. Since `analyze_text()` is now supposed to return two values, we'll have it return a tuple with line count in the first position and character count in the second. Our new test looks like this:

```python
# text_analyzer.py

class TextAnalysisTests(unittest.TestCase):
    . . .
    def test_character_count(self):
        "Check that the character count is correct."
        self.assertEqual(analyze_text(self.filename)[1], 131)
```

And it fails as expected:

```
% python text_analyzer.py
E..
======================================================================
ERROR: test_character_count (__main__.TextAnalysisTests)
----------------------------------------------------------------------
Traceback (most recent call last):
  File "text_analyzer.py", line 32, in test_character_count
    self.assertEqual(analyze_text(self.filename)[1], 131)
TypeError: 'int' object has no attribute '__getitem__'


----------------------------------------------------------------------
Ran 3 tests in 0.004s

FAILED (errors=1)
```

This result is telling us that it can't index into the integer returned by `analyze_text()`. So let's fix `analyze_text()` to return the proper tuple:

```
# text_analyzer.py

def analyze_text(filename):
    """Calculate the number of lines and characters in a file.

    Args:
        filename: The name of the file to analyze.

    Raises:
        IOError: If ``filename`` does not exist or can't be read.

    Returns: A tuple where the first element is the number of lines in
        the files and the second element is the number of characters.

    """
    lines = 0
    chars = 0
    with open(filename, 'r') as f:
        for line in f:
            lines += 1
            chars += len(line)
    return (lines, chars)
```

This fixes our new test, but we find we've broken an old one:

```
% python text_analyzer.py
..F
=======================================================================
FAIL: test_line_count (__main__.TextAnalysisTests)
-----------------------------------------------------------------------
Traceback (most recent call last):
  File "text_analyzer.py", line 34, in test_line_count
    self.assertEqual(analyze_text(self.filename), 4)
AssertionError: (4, 131) != 4


-----------------------------------------------------------------------
Ran 3 tests in 0.004s

FAILED (failures=1)
```

Fortunately that's easy enough to fix because all we need to do is account for the new return type in our earlier test:

```
# text_analyzer.py

class TextAnalysisTests(unittest.TestCase):
    . . .
    def test_line_count(self):
        "Check that the line count is correct."
        self.assertEqual(analyze_text(self.filename)[0], 4)
```

Now everything is passing again:

```
% python text_analyzer.py
...
-----------------------------------------------------------------------
Ran 3 tests in 0.004s

OK
```

Testing for exceptions

Another thing we want to test for is that `analyze_text()` raises the correct exception when it is passed a non-existent file name, which we can test like this:

```
# text_analyzer.py

class TextAnalysisTests(unittest.TestCase):
    . . .
    def test_no_such_file(self):
        "Check the proper exception is thrown for a missing file."
        with self.assertRaises(IOError):
            analyze_text('foobar')
```

Here we use the `TestCase.assertRaises()` assertion. This assertion checks that the specified exception type — in this case `IOError` — is thrown from the body of the `with`-block.

Since `open()` raises `IOError` for non-existent files, our test already passes with no further implementation:

```
% python text_analyzer.py
....
----------------------------------------------------------------------
Ran 4 tests in 0.004s

OK
```

Testing for file existence

Finally, we can see one more very useful type of assertion by writing a test to verify that `analyze_text()` doesn't delete the file — a reasonable requirement for the function!:

```
# text_analyzer.py

class TextAnalysisTests(unittest.TestCase):
    . . .
    def test_no_deletion(self):
        "Check that the function doesn't delete the input file."
        analyze_text(self.filename)
        self.assertTrue(os.path.exists(self.filename))
```

The `TestCase.assertTrue()` function simply checks that the value passed to it evaluates to True. There is an equivalent `assertFalse()` which does the same test for false values.

As you probably expect, this test passes already as well:

```
% python text_analyzer.py
.....
----------------------------------------------------------------------
Ran 5 tests in 0.002s

OK
```

So now we've got a useful, passing set of tests! This example is small, but it demonstrates many of the important parts of the `unittest` module. There are `many more parts to the unittest module`, but you can get quite far using just the techniques we've seen here.

Moment of zen

Moment of zen: In the face of ambiguity, refuse the temptation to guess:

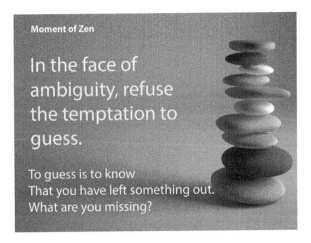

Figure 10.1: Moment of Zen

The temptation to guess, or to ignore ambiguity with wishful thinking, can lead to short term gains. But it can often lead to confusion in the future, and to bugs which are difficult to understand and fix. Before you make that next quick fix, ask yourself what information you need to do it correctly.

Summary

- The `unittest` module is a framework for developing reliable automated tests.
- You define *test cases* by subclassing from `unittest.TestCase`.
- The `unittest.main()` function is useful for running all of the tests in a module.
- The `setUp()` and `tearDown()` fixtures are used to run code before and after each test method.
- Test methods are defined by creating method names that start with `test_` on test case objects.
- The various `TestCase.assert...` methods can be used to make a test method fail when the right conditions aren't met.
- Use `TestCase.assertRaises()` in a `with`-statement to check that the right exceptions are thrown in a test.

1. Test-driven development, or simply TDD, is a form of software development where tests are written first, That is, before you write the actual functionality to be tested. This may seem backwards at first, but it can be a surprisingly powerful technique. You can learn more about TDD here.

2. Note that we don't actually try to test any functionality yet. This is just the initial skeleton of our test suite that lets us verify that the test method executes.

3. A tenet of TDD is that your tests should fail before they pass, and you should only ever write enough implementation code to make you tests pass. In this way, your tests stand as a complete description how your code should behave.

4. You may have noticed that the `setUp()` and `tearDown()` method names aren't in line with what PEP 8 prescribes. This is because the `unittest` module predates those parts of PEP 8 which specify the convention of function names being in lower case with underscores. There are several such cases in the Python standard library but most new Python code follows the PEP 8 style.

5. If we were strictly interpreting TDD here, this amount of implementation would have been too much. To make our existing test pass, we didn't need to actually implement line counting; we just needed to return the value 4. Subsequent tests would have then forced us to continually "update" our implementation as they described a more complete version of the analysis algorithm. We think you'll agree that such a dogmatic approach would be inappropriate here and, frankly, in real development as well.

11
Debugging with PDB

Even with a comprehensive automated test suite, we can still get into situations where we need a debugger to figure out what's going on. Fortunately, Python includes a powerful debugger with the standard library: PDB. PDB is a command-line debugger, and if you're familiar with tools like GDB then you'll already have a good idea of how to use PDB.

The key advantage of PDB over other Python debuggers is that, being part of Python itself, PDB is available pretty much anywhere that Python is, including specialized environments where the Python language has been embedded into larger systems, such as ESRI's *ArcGIS* Geographical Information System. That said, it can be much more comfortable to use a

so-called *graphical* debugger, such as the ones included with products such as *Jetbrains'* *PyCharm* or *Microsoft's* *Python Tools for Visual Studio*. You should feel free to skip this chapter until such time that familiarity with PDB becomes more pressing; you won't be missing anything we rely on later in this book or in *The Python Journeyman* or *The Python Master*.

PDB is different from many debugging tools in that it's not really a separate program but rather a module just like any other Python module. You can import pdb into any program and start the debugger using the set_trace() function call. This function simply starts the debugger at whatever point you are at in the program's execution.

For our first look at PDB, let's use a REPL and start the debugger with set_trace():

```
>>> import pdb
>>> pdb.set_trace()
--Return--
> <stdin>(1)<module>()->None
(Pdb)
```

You'll see that after you execute set_trace() your prompt changes from the triple-chevron to (Pdb) – this is how you know you're in the debugger.

Debugging commands

The first thing we'll do is simply see what commands are available in the debugger by typing help:

```
(Pdb) help

Documented commands (type help <topic>):
========================================
EOF      cl         disable   interact   next      return    u           where
a        clear      display   j          p         retval    unalias
alias    commands   down      jump       pp        run       undisplay
args     condition  enable    l          print     rv        unt
b        cont       exit      list       q         s         until
break    continue   h         ll         quit      source    up
bt       d          help      longlist   r         step      w
c        debug      ignore    n          restart   tbreak    whatis

Miscellaneous help topics:
==========================
pdb   exec
```

This lists a few dozen commands, some of which you'll use in almost every debugging session, and some of which you may never use at all.

You can get specific help on a command by typing help followed by the command name. For example, to see what continue does, type `help continue`:

```
(Pdb) help continue
c(ont(inue))
Continue execution, only stop when a breakpoint is encountered.
```

The curious parentheses in the command name tell you that `continue` can be activated by typing `c`, `cont`, or the full word continue. Knowing the shortcuts for common PDB commands can greatly increase your comfort and speed at debugging.

Palindrome debugging

Rather than simply list all of the commonly useful PDB commands, we're going to instead debug a simple function. Our function – `is_palindrome()` – takes in an integer and determines if the digits of the integer are a palindrome or not. A palindrome is a sequence which is the same both forwards and backwards.

The first thing we'll do is create a new file, `palindrome.py`, with this code:

```python
import unittest

def digits(x):
    """Convert an integer into a list of digits.

    Args:
      x: The number whose digits we want.

    Returns: A list of the digits, in order, of ``x``.

    >>> digits(4586378)
    [4, 5, 8, 6, 3, 7, 8]
    """

    digs = []
    while x != 0:
        div, mod = divmod(x, 10)
        digs.append(mod)
        x = mod
    return digs

def is_palindrome(x):
    """Determine if an integer is a palindrome.

    Args:
      x: The number to check for palindromicity.

    Returns: True if the digits of ``x`` are a palindrome,
      False otherwise.

    >>> is_palindrome(1234)
    False
    >>> is_palindrome(2468642)
    True
    """
    digs = digits(x)
    for f, r in zip(digs, reversed(digs)):
        if f != r:
            return False
    return True

class Tests(unittest.TestCase):
    """Tests for the ``is_palindrome()`` function."""
    def test_negative(self):
        "Check that it returns False correctly."
        self.assertFalse(is_palindrome(1234))
```

```
    def test_positive(self):
        "Check that it returns True correctly."
        self.assertTrue(is_palindrome(1234321))

    def test_single_digit(self):
        "Check that it works for single digit numbers."
        for i in range(10):
            self.assertTrue(is_palindrome(i))

if __name__ == '__main__':
    unittest.main()
```

As you can see, our code has three main parts:

- The first is the `digits()` function which converts an integer into a list of digits.
- The second is the `is_palindrome()` function which first calls `digits()` and then checks if the resulting list is a palindrome.
- The third part is a set of unit tests. We'll use these tests to drive the program.

As you might expect, this being a section on debugging, there's a bug in this code. We're going to first run the program and notice the bug, and then we'll see how to use PDB to find the bug.

Bug hunting with PDB

So, let's simply run the program. We have three tests that we expect to run, and since this is a relatively simple program we expect it run very quickly:

```
$ python palindrome.py
```

Instead of running quickly, we see that this program seems to run forever! And if you look at its memory usage, you'll also see that it grows in size the longer it runs. Clearly something is wrong, so let's use *Ctrl+C* to kill the program.

Let's use PDB to try to understand what's going on here. Since we don't know where our problem might lie, we don't know where to put a `set_trace()` call. So we're going to instead start the program under the control of PDB using a command-line invocation:

```
$ python -m pdb palindrome.py
> /Users/sixty_north/examples/palindrome.py(1)<module>()
-> import unittest
(Pdb)
```

Here we're using the -m argument which tells Python to execute the specific module – in this case PDB – as a script. The remaining arguments are passed to that script. So here we're telling Python to execute the PDB module as a script, and we're passing the name of our broken file to it.

What we're seeing is that we're immediately taken to a PDB prompt. The arrow pointing to `import unittest` is telling us that this is the next statement that will be executed when we continue. But where is that statement?

Let's use the where command to find out:

```
(Pdb) where
/Library/Frameworks/Python.framework/Versions/3.5/lib/python3.5/bdb.py(387)
run()
-> exec cmd in globals, locals
  <string>(1)<module>()
> /Users/sixty_north/examples/palindrome.py(1)<module>()
-> import unittest
```

The where command reports our current call stack, with the most recent frames at the bottom, and we can see that PDB has paused execution at the very first line of `palindrome.py`. This reinforces an important aspect of Python execution which we've discussed before: everything is evaluated at runtime. In this case, we've paused execution right before an import statement.

We can execute this import by running to the next statement using the next command:

```
(Pdb) next
> /Users/sixty_north/examples/palindrome.py(3)<module>()
-> def digits(x):
(Pdb)
```

We see that this takes us to the `def` call for the `digits()` function. When we execute another next, we move to the definition of the `is_palindrome()` function:

```
(Pdb) next
> /Users/sixty_north/examples/palindrome.py(12)<module>()
-> def is_palindrome(x):
(Pdb)
```

You may be wondering why the debugger didn't step into the body of digits. After all, isn't it evaluated at runtime like everything else? The answer is that the body of the function can only be evaluated when there are arguments supplied to it, so it will be run only when the function is called. The bodies of functions *are* checked for proper syntax when they're imported, but PDB doesn't let us debug that part of the process.

Finding infinite loops with sampling

We could continue using next to move through our program's execution, but since we don't know where the bug lies this might not be a very useful technique. Instead, remember that the problem with our program is that it seemed to be running forever. This sounds a lot like an infinite loop!

So rather than stepping through our code, we'll simply let it execute and then we'll use *Ctrl+C* to break back into the debugger when we think we might be in that loop:

```
(Pdb) cont
^C
Program interrupted. (Use 'cont' to resume).
> /Users/sixty_north/examples/palindrome.py(9)digits()
-> x = mod
(Pdb)
```

After letting the program run for a few seconds, we press *Ctrl+C* which halts the program and shows us that we're in the the digits() function of palindrome.py. If we want to see the source code at that line, we can use the PDB command list:

```
(Pdb) list
  4          "Convert an integer into a list of digits."
  5          digs = []
  6          while x != 0:
  7              div, mod = divmod(x, 10)
  8              digs.append(mod)
  9  ->          x = mod
 10          return digs
 11
 12  def is_palindrome(x):
 13          "Determine if an integer is a palindrome."
 14          digs = digits(x)
(Pdb)
```

We see that this is indeed inside a loop, which confirms our suspicion that an infinite loop might be involved.

We can use the return command to try to run to the end of the current function. If this doesn't return, we'll have very strong evidence that this is an infinite loop:

```
(Pdb) r
```

We let this run for a few seconds to confirm that we never exit the function, and then we press *Ctrl+C*. Once we get back to a PDB prompt, let's exit PDB with the quit command:

```
(Pdb) quit
%
```

Setting explicit breaks

Since we know the problem lies in `digits()`, let's set an explicit breakpoint in there using the `pdb.set_trace()` function mentioned earlier:

```python
def digits(x):
    """Convert an integer into a list of digits.

    Args:
      x: The number whose digits we want.

    Returns: A list of the digits, in order, of ``x``.

    >>> digits(4586378)
    [4, 5, 8, 6, 3, 7, 8]
    """

    import pdb; pdb.set_trace()

    digs = []
    while x != 0:
        div, mod = divmod(x, 10)
        digs.append(mod)
        x = mod
    return digs
```

Remember that the `set_trace()` function will halt execution and enter the debugger.

So now we can just execute our script without specifying the PDB module:

```
% python palindrome.py
> /Users/sixty_north/examples/palindrome.py(8)digits()
-> digs = []
(Pdb)
```

And we see that we almost immediately go to a PDB prompt with execution halted at the beginning of our `digits()` function.

To verify that we know where we are, let's use where to see our call stack:

```
(Pdb) where
  /Users/sixty_north/examples/palindrome.py(35)<module>()
-> unittest.main()
  /Library/Frameworks/Python.framework/Versions/3.5/lib/python3.5/un\
ittest/main.py(95)__init__()
-> self.runTests()
  /Library/Frameworks/Python.framework/Versions/3.5/lib/python3.5/uni\
ttest/main.py(229)runTests()
-> self.result = testRunner.run(self.test)
  /Library/Frameworks/Python.framework/Versions/3.5/lib/python3.5/uni\
ttest/runner.py(151)run()
-> test(result)
  /Library/Frameworks/Python.framework/Versions/3.5/lib/python3.5/uni\
ttest/suite.py(70)__call__()
-> return self.run(*args, **kwds)
  /Library/Frameworks/Python.framework/Versions/3.5/lib/python3.5/uni\
ttest/suite.py(108)run()
-> test(result)
  /Library/Frameworks/Python.framework/Versions/3.5/lib/python3.5/uni\
ttest/suite.py(70)__call__()
-> return self.run(*args, **kwds)
  /Library/Frameworks/Python.framework/Versions/3.5/lib/python3.5/uni\
ttest/suite.py(108)run()
-> test(result)
  /Library/Frameworks/Python.framework/Versions/3.5/lib/python3.5/uni\
ttest/case.py(391)__call__()
-> return self.run(*args, **kwds)
  /Library/Frameworks/Python.framework/Versions/3.5/lib/python3.5/uni\
ttest/case.py(327)run()
-> testMethod()
/Users/sixty_north/examples/palindrome.py(25)test_negative()
-> self.assertFalse(is_palindrome(1234))
/Users/sixty_north/examples/palindrome.py(17)is_palindrome()
-> digs = digits(x)
> /Users/sixty_north/examples/palindrome.py(8)digits()
-> digs = []
```

Remember that the most recent frames are at the end of this listing. After a lot of `unittest` functions, we see that we are indeed in the `digits()` function, and that it was called by `is_palindrome()`, just as we expected.

Stepping through execution

What we want to do now is watch execution and see why we never exit this function's loop. Let's use next to move to the first line of the loop body:

```
(Pdb) next
> /Users/sixty_north/examples/palindrome.py(9)digits()
-> while x != 0:
(Pdb) next
> /Users/sixty_north/examples/palindrome.py(10)digits()
-> div, mod = divmod(x, 10)
(Pdb)
```

Now lets look at the values of some of our variables and try to decide what we expect to happen. We can examine values by using the print command:

```
(Pdb) print(digs)
[]
(Pdb) print x
1234
```

This looks correct. The `digs` list — which will contain the sequence of digits in the end — is empty, and x is what we passed in. We expect the `divmod()` function to return 123 and 4, so let's try that:

```
(Pdb) next
> /Users/sixty_north/examples/palindrome.py(11)digits()
-> digs.append(mod)
(Pdb) print div,mod
123 4
```

This looks correct: The `divmod()` function has clipped off the least significant digits from our number, and the next line puts that digit into our results list:

```
(Pdb) next
> /Users/sixty_north/examples/palindrome.py(12)digits()
-> x = mod
```

If we look at `digs`, we'll see that it now contains mod:

```
(Pdb) print digs
[4]
```

The next line will now update x so that we can continue clipping digits from it:

```
(Pdb) next
> /Users/sixty_north/examples/palindrome.py(9)digits()
-> while x != 0:
```

We see that execution goes back up to the `while`-loop as we expected. Let's look at x to make sure it has the right value:

```
(Pdb) print x
4
```

Wait a second! We expect x to hold the digits that aren't already in the results list. Instead, it contains *only* the digit in the results list. Clearly we've made a mistake in updating x!

If we look at our code, it quickly becomes apparent that we should have assigned `div` rather than mod to x. Let's exit PDB:

```
(Pdb) quit
```

Note that you may have to run quit a few times because of how PDB and `unittest` interact.

Fixing the bug

After you're out of PDB, let's remove the `set_trace()` call and modify `digits()` to fix the problem we found:

```
def digits(x):
    """Convert an integer into a list of digits.

    Args:
      x: The number whose digits we want.

    Returns: A list of the digits, in order, of ``x``.

    >>> digits(4586378)
    [4, 5, 8, 6, 3, 7, 8]
    """

    digs = []
```

```
    while x != 0:
        div, mod = divmod(x, 10)
        digs.append(mod)
        x = div
    return digs
```

If we run our program now, we see that we're passing all tests, and it runs very quickly:

```
$ python palindrome.py
...
----------------------------------------------------------------------
Ran 3 tests in 0.001s

OK
```

So that's a basic PDB session, and it demonstrates some of the core features of PDB. PDB has many other commands and features, however, and the best way to learn them is to simply start using PDB and trying out the commands. This palindrome program can serve as a good example for learning most of the features of PDB.

Summary

- Python's standard debugger is called PDB.
- PDB is a standard command-line debugger.
- The `pdb.set_trace()` method can be used to stop program execution and enter the debugger.
- Your REPL's prompt will change to (Pdb) when you're in the debugger.
- You can access PDB's built-in help system by typing `help`.
- You can use python -m pdb followed by a script name to run a program under PDB from the start.
- PDB's `where` command shows the current call stack.
- PDB's `next` command lets execution continue to the next line of code.
- PDB's `continue` command lets program execution continue indefinitely, or until you stop it with *Ctrl+C*.
- PDB's `list` command shows you the source code at your current location.
- PDB's `return` command resumes execution until the end of the current function.
- PDB's `print` command lets you see the values of objects in the debugger.
- Use the `quit` command to exit PDB.

Along the way we found that:

- The `divmod()` function calculates the quotient and remainder for a division operation at one time.
- The `reversed()` function can reverse a sequence.
- You can pass –m to your Python command to have it run a module as a script.
- Debugging makes it clear that Python is evaluating everything at run time. Notice that we can use print with or without parentheses. Don't be alarmsed – we haven't regressed to Python 2. In this context print is a PDB *command* rather than a Python 3 *function*.

Afterword: Just the Beginning

As we said at the beginning, Python is a big language. Our goal with this book is get you started in the right direction, to give you the foundation you need to not just program Python effectively but direct your own growth with the language. Hopefully, we've done our job!

We encourage you to use what you've learned here whenever you can. Practicing these skills really is the only way to master them, and we're sure that your appreciation for Python will deepen as you put the language to use. Perhaps you can use Python immediately in your job or school work, but if not there are countless open-source projects that would love to have your help. Or you could start your own project! There are so many ways to get experience with Python that the real problem may be finding the one that suits you best.

There is, of course, a great deal to Python that is not covered in this book. Our forthcoming books `The Python Journeyman` and `The Python Master` will look at many of the more advanced topics that weren't covered here, so give them a look when you're ready to learn more. Or if you're interested in learning Python in other forms be sure look at the Python courses on PluralSight, `Python Fundamentals`, `Python: Beyond the Basics`, and "Advanced Python" (coming soon). We also offer `in-house Python training` and `consulting` through our company Sixty North if you have more substantial needs.

Whatever your journey with Python becomes, we sincerely hope you've enjoyed this book. Python is a wonderful language with a great community, and we want you to get as much joy from it as we have. Happy programming!

Appendix A
Virtual Environments

A *virtual environment* is a light-weight, self-contained Python installation. The main motivation for virtual environments is to allow different projects to have control over the versions of installed Python packages, without interfering with other Python projects installed on the same host. A virtual environment consists of a directory containing a symbolic link to (Unix), or a copy of (Windows), an existing Python installation, together with an empty site-packages directory into which Python packages specific to this virtual environment can be installed. A second motivation for virtual environments is that users can create a virtual environment without needing administrator rights on their system, making it easy for them to install packages locally. A third motivation is that different virtual environments can be based on different versions of Python, making it easier to test code on say Python 3.4 and Python 3.5 on the same computer.

If you're using Python 3.3 or later, then you should already have a module called venv installed on your system. You can verify this by running it from the command line:

```
$ python3 -m venv
usage: venv [-h] [--system-site-packages] [--symlinks | --copies]\
            [--clear] [--upgrade] [--without-pip]
            ENV_DIR [ENV_DIR ...]
venv: error: the following arguments are required: ENV_DIR
```

If you don't have `venv` installed, there is another tool

- The `virtualenv` environment variable - which works very similarly. You can get it from the `Python Package Index (PyPI)`. We explain how to install packages from PyPI in `Appendix C`, *Installing Third-Party Packages*. You can use either `venv` or `virtualenv`, though we'll use `venv` here, since it is built in to recent versions of Python.

Creating a virtual environment

Using `venv` is very simple: You simply specify the path of a directory which is to contain the new virtual environment. The tool creates the new directory and populates it with the installation:

```
$ python3 -m venv my_python_3_5_project_env
```

Activating a virtual environment

Once the environment is created you can *activate* it by using the activate script in the environment's bin directory. On Linux or macOS you have to source the script:

```
$ source my_python_3_5_project_env/bin/activate
```

And on Windows you simply run it:

```
> my_python_3_5_project_env\bin\activate
```

Once you do this your prompt will change to remind you that you're in a virtual environment:

```
(my_python_3_5_project_env) $
```

The Python that will execute when you run python is from the virtual environment. In fact, using virtual environments is by far the best way to get a predictable version of Python when you invoke python rather than having to remember to use python for Python 2 and python3 for Python 3.

Once in the virtual environment you can work as normal, secure in the knowledge that package installations are isolated from the system Python and other virtual environments.

Deactivating a virtual environment

To leave a virtual environment use the deactivate command, which will return you to the parent shell from which the virtual environment was activated:

```
(my_python_3_5_project_env) $ deactivate
$
```

Other tools for working with virtual environments

If you work with virtual environments a lot — we would advocate that you should almost always be working within one — managing a plethora of environments can itself become something of a chore. Integrated Development Environments such as *JetBrains' PyCharm* contain excellent support for creating and using virtual environments. On the command line, we recommend a tool called `virtualenv wrapper` which makes switching between projects which rely on different virtual environments almost trivial, once you've done some initial configuration.

Appendix B
Packaging and Distribution

Packaging and distributing your Python code can be a complex and sometimes confusing task, especially if your projects have lots of dependencies or involve components more exotic than straight Python code. However, for many cases it's very straightforward to make your code accessible to others in a standard way, and we'll see how to do that using the standard `distutils` module in this section. The main advantage of `distutils` is that it's included in the Python Standard Library. For much beyond the simplest packaging requirements you'll probably want to look at setup tools instead, which has capabilities beyond those of `distutils`, but which is correspondingly more confusing.

The `distutils` module allows you to write a simple Python script which knows how to install your Python modules into any Python installation, including one hosted in a virtual environment. By convention this script is called `setup.py` and it exists at the top level of your project structure. This script can then be executed to perform the actual installation.

Configuring a package with distutils

Let's see a simple example of `distutils`. We'll create a basic `setup.py` installation script for the palindrome module we wrote in the Chapter 11, *Debugging with PDB*.

The first thing we want to do is to create a directory to hold our project. Let's call this `palindrome`:

```
$ mkdir palindrome
$ cd palindrome
```

Let's put a copy of our `palindrome.py` in this directory:

```
"""palindrome.py - Detect palindromic integers"""

import unittest

def digits(x):
    """Convert an integer into a list of digits.

    Args:
      x: The number whose digits we want.

    Returns: A list of the digits, in order, of ``x``.

    >>> digits(4586378)
    [4, 5, 8, 6, 3, 7, 8]
    """

    digs = []
    while x != 0:
        div, mod = divmod(x, 10)
        digs.append(mod)
        x = div
    return digs

def is_palindrome(x):
    """Determine if an integer is a palindrome.

    Args:
      x: The number to check for palindromicity.

    Returns: True if the digits of ``x`` are a palindrome,
        False otherwise.

    >>> is_palindrome(1234)
    False
    >>> is_palindrome(2468642)
    True
    """
    digs = digits(x)
    for f, r in zip(digs, reversed(digs)):
        if f != r:
            return False
    return True

class Tests(unittest.TestCase):
    "Tests for the ``is_palindrome()`` function."
    def test_negative(self):
```

```
        "Check that it returns False correctly."
        self.assertFalse(is_palindrome(1234))

    def test_positive(self):
        "Check that it returns True correctly."
        self.assertTrue(is_palindrome(1234321))

    def test_single_digit(self):
        "Check that it works for single digit numbers."
        for i in range(10):
            self.assertTrue(is_palindrome(i))

if __name__ == '__main__':
    unittest.main()
```

And finally let's create the `setup.py` script:

```
from distutils.core import setup

setup(
    name = 'palindrome',
    version = '1.0',
    py_modules  = ['palindrome'],

    # metadata
    author = 'Austin Bingham',
    author_email = 'austin@sixty-north.com',
    description = 'A module for finding palindromic integers.',
    license = 'Public domain',
    keywords = 'palindrome',
    )
```

The first line in the file imports the functionality we need from the `distutils.core` module, namely the `setup()` function. This function does all of the work of installing our code, so we need to tell it about the code we're installing. We do this, of course, with the arguments we pass to the function.

The first thing we tell `setup()` is the name of this project. We've chosen palindrome in this case, but you can choose any name you like. In general, though, it's simplest to just keep the name the same as your project name.

The next argument we pass to `setup()` is the version. Again, this can be any string you want. Python doesn't rely on the version to follow any rules.

The next argument, `py_modules`, is probably the most interesting. We use this to specify the Python modules we want to install. Each entry in this list is the name of the module without the `.py` extension. The `setup()` function will look for a matching `.py` file and install it. So, in our example, we've asked `setup()` to install `palindrome.py` which, of course, is a file in our project.

The rest of the arguments we're using here are fairly self-explanatory and are there mostly to help people to use your module correctly and to know who to contact if they have problems.

Before we start using our `setup.py`, we first need to create a virtual environment into which we'll install our module. In your palindrome directory, create a virtual environment called `palindrome_env`:

```
$ python3 -m venv palindrome_env
```

When this completes, activate the new environment. On Linux or macOS, source the activate script:

```
$ source palindrome_env/bin/activate
```

Or on Windows call the script directly:

```
> palindrome_env\bin\activate
```

Installing with distutils

Now that we've got our `setup.py`, we can use it to do a number of interesting things. The first, and perhaps most obvious, thing we can do is install our module into our virtual environment! We do this by passing the install argument to `setup.py`:

```
(palindrome_env)$ python setup.py install
running install
running build
running build_py
copying palindrome.py -> build/lib
running install_lib
copying build/lib/palindrome.py ->
/Users/sixty_north/examples/palindrome/palindrome_env/lib/python3.5/site-
packages
byte-compiling
/Users/sixty_north/examples/palindrome/palindrome_env/lib/python3.5/site-
packages/palindrome.py to palindrome.cpython-35.pyc
running install_egg_info
```

```
Writing
/Users/sixty_north/examples/palindrome/palindrome_env/lib/python3.5/site-
packages/palindrome-1.0-py3.5.egg-info
```

When invoked `setup()` prints out a few lines to tell you about its progress. The most important line for us is where is actually copies `palindrome.py` into the installation folder:

```
copying build/lib/palindrome.py ->
/Users/sixty_north/examples/palindrome/palindrome_env/lib/python3.5/site-
packages
```

The `site-packages` directory of a Python installation is where third-party packages such as ours are normally installed. So it looks like the installation worked properly.

Let's verify this by running Python and seeing that our module can be imported. Note that we want to change directories before we do this, otherwise when we import palindrome Python will simply load the source file in our current directory:

```
(palindrome_env)$ cd ..
(palindrome_env)$ python
Python 3.5.2 (v3.5.2:4def2a2901a5, Jun 26 2016, 10:47:25)
[GCC 4.2.1 (Apple Inc. build 5666) (dot 3)] on darwin
Type "help", "copyright", "credits" or "license" for more information.
>>> import palindrome
>>> palindrome.__file__
'/Users/sixty_north/examples/palindrome/palindrome_env/lib/python3.5/site-
packages/palindrome.py'
```

Here we use the `__file__` attribute on the module to see where it was imported from, and we see that we're importing it from our virtual environment's `site-packages`, which is exactly what we wanted.

Don't forget to switch back to your source directory after exiting the Python REPL:

```
(palindrome_env)$ cd palindrome
```

Packaging with distutils

Another useful feature of `setup()` is that it can create various types of "distribution" formats. It will take all of the modules you've specified and bundle them up into packages that are easy to distribute to others. You can do this with the `sdist` command (which is shorthand for 'source distribution'):

```
(palindrome_env)$ python setup.py sdist --format zip
running sdist
```

```
running check
warning: check: missing required meta-data: url

warning: sdist: manifest template 'MANIFEST.in' does not exist (using
default file list)

warning: sdist: standard file not found: should have one of README,
README.txt

writing manifest file 'MANIFEST'
creating palindrome-1.0
making hard links in palindrome-1.0...
hard linking palindrome.py -> palindrome-1.0
hard linking setup.py -> palindrome-1.0
creating dist
creating 'dist/palindrome-1.0.zip' and adding 'palindrome-1.0' to it
adding 'palindrome-1.0/palindrome.py'
adding 'palindrome-1.0/PKG-INFO'
adding 'palindrome-1.0/setup.py'
removing 'palindrome-1.0' (and everything under it)
```

If we look, we'll see that this command created a new directory, dist, which contains the newly generated distribution file:

```
(palindrome_env) $ ls dist
palindrome-1.0.zip
```

And if we unzip that file we'll see that it contains our project's source code, including the setup.py:

```
(palindrome_env)$ cd dist
(palindrome_env)$ unzip palindrome-1.0.zip
Archive:  palindrome-1.0.zip
  inflating: palindrome-1.0/palindrome.py
  inflating: palindrome-1.0/PKG-INFO
  inflating: palindrome-1.0/setup.py
```

So now you can send this zip file to anyone who wants to use your code, and they can use the setup.py to install it into their system. Very convenient!

Note that the `sdist` command can produce distributions of various types. To see the available options, you can use the `--help-formats` option:

```
(palindrome_env) $ python setup.py sdist --help-formats
List of available source distribution formats:
  --formats=bztar  bzip2'ed tar-file
  --formats=gztar  gzip'ed tar-file
  --formats=tar    uncompressed tar file
  --formats=zip    ZIP file
  --formats=ztar   compressed tar file
```

This section really just touches on the very basics of `distutils`. You can find out more about how to use `distutils` by passing `--help` to `setup.py`:

```
(palindrome_env) $ python setup.py --help
Common commands: (see '--help-commands' for more)

  setup.py build      will build the package underneath 'build/'
  setup.py install    will install the package

Global options:
  --verbose (-v)      run verbosely (default)
  --quiet (-q)        run quietly (turns verbosity off)
  --dry-run (-n)      don't actually do anything
  --help (-h)         show detailed help message
  --command-packages  list of packages that provide distutils commands

Information display options (just display information, ignore any commands)
  --help-commands     list all available commands
  --name              print package name
  --version (-V)      print package version
  --fullname          print <package name>-<version>
  --author            print the author's name
  --author-email      print the author's email address
  --maintainer        print the maintainer's name
  --maintainer-email  print the maintainer's email address
  --contact           print the maintainer's name if known, else the
author's
  --contact-email     print the maintainer's email address if known, else
the
                      author's
  --url               print the URL for this package
  --license           print the license of the package
  --licence           alias for --license
  --description       print the package description
  --long-description  print the long package description
  --platforms         print the list of platforms
  --classifiers       print the list of classifiers
```

```
    --keywords            print the list of keywords
    --provides            print the list of packages/modules provided
    --requires            print the list of packages/modules required
    --obsoletes           print the list of packages/modules made obsolete

usage: setup.py [global_opts] cmd1 [cmd1_opts] [cmd2 [cmd2_opts] ...]
   or: setup.py --help [cmd1 cmd2 ...]
   or: setup.py --help-commands
   or: setup.py cmd --help
```

For many simple projects you'll find that what we've just covered is almost all you need to know.

Appendix C

Installing Third-Party Packages

Packaging in Python has had a troubled and confusing history. Thankfully, the situation has settled down and a tool called pip has emerged as the clear front-runner among package installation tools for general purpose Python use. For more specialist uses such as numerical or scientific computing which rely on the *Numpy* or *Scipy* packages you should consider *Anaconda* as a strong alternative to pip.

Installing pip

In this appendix we'll focus on pip as it is officially blessed by the core Python developers and comes with support out of the box. Although pip is not distributed with Python, a tool to install pip called ensurepip is included. It was done this way to allow pip to evolve at a different rate to the Python language and standard library.

It shouldn't usually be necessary to install pip with recent Python releases, as ensurepip is invoked automatically when Python is installed or when a new virtual environment is created. If for some reason you need to install pip manually, you can simply issue this command:

```
$ python -m ensurepip
```

The `ensurepip` module will do the rest. Bear in mind though, that pip will be installed into the environment corresponding to the python interpreter you invoke in this call.

The Python Package Index

The pip tool can search for packages in a central repository — the *Python Package Index*, or *PyPI*, also known by the nickname "Cheeseshop" — and then download and install them along with their dependencies. You can browse the PyPI at `https://pypi.python.org/pyp i`. This is an extremely convenient way to install Python software, so it's good to understand how to use it.

Installing with pip

We'll demonstrate how to use pip by installing the nose testing tool. The `nose` command is a sort of power-tool for running `unittest` based tests such as those we developed in `Chapter 10`, *Unit testing with the Python standard library*. One really useful thing it can do is *discover* all of your tests and run them. This means that you don't need to add `unittest.main()` into your code; you can just use `nose` to find and run your tests.

First though, we need to do some groundwork. Let's create a virtual environment (see `Appendix B`, *Pakaging and Distribution*) so we don't inadvertently install into our system Python installation. Create a virtual environment using `pyenv`, and activate it:

```
$ python3 -m venv test_env
$ source activate test_env/bin/activate
(test_env) $
```

As `pip` is updated much more frequently than Python itself, it's good practice to upgrade `pip` in any new virtual environment, so let's do that. Fortunately, `pip` is capable of updating itself:

```
(test_env) $ pip install --upgrade pip
Collecting pip
  Using cached pip-8.1.2-py2.py3-none-any.whl
Installing collected packages: pip
  Found existing installation: pip 8.1.1
    Uninstalling pip-8.1.1:
      Successfully uninstalled pip-8.1.1
Successfully installed pip-8.1.2
```

If you don't upgrade pip it will give you warnings every time you use it, if a new version has become available since you last upgraded.

Now let's use pip to install nose. pip uses subcommands to decide what to do, and to install modules you use `pip install package-name`:

```
(test_env) $ pip install nose
Collecting nose
  Downloading nose-1.3.7-py3-none-any.whl (154kB)
     100% |████████████████████████████████| 163kB
2.1MB/s
Installing collected packages: nose
Successfully installed nose-1.3.7
```

If this succeeds, nose is ready to use in our virtual environment. Let's check that it's available by trying to import it at the REPL and instrospecting the path at which it is installed:

```
(test_env) $ python
Python 3.5.2 (v3.5.2:4def2a2901a5, Jun 26 2016, 10:47:25)
[GCC 4.2.1 (Apple Inc. build 5666) (dot 3)] on darwin
Type "help", "copyright", "credits" or "license" for more information.
>>> import nose
>>> nose.__file__
'/Users/sixty_north/.virtualenvs/test_env/lib/python3.5/site-
packages/nose/__init__.py'
```

As well as installing a module, `nose` installs the `nosetests` program in the bin directory of the virtual environment. To really put the icing on the cake, let's use `nosetests` to run the tests from `palindrome.py` from Chapter 11, *Debugging with PDB*:

```
(test_env) $ cd palindrome
(test_env) $ nosetests palindrome.py
...
----------------------------------------------------------------------
Ran 3 tests in 0.001s

OK
```

Installing Local Packages with pip

You can also use pip to install from local packages in files rather than from the Python Package Index. To do this, simply pass the filename of the packaged distribution to `pip` install. For example, in `Appendix B`, *Packaging and Distribution* we showed how to build a so called source distribution using `distutils`. To install this using `pip`, do:

```
(test_env) $ palindrome/dist
(test_env) $ pip install palindrome-1.0.zip
```

Uninstalling Packages

A key advantage to installing packages with pip rather than directly invoking `setup.py` of the source distribution is that pip knows how to uninstall packages. Simply use the `uninstall` subcommand:

```
(test_env) $ pip uninstall palindrome-1.0.zip
Uninstalling palindrome-1.0:
Proceed (y/n)? y
Successfully uninstalled palindrome-1.0
```

Index

.

.py file
  code, organizing 66

A

Aircraft class
  refactoring 245, 248
aircraft
  seats, booking 231
argument passing semantics
  external objects, modifying in function 97, 99
  new objects, binding in function 99, 100
  pass by object-reference 97
  reference binding 101
assertions 286
assertions, for testing behavior
  about 292
  characters, counting 293
  lines, counting 293

B

binary files
  about 269
  bitwise operator 274
  BMP file format 269, 271
  BMP file, writing 274
  reading 276
BMP image file
  fractal images, generating 275
  generating 274
BoardingCardPrinter class 242
bool 27, 31

C

class invariants 226
classes

defining 222
clean-up actions 190
code organization, .py file
  about 66
  modules, importing into REPL 67
  Python programs, running from operating system
    shell 66
code structure 17
collection protocols
  about 166
  container protocol 167
  iterable protocol 167
  other protocols 168
  sequence protocol 168
  sized protocol 167
command line argument
  accepting 77
comments 83
comprehensions
  about 195
  dictionary comprehension 198
  filtering clause 199
  filtering, combining with transformation 200
  list comprehension 196
  set comprehension 197
conditional control flow
  if-statement 33
  if...elif...else statement 35
  if...else statement 34
container protocol 167
context managers
  about 264, 266
  resources, managing with 266
  with-blocks 267
control flows 33

D

debugging, with PDB
  about 299
  commands 300
  palindrome debugging 300
dictionaries
  about 151, 152
  copying 153
  dictionary keys, iterating over 154
  dictionary values, iterating over 155
  items, removing 157
  key-value pairs, iterating over 156
  membership testing, for dictionary keys 156
  mutability 157
  pretty printing 158
  updating 154
dictionary comprehension
  about 198
  complexity 199
distutils module
  about 317
  installing with 320
docstrings 80
duck typing 244, 245

E

Easier to Ask for Forgiveness than for Permission
  (EAFP)
  about 188
  versus LBYL 188
empty blocks 176
enumerate() 132
exception handling 171
exception objects 177
exception types
  about 186
  IndexError 186
  KeyError 186
  ValueError 186
exceptions
  about 172, 185
  catching 182
  control flow 172
  handling 173

  part of function's API 180, 181
  part of protocols 185
  raised by Python 181
  raising explicitly 182
  re-raising 179
  testing for 296
executable Python programs
  on Linux 83
  on Mac 83
  on Windows 84
execution models
  about 72
  modules 73
  programs 73
  scripts 73

F

file-like objects
  about 278
  using 278
files
  about 256
  appending to 262
  binary mode 256
  closing 259
  encoding 256
  existence, testing 296, 297
  file objects, as iterators 263
  file outside, of Python 259
  opening, in write mode 257
  reading 260
  reading line by line 261
  reading multiple lines at once 261
  text mode 256
  writing to 258
fixtures
  about 286
  new fixtures, using 290
  used, for creating temporary files 289
Flight class
  make_boarding_cards(), adding 243
float
  about 27, 29
  promotion to float 30
  special floating point values 30

function arguments
  about 102
  default arguments, evaluating 104, 106
  default parameter values 103
  keyword arguments 104
functions
  defining 68
  used, for organizing words module 69

G

generator expressions
  about 211
  generator object, running once 212
  if-clause, using 213
  iteration, without memory 213
  optional parentheses 213
generator functions
  about 204, 209
  distinct() 208
  explicit state, maintaining 207
  generator code, executing 206
  infinite 210
  iterators 205
  laziness 210
  lazy generator pipelines 209
  Lucas series, generating 210
  take() 207
  yield keyword 204
generators 219
guard clauses 184

H

help() function
  using 23

I

if-statement 33
if...elif...else statement 35
if...else statement 34
implementation sharing
  Aircraft, inheriting from 249
  base class, for aircraft 248
  common functionality, hosting into base class
    250
imprudent return codes 178

index() method 146
inheritance
  about 248
instance initializers
  about 224
  lack, of access modifiers 225
instance methods 223
int 27
invariants 226
iterable protocol 167
iteration protocols
  about 202
  example 202
  practical example 203
iteration tools
  about 213, 219
  booleans sequences 215
  itertools 214
  sequences, concatenating lazily with chain() 217
  sequences, merging with zip() 215, 216

L

LEGB rule
  about 108
  built-in 109
  enclosing 109
  global 109
  local 109
Linux
  Python 3, installing 14
list comprehension
  about 196
  elements 197
  syntax 196
list
  concatenating 149
  copying 138
  elements by index, removing with del 147
  elements by value, removing with remove() 148
  elements, finding with index() 146
  elements, rearranging 149
  implementing 133
  items, inserting into 148
  membership testing, with count() and in 147
  negative indexing 134, 135

out-of-place rearrangement 150
repeating 144, 145
shallow copies 139, 140, 141, 142, 144
slicing 135, 136, 137
literal tuples 120
local packages
installing, with pip 328
Look Before you Leap (LBYL) 188
loop
exiting, with break statement 38
while-loop 36
Lucas series
generating 210

M

macOS
Python 3, installing 13
main function, with command line argument
setting up 73, 76
math.factorial() function
using 25
modularity 65
modules
executing, from command line 70
multiple exceptions
handling 174

N

naming methods
for implementation details 238
relocate_passenger(), implementing 239, 240
NaN (Not a Number) 30
nested tuples 121
nominal sub-typing 245
number
types 26

O

Object-Oriented Programming (OOP) 222
object
about 112
function, inspecting 113

P

package
configuring, with distutils 317, 320
uninstalling 328
packaging
about 317
with distutils 321
palindrome debugging
about 300
bug hunting, with PDB 302
bug, fixing 308
explicit breaks, setting 305
infinite loops, finding with sampling 304
stepping, through execution 307
pass statement 176
PDB 299
phenylthiocarbamide (PTC) 166
pip
installing 325
platform-specific code 191
polymorphism 244
pprint 158
programmer errors 175
protocol 166
Python 2.7
reference 11
Python 3.5
reference 11
Python 3
installing 11
installing, on Linux 14
installing, on macOS 13
installing, on Windows 12
obtaining 11
reference 12, 13
Python code
distributing 317
Python command line REPL
starting 15
Python indentation
rules 21
Python object references
about 87
assigning, to another 89, 90

equality of identity, testing with is function 91
equality of value, versus equality of identity 96,
    97
mutating, without mutating 91, 92, 93, 94
reassigning 88
to mutable objects 94, 95
value versus identity, exploring with id() 90
Python Package Index
    about 326
    installing, with pip 326
Python programs
    running, from operating system shell 66
Python return semantics 102
Python type system
    about 107
    dynamic typing 107
    strong typing 108
Python
    approach, to whitespaces 20
    culture 21, 23

R

range
    about 130
    enumerate() function 132
    starting value 131
    step argument 132
relational operators
    about 32
    comparison operators 33
REPL
    exiting 16
    exiting, on Unix 17
    exiting, on Windows 17
    modules, importing 67
resources
    other resources 280

S

scalar data types
    bool 27, 31
    float 27, 29
    int 27
    none 30
    None 27

scopes
    global keyword 111
    identical names, in global and local scope 110
    implementing 109
    LEGB rule 108
scoping 108
seating plan, aircraft
    about 233, 234
    available seats, counting 241
    seats, allocating to passengers 235, 236, 238
second class, aircraft
    adding 227, 229
sequence protocol 168
set comprehension 197
sets
    about 158
    algebra operations 162
    copying 162
    difference 164
    elements, adding to 161
    elements, removing from 162
    intersection 164
    iterating over 160
    membership testing 161
    set constructor 160
    subset relationships 165
    symmetric difference 164
    union 163
shallow copy 139
shebang 83
significant indentation 18
single-element tuples
    about 122
    creating 122
sized protocol 167
standard library modules
    importing 23
string methods 130
strings
    capabilities 125
    concatenating 125, 126
    formatting 129
    joining 127
    length 125
    partitioning 128

splitting 127

T

tuple constructor
  about 124
  membership tests 124
tuples
  about 120
  concatenating 121
  elements, accessing 120
  empty tuples 122
  iterating over 121
  length, determining 120
  literal tuples 120
  nested tuples 121
  parentheses 122
  repetition 121
  returning 123
  single-element tuples 122
  unpacking 123
  variables, swapping with tuple unpacking 124
TypeError
  not protecting against 187, 188

U

unit testing example
  failing test, fixing 288
  initial tests, running 288
  text analysis 286
unittest module 285

V

validation 226
variable declaration 108
virtual environment
  about 313
  activating 314
  creating 314
  deactivating 315
  working with 315

W

while-loop 33, 36
Windows
  Python 3, installing 12
  REPL, exiting 17
with-block syntax 268
words module
  organizing, functions used 69

Made in the USA
Middletown, DE
09 October 2020